>>>>>>>>>> PLAYS OF IMPASSE <<<<<<<<<<

>>>>>>>>>>>>>>>> <<<<<<<<<<<<<<<<

PLAYS OF IMPASSE

CONTEMPORARY DRAMA
SET IN CONFINING INSTITUTIONS

BY

CAROL ROSEN

>>>>>>>>>>>>>>>> <<<<<<<<<<<<<<<<

PRINCETON UNIVERSITY PRESS
PRINCETON, NEW JERSEY

Published by Princeton University Press, 41 William Street, Princeton,
New Jersey
In the United Kingdom: Princeton University Press,
Guildford, Surrey

Library of Congress Cataloging in Publication Data will be
found on the last printed page of this book

This book has been composed in Linotron Baskerville

Clothbound editions of Princeton University Press books
are printed on acid-free paper, and binding materials are
chosen for strength and durability.

Printed in the United States of America by Princeton
University Press, Princeton, New Jersey

IN MEMORY OF

BARBARA ROSEN AND FRANCES ROSEN KING

WITH GRATITUDE FOR THEIR JOY OF LIFE

>>>>>>>>>>>>> CONTENTS <<<<<<<<<<<<<

CONTENTS

I know of one acid test in the theatre. It is literally an acid test. When a performance is over, what remains? Fun can be forgotten, but powerful emotion also disappears and good arguments lose their thread. When emotion and argument are harnessed to a wish from the audience to see more clearly into itself—then something in the mind burns. The event scorches on to the memory an outline, a taste, a trace, a smell—a picture. It is the play's central image that remains, its silhouette, and if the elements are rightly blended this silhouette will be its meaning, this shape will be the essence of what it has to say.

Peter Brook, *The Empty Space*

THIS BOOK is the result of the encouragement and generosity of many. The Princeton University Department of English, chaired by A. Walton Litz, Jr., supported my research through several drafts, notably with a Tuck Fund Grant for research in London. Support for the writing of the book came through the assistance of the National Endowment for the Humanities, which granted me a fellowship for 1979–1980.

I wish to thank several scholars in the field of drama. I owe a special debt of thanks to Bernard Beckerman. Many of the ideas in this book began to take shape at a 1976 N.E.H. seminar that he led, and more recently, he gave me the benefit of his close, searching reading of the text. I am grateful to Theodore Shank and Alvin Kernan for comments on the text and for their ideas about dramatic form in general. I am glad I got to benefit from Daniel Seltzer's advice and his presence. His performance as Hamm in Joseph Chaikin's production of *Endgame* inspired my discussion of that play and enriched my life.

Other perspectives have also contributed to this book. David Rothman's knowledge of the history of institutions proved invaluable in the early stages of research. So did my sister Sharon Rosen's special knowledge of medical sociology and my sister Frances Rosen King's heartening faith in the project. Arnold Wesker kindly shared his thoughts on the subject of this book, and Iain Reid of the Greater London Arts Association was generous with his time, friendship, and knowledge of experimental theater in London. Most recently, Jonathan Levy's encouragement, good sense, and grace have taught me much.

Many have helped me as well in the preparation of this book for publication. Jerry Sherwood at Princeton University Press demonstrated awesome patience and good will.

Carolyn Dinshaw provided common sense and imagination as well as expert research assistance. Alice Calaprice was a meticulous and thoughtful editor. Marilyn Walden typed up a storm. Thanks are also due to the editors of *Modern Drama* for granting permission to include here the discussion of David Storey's *Home*, which appeared in slightly different form in that journal, and to the Princeton University Library and the New York Public Library Theater Collection at Lincoln Center.

Deep thanks go to my ever-so-serious graduate students at Columbia University in Fall 1980 and at Princeton, and to my feisty, exuberant undergraduates in "Problems in the Drama: Contemporary Drama" over the years at Princeton. Their intelligent challenges, wonder, and pleasure at the poetry of the theater have delighted me and nourished this book beyond words.

I am most grateful for the strength and insights I have gained from Martin Meisel and Michael Goldman. I have had more than my share of luck in meeting, studying with, and later teaching with these two exemplary scholars, critics, and teachers. Both are responsible for a great many perceptions I often fancy are my own. Both willed this book to completion, offered valuable suggestions at every step, and inspire my work. What I know about drama I owe in great measure to them.

For whatever I know of other matters, I thank Jack Carden, my husband, my dearest friend, and my most astute critic. My deepest debt is to this terrific man who wanted a sensible life and chose to share one with me instead.

May 1982

>>>>>>>>>> PLAYS OF IMPASSE <<<<<<<<<<

INTRODUCTION

The Contemporary Dramatic Mode

RECENT THEATER SEASONS have been among the most exciting yet depressing in memory. Major Broadway productions have been mounted of *The Elephant Man, Whose Life Is It Anyway?*, and *Wings,* all three of which revolved around a debilitated character living in a hospital. Also on Broadway in 1979 was *G. R. Point* which, along with a rock musical version of *Dispatches* downtown at the New York Shakespeare Festival Public Theater, took a close look at free-floating terror in Vietnam and in combat zone barracks. The anguish of characters in such dramas puzzled many theater speculators, who would have predicted the out-of-town mercy killing of many such plays. But there was no stopping this avalanche of plays in which a longing for individual freedom was walled in by a social institution. Even Tom Stoppard, always good for a philosophical guffaw, set his most recent pun drama, *Every Good Boy Deserves Favour,* presented with full orchestra at the Metropolitan Opera House, in a bleak Soviet insane asylum. The sudden crush of such plays right on mainstream Broadway—this slew of highly visible plays set in contemporary society's dead ends—has heralded a major mode in contemporary drama to a wider audience than ever before.

Responding to what seemed suddenly to emerge as a trend, critics offered up hypotheses in the Sunday *New York Times.* Walter Kerr first astutely observed the contemporary theater's "increasing preoccupation with illness and age, with senility and death"; he pointed out the recurring set of the hospital, sanatorium, and nursing home in recent plays; and most important, he asked, "Why, in these past

3

few years, should the renewed, determined effort to reach out, get in touch, *make* contact turn up almost exclusively in plays devoted to those whose brains and bodies are on the verge of flickering out? Why the intense focus on this single, very late moment in the time of our lives?" Kerr went on to suggest that these are plays "of last-minute awakening, last-ditch drives for a breakthrough."[1]

About a year later, Roger Copeland wrote in the *Times* about the "utter indifference to public life" in recent plays obsessed with the self. Contrasting the "obsession with the private sanctum" in new American plays with what he called "the essentially public nature of the theater," Copeland discussed the solipsistic nature of *Wings*, for example, and he went on to consider how "a number of recent American plays have dealt, in one way or another, with the public trauma of Vietnam; but none has examined or even raised the issues of public policy related to our experience in Southeast Asia." Copeland cited in particular *Dispatches* and *G. R. Point*, and to a lesser degree, David Rabe's Vietnam trilogy, as plays set in the military that "manage effectively to evoke the hallucinatory quality of the war for those who fought it; and . . . dramatize the moral dilemma experienced by presumably civilized people who discover that they feel strangely 'alive' on the battlefield . . . but . . . focus on the way individual characters react to the war, rather than on the war itself (and as a result, Vietnam tends to become merely a metaphor for 'War' as opposed to a particular war fought for particular reasons)."[2]

Finally, Mel Gussow described the phenomenon of the incapacitated, wounded hero, and focusing on the many hospital beds cluttering the Broadway stage, he proposed that "the existence of these plays would seem to be no coincidence. There is a reason why playwrights and theatergoers are increasingly concerned with such problems." Gussow proceeded to ask some prominent social observers for their opinions about the now apparent proliferaton of plays centered on brittle, broken people often institutionalized, always at the edge. Leslie Fiedler, author of *Freaks*, suggested that there is a growing interest in "beings who seem to be at the margin of everything called normal. They seem to be moving into the center of our imaginations. More and more stories deal with these people. It's an overwhelming metaphor for what people think of their own condition, a reigning metaphor of our age."

Professor of psychiatry Robert Jay Lifton said:

> What we so broadly speak of as narcissism in our culture is often more basically the self-absorption people resort to because of their sense of being threatened or of falling apart. In these plays there is the metaphor of the single life. It is not so easy for a playwright to write about nuclear dangers and weapons without making it a propaganda tract. If you feel the danger of holocaust, you're not just talking about death and dying, but about premature death. These plays would seem to reflect the use of what I call 'death equivalents' as creative metaphor. The plays seem to express death equivalents very strongly through the metaphor of a particular kind of illness. By no means are the plays despairing. One can use death imagery—in the direction of renewal.

And sociologist Amitai Etzioni pointed out a third angle; he saw this dramatic trend developing out of a "black period in society—a society depressed," and he, too, described incapacitated characters as a metaphor for contemporary civilization. "The body society is impaired," he said. "Nothing works anymore. Energy doesn't work. The economy doesn't work. We used to think we could fight inflation by tightening our belts. Now, no matter what you do, inflation gets worse. It is as if we are surrounded by a congenital disease. Society responds as if it were a dead body."[3]

These comments apply not only to hospital-based contemporary plays, but equally well to the shape and movement of contemporary drama as a whole. Fiedler's notion of such plays as a metaphor for abnormality in our age, Lifton's vision of them as an apocalyptic metaphor for the

5

threatened individual in post-World War II society, and Etzioni's concept of "the body society" as ill are all valuable commentaries on the cause of what must be reckoned with as the major mode of contemporary drama: a mode of serious plays relentlessly depicting characters at the edge of despair; characters lost in a situation of pain, anguish, and powerlessness; characters cornered, subjugated to the will of an overwhelming social setting.

This contemporary mode of drama is, as this book will show, by no means just this year's trend, and it is by no means simply a trend of exposing the pain, deformities, wounds, inertia, and drudgery of claustrated souls onstage. Rather, the success of such recent plays, which have won some commercial as well as artistic prestige—*Whose Life Is It Anyway?*, *The Elephant Man*, and *Wings* have all won major awards—indicates the commercial theater's and the public's recent, rather grudging acceptance of a mode of drama which, in fact, has been developing since the end of World War II. This new mode of drama reflects life in an age George Steiner has eerily called a "post-culture," shaken by the revelation that during World War II there was a "transference of Hell from below the earth to its surface."[4]

In an essay exploring how prison imagery is closely woven into the philosophical texture of Sartre's plays, "not as an illustration but as a metaphoric embodiment of a philosophical dilemma," Victor Brombert finds that Sartre's works "betray metaphorically an obsession with images of confinement, enclosure, and immurement. They communicate a sense of the walled-in quality of human consciousness and human existence. Bounded by external contingencies or by the imperatives of a dilemma, the Sartrean hero often appears inextricably jammed-in." Sartre himself writes, "Each situation is a trap, there are walls everywhere," in *Situations II*, cited by Brombert. Why does Sartre call for "a new dramaturgy of *situations*, which he conceives in fact as a theater of entrapment"?

Sartre asserts that the post-World War II generation has been "driven to create a literature of historicity." As Brombert sees it, "Sartre's generation had indeed learned that this was no longer a time to toy with aesthetic problems or to seek private salvation through art—that private salvation was no longer possible, that man was involved in a collective tragedy, and that the very meaning of traditional Humanism was being seriously challenged. The era of concentration camps (*l'ère concentrationnaire*, as it came to be called) reminded the writer that even imprisonment was no longer a private affair."

It should be argued that Sartre's concern with protagonists as "entrapped freedoms"—directly expressed in *No Exit*—is fundamental not only to the philosophical texture of post-World War II drama, but even more fundamental to the formal mode that has taken the contemporary stage. Nevertheless, one *could* argue that the action of plays of many periods is propelled by the yearning to escape. To extricate oneself, to liberate oneself, to get out—these are all serviceable "spines" for action in plays from Euripides' time to our own. But today's drama is harnessed to this spine in a way different from ever before. As Brombert suggests:

> The theater, to be sure, lends itself to the prison image. The epic form—whether in the classical epic or in modern fiction—allows and even calls for movement in time and space. Tragedy, especially in the French tradition with its "unities," most often focuses on a crisis in which the protagonists have reached a seeming impasse. Racine's antechambers are not so different from Sartre's cell where characters are locked together in a death dance. And one could easily show that Greek tragedy is filled with images of restriction and confinement: the chains of Prometheus, the fatal webs and nets in *Agamemnon*, the meshes of fate and the trap of intellect in *Oedipus*. The modern stage, with its three walls—the fourth wall being the inexorable eye of the public—may be said to symbolize an issueless situation.

These are no doubt permanent features of the tragic

theater. But in Sartre's plays, the prison motif is closely bound up with psychological obsessions as well as with philosophical themes.[5]

That final point is crucial to this study. For when Martin Esslin, in his excellent survey of drama since Beckett, dubs contemporary playwrights members of "the theater of the absurd," the emphasis is on the philosophical theme of existentialism; the focus is on the plight of characters condemned to Camus's desert of freedom, where man must first of all invent himself. The present study aims to go beyond the philosophical theme of enclosure by exploring the form and effect of contemporary plays. These plays objectify a psychological and social state of entrapment in a world that feels airless.

To understand more fully how special to our age is this sense of claustration, this Sartrean dramaturgy of situations, it helps to compare the felt predicament of contemporary characters with the predicament faced by their immediate theatrical predecessors. For the world realized onstage in contemporary plays is highly distinct from the stage worlds of modern dramatists such as Ibsen, Strindberg, and Chekhov. In plays by Ibsen, Strindberg, and Chekhov, even if characters cannot escape from the emptiness they find at the heart of their lives—an emptiness which defies their longings for self-fulfillment and for the joy of life—such trapped characters can at least find symbolic referents for their condition in the world engulfing them. Even at a moment when action becomes impossible, Ibsen's Oswald can still cry out for the sun, Strindberg's dreamers can still express anguish through interior journeys and images of vampirism, and Chekhov's Nina can still identify her situation with that of a seagull.

But in the contemporary dramatic mode, in what I identify as plays of impasse, the world onstage has been emptied of consistent symbolic referents; symbols are autonomous; everyday activities and attempts to endure life in a parenthesis are vacated of traditional social or moral meaning.

Contemporary plays of impasse tend to zero in on a claustrophobic, no-exit situation, and to explore with a camera's precision the nuances of everyday behavior by characters clinging to a hard life. They depict life with documentary exactness, and they turn that bitter life into a metaphor for the way things are. Plays of impasse tend to focus on the setting engulfing the individual, rather than on the individual himself, and they tend to find that setting reductive, at once diminishing and intensifying the experience of survival within bounds, against odds. The pain of this kind of survival, spatially fixed, demanding isolation and loss, is, for example, at the heart of Beckett's *Endgame*, an extreme instance of this mode of drama at the edge of existence—the tasks nearly finished, the bleak world onstage nearly empty—when choice is limited to simple, small, yet risky moves. What remains is a burning ember of action, a pure image of life at the edge.

My concern, then, is the shape of plays of impasse: their form and their effect on a contemporary audience. This form is most pronounced in plays set in what sociologist Erving Goffman identified as "total institutions," by far the predominant contemporary stage setting. The correlation between the setting in a total institution, which becomes, in stage poetry, an overdetermined Structure, and the dynamic of impasse is the subject of this study.

Total Institutions

First, a definition. In his study of contemporary *Asylums*, Erving Goffman discovered that institutions established to pursue different goals share characteristics that govern interaction. First, Goffman groups total institutions according to their ostensible purpose in society:

> First, there are institutions established to care for persons felt to be both incapable and harmless; these are the homes for the blind, the aged, the orphaned, and the indigent. Second, there are places established

to care for persons felt to be both incapable of looking after themselves and a threat to the community, albeit an unintended one: TB sanitaria, mental hospitals, and leprosaria. A third type of total institution is organized to protect the community against what are felt to be intentional dangers to it, with the welfare of the persons thus sequestered not the immediate issue: jails, penitentiaries, P.O.W. camps, and concentration camps. Fourth, there are institutions purportedly established the better to pursue some worklike task and justifying themselves only on these instrumental grounds: army barracks, ships, boarding schools, work camps. . . . Finally, there are those establishments designed as retreats from the world even while often serving also as training stations for the religious; examples are abbeys, monasteries, convents, and other cloisters.

Once he points out these teleological distinctions, however, Goffman undermines their significance: he demonstrates that although total institutions differ in cause, their effect on inmates is essentially the same. All these subtly related establishments are finally "forcing houses for changing persons; each is a natural experiment on what can be done to the self." The split between inmates and staff; the process of initiation, mortification, and subjugation of the self to the institution; the adherence to regimentation and routine; and the system of sanctions controlling inmate behavior—all these characteristics cluster together in a single configuration common to apparently unrelated institutional worlds. Hospitals and prison camps, for example, which are presumably worlds apart, are linked in Goffman's overview as two total institutions, both of them concerned primarily with "the management of men."[6]

Goffman defines the central feature common to all total institutions as a breakdown of the barriers ordinarily separating the sleep, work, and play spheres of human existence. He explains:

First, all aspects of life are conducted in the same place and under the same single authority. Second, each phase of the member's daily activity is carried on in the immediate company of a large batch of others, all of whom are treated alike and required to do the same thing together. Third, all phases of the day's activities are tightly scheduled, with one activity leading at a prearranged time into the next, the whole sequence of activities being imposed from above by a system of explicit formal rulings and a body of officials. Finally, the various enforced activities are brought together into a single rational plan purportedly designed to fulfill the official aims of the institution.[7]

In the controlled environment of a total institution, then, inmates act out a script in which thay are typecast. Yet even within the coercive conventions of model behavior, inmates may find space for existential improvisations: some may embrace their roles in the institutional system while others may establish an inner distance between self and role-playing. According to Goffman's model, inmates of total institutions follow the rules of a ritualistic game, planned and imposed on them by the hierarchy above.

This phenomenon of role-playing among inmates and staff in a total institution, further explored by Goffman in *Strategic Interaction* (1972), suggests the strong element of performance as a way of life in a total institution. Elsewhere, particularly in his seminal work, *The Presentation of Self in Everyday Life* (1959), and in "Role Distance" (1961), *Interaction Ritual* (1967), and *Frame Analysis* (1974), works to which I will return throughout this study, Goffman has illuminated, with what commentators have dubbed Dickensian particularity, our behavior in social situations by means of a theatrical metaphor, the idiom of performance.

Various separate societies of role-players, then—whether aimed at cure, care, comfort, punishment, or protection—are linked in *Asylums* by their mutual modus operandi; their treatment of inmates, techniques, and effects are alike. Similarly, seemingly unrelated dramas—set in total institutions such as hospitals, insane asylums, prisons, or military training camps—may be linked by their treatment of ideas, their self-conscious theatricalism, and their effect as psychological and social metaphors.

STRUCTURES ONSTAGE AND THE NEW NATURALISM

Just as Goffman's concept of the total institution illuminates similarities overshadowed by obvious differences, so, too, the idea of contemporary plays of impasse links and clarifies seemingly dissimilar dramas which are actually all in the same mode. For the many contemporary plays which dwell both naturalistically and symbolically on our civilizations within civilizations, on the self governed by the Structure, are indeed all closely related in three ways: (1) the Structure depicted—an extremely naturalistic model of impingement; (2) the thematic metaphor—the world as it is, an overdetermined, ironically presented institution; and (3) the controlling image—impasse. Since the terms Structure and naturalism will be used throughout this book, I wish to present my definitions of them specifically at the outset.

Discussing The Living Theatre's production of *The Brig*, Judith Malina, the play's director, characterizes the set, the Structure depicted, as an overdetermined institution, a closed system:

> The Brig is a structure. The precision of the description of this structure is the key to *The Brig*.
>
> The Immovable Structure is the villain. Whether that structure calls itself a prison or a school or a factory or a family or a government or The World As It Is. That structure asks each man what he can do for it, not what it can do for him, and for those who do not do for it, there is the pain of death or imprisonment, or social degradation, or the loss of animal rights.
>
> The men placed inside the structure are intended to become part of this structure, and the beauty and

terror of *The Brig* is seeing how it succeeds and how it fails in incorporating those whom it has imprisoned into its own corporeal being. . . .

    The Brig is a Constructivist play. The construction of the set dictates and directs the action by the power of its vectors and its centers of gravity. It was designed by the architects of ancient military prisons, Masonic craftsmen of dungeons and towers. From these fearsome structures the utility of minimal construction and maximum security is in direct descent.[8]

Here, the staged institution becomes a sort of cage. According to Goffman, the "total" nature of society's institutions is "symbolized by the barrier to social intercourse with the outside and to departure that is often built right into the physical plant, such as locked doors, high walls, barbed wire, cliffs, water, forests, or moors."[9] Some plays, like the barbed-wire-enclosed *Brig*, now incorporate such concrete barriers into their designs, as if to keep the actors in and the audience out by means of a physical reminder of the limits of characters' mobility, the limits of play.

For the more documentary-like plays, then, the Structure may furnish its own boundary. The barbed wire between the audience and the action of *The Brig*, for example, objectively quarantines the Structure most emphatically. In other plays, such as Weiss's *Marat/Sade*, Storey's *Home*, or Kopit's *Wings*, the boundary is blurred. And elsewhere, as in Nichols's *The National Health* or Arden's *The Happy Haven*, the fourth wall is broken by means of direct address to the audience, treating us as visitors, observers at an institution. Some plays of impasse finally lurch beyond the frame of performance into an actual presentation, as in the pass-out parade at the end of Arnold Wesker's *Chips With Everything*. Always, the power of the setting—of the institutional Structure—to engulf *and* to exclude at will is central. People become stage properties, reacting to a situation, to an encompassing environment, instead of initiating action themselves. The pervasive set emerges as protagonist. So I am using Structure as a specific term, not as a synonym for form, edifice, space, or institution, but as Malina defines it, a massive, de-energizing social model.

Within the overwhelming Structure emerges the thematic metaphor of the world as it is, an extremely naturalistic model of impingement. The individual character is subjugated to his setting in these plays: no longer certain of his rights and choices, no longer secure in his judgments, no longer trusting his state, the contemporary player is wary of the setting which surrounds him. Structures such as hospitals, insane asylums, prisons, and barracks train inmates to survive in an imposing world like our own. But they also segregate their inmates in secret societies from which we are normally excluded. Again, *The Brig*, far from the best, but probably the clearest instance of the mode I am describing, illuminates the second characteristic of plays of impasse. The Structure of *The Brig*, its meticulously detailed, accurately rendered set, is meant to serve, writes Julian Beck, "in the scrutiny of actuality." Beck goes on:

> "Poetry of the theatre," says Cocteau, not meaning meter; the phrase turned on the line, that kind of thing, but something else, which in the work of Brown . . . emerges as the distillation, extraction, representation of exact words and action of life as it is lived, honest, uncompromisingly honest, and by being life itself and not sham is some kind of poetry . . .
>
> A resurgence of realism was needed: what had been passing for realism was not real.[10]

Throughout this study we will come across plays that go beyond Zola's principles of *Le Naturalism au théâtre* (1882) in their rigorous demand for clinical reconstructions, documentary accuracy, photographic images of social institutions transplanted to the stage. This is a self-conscious naturalism, reflecting on its purity of style, calling attention to its detailed setting, its sense of the minutiae of daily life, its episodic form.

Like George Segal's uncanny sculptures of public places—

gas stations, subway cars, diners, butcher shops—inhabited by white plaster specters of humankind, these plays transcend the tradition of naturalism by making the convention of naturalism part of the subject of drama. Play after play presents naturalistically an irremediable state of being. In hospital-set plays, we see gleaming models of medical endgames; in asylum-set plays, we see elaborate measures taken to mask the divided self; in prison-set plays, we see the most direct and natural expression of lost freedom on a cul-de-sac stage; and in military-set plays, we see how machine-like man himself can become when he loses himself to the rigor and beauty of the Structure. And always, there is the sense of character as a ghost stalking these plays, like those pale plaster shadows haunting George Segal's petrified worlds.

In his essay "Notes on Naturalism: Truth is Stranger as Fiction," Stanley Kauffmann posits a "new naturalism," a term to which I will return in the discussion of David Storey's *Home*. Kauffmann recalls Jonathan Marks's apt analogy for the style of Storey's plays. This analogy suits not only Storey's plays, but many plays of impasse in general. "The Disney Studios have artists who do foregrounds—the story elements—and artists who do backgrounds. It is as if the foreground men had little to do in *The Contractor* and weren't used at all for *The Changing Room*," he writes. Now that "the Disney story men have gone home, naturalism becomes perforce as sheerly aesthetic a mode as any that would have pleased Pater or Wilde." Kauffmann now goes on to clarify the self-consciousness, the transparency, of the "new naturalism." He writes:

> The pleasure in watching *The Changing Room* was a pleasure in abstraction, not in reproduction; in stylistic exercise, not in any of the historical "scientific" aims of naturalism. And thus that pleasure, rather than being dusty with century-old courage, became ultra-contemporary and free: The creation of a para-world that merely resembles, more than is usual in the theater,

obvious play of impasse in which the shape of Pinter's drama is directly expressed. In fact, after seeing this play, an uproariously funny send-up of an institution where methodical depersonalization and torture happen every day, we can understand why the playwright's first impulse was to stash this one away in a drawer. As Pinter has said,

> Wrote the whole damn thing in three drafts. It was called *The Hothouse* and was about an institution in which patients were kept: all that was presented was the hierarchy, the people who ran the institution; one never knew what happened to the patients or what they were there for or who they were. It was heavily satirical and it was quite useless. I never began to like any of the characters, they really didn't live at all. So I discarded the play at once. The characters were so purely cardboard. I was intentionally—for the only time, I think—trying to make a point, an explicit point, that these were nasty people and I disapproved of them. And therefore they didn't begin to live.[14]

Although Pinter is being his own harshest critic here, he is quite right in saying he was trying "for the only time" in his career as a playwright "to make a point, an explicit point." For *The Hothouse* is a sketchy, heavy-handed version of Pinter's more subtle, fleshed-out plays of closed circuits, empty phrases, institutional jargon, hopelessly gummed-up works, and seductions by a forceful idea of a woman. Here, in an insane asylum so bizarre that it might very well be where *The Cocktail Party*'s poor Celia was sent, Pinter plays with the idea of inmates massacring a complacent staff at Christmas time. Roote and Gibbs, administrators with a tension between them as thick as that between Lenny and Teddy in *The Homecoming*, talk about "taking the piss" out of each other,[15] a pastime many of Pinter's characters happily engage in for hours on end. Language is used as a cutting weapon here ("I mean, not only are you a scientist, but you have literary ability, musical ability, knowledge of most schools of philosophy, philology, photography, anthropology, cosmology, theology, phytology, phytonomy, phytotomy—" says Lush; "Oh, no, no, not phytotomy," Roote answers [p. 88]). A volunteer employee, the eager Lamb, undergoes an interview and torture in a soundproof booth. His interrogation is a less resonant double of Stanley's word-whipping in *The Birthday Party*. Here the interrogator is the luscious Miss Cutts:

> CUTTS. Are you virgo intacta?
> LAMB. Yes, I am, actually. I'll make no secret of it.
> CUTTS. Have you always been virgo intacta?
> LAMB. Oh yes, always. Always.
> CUTTS. From the word go?
> LAMB. Go? Oh yes. From the word go.
> GIBBS. What is the law of the Wolf Cub Pack? . . .
>
> (pp. 73–74)

There is a parodic version of the kind of remembered love that vivifies the shadows of *No Man's Land*, *Landscape*, and *Silence*:

> Do you remember the first time we met? On the beach? In the night? All those people? And the bonfire? And the waves? And the spray? And the mist? And the moon? Everyone dancing, somersaulting, laughing? And you—standing silent, staring at a sandcastle in your sheer white trunks. The moon was behind you, in front of you, all over you, suffusing you, consuming you, you were transparent, translucent, a beacon. I was struck dumb, dumbstruck. . . . (p. 143)

And there is a mystery about who has died, and who has fathered a patient's newborn babe, the kinds of questions Pinter's characters never seem to know the answers to.

Most important, *The Hothouse* is quite clearly about the breakdown of a malevolent order, and the renewing of that order after the mess has been cleaned up. Like Arden's *The Happy Haven*, *The Hothouse* is ostensibly about a sanatorium where a dead patient's mother may be asked dead-pan:

Didn't you come down for Mother's Day, or Thanksgiving Day, or for the annual summer picnic for patients, staff, relatives and friends? Weren't you invited to the Halloween Feast, the May Dance, the October Revival, the Old Boys and Girls supper and social? Dancing on the lawn, cold buffets on the flat roof, midnight croquet, barbecued boar by the lake? None of this? ... (p. 56)

But at bottom, the form of Pinter's less skeletal metaphysical farces and the redundant movements of his more searching plays of memory, desire, and conquest, going round and round without end, may be discerned in *The Hothouse*. Two moments stand out in particular: at one point, a woman languidly lies in an armchair, tossing a ping-pong ball in the air, while offstage a sigh, a keen, and then a laugh are heard; at another point, two men stand frozen with knives raised (pp. 117, 135). Such are the shapes of impasse that characterize Pinter's masterworks—silhouettes of inquietude and sexual energy contained—present even in this sketchy play, set by no less than Pinter in a zany, merciless total institution.

PLAYWRIGHTS' STYLISTIC APPROACHES TO IMPASSE

The dominant image of contemporary drama seems to me to be impasse, and the dominant way of expressing this core of meaning, at once naturalistically and symbolically, is the total institution. Plays set in hospitals, insane asylums, prisons, and the military turn up with an uncanny frequency. The plays I have chosen to explicate—to consider their effect on their audiences as they move from photographic immersions in an institution towards an image of a state of social and spiritual impasse—are the ones that strike me as the clearest examples of the contemporary mode.

Within the contemporary mode, three distinct stylistic emphases emerge:

20

1. Plays that strive for objectivity, moving forward linearly, but subordinating plot to a depiction of a total institution with naturalistic, almost documentary accuracy as a kinetic *objet trouvé*;

2. Satiric, parodic treatments of total institutions, using these settings as entertaining and often grimly funny vehicles for social commentary and for a play of ideas; and

3. Imagistic, reductive, interior plays that suggest the total institution as they focus on the individual lost in a world he did not make and cannot control.

Each chapter in this study is devoted to plays set in a single total institution, examining three plays typical of the stylistic approaches to a Structure of impasse. In each chapter, then, one of the plays chosen is primarily photographic, exterior in its bias; the second play clearly expresses a satirical point of view, a commentary on the Structure as a metaphor for society gone haywire; and the third play is subdued, tending towards lyricism, indicating by means of props, sounds, and spaces an inner isolation, a personal stalemate within the larger, implied Structure.

In each chapter, the plays chosen in each of the three styles complement each other as powerful instances of the contemporary mode set in total institutions. Let me indicate how by enumerating styles here as above:

Hospitals: 1. Peter Nichols's *The National Health (or Nurse Norton's Affair)*
2. John Arden's *The Happy Haven*
3. Arthur Kopit's *Wings*

Insane Asylums: 1. Peter Weiss's *Marat / Sade*
2. Friedrich Dürrenmatt's *The Physicists*
3. David Storey's *Home*

21

Prisons:	1. Kenneth H. Brown's *The Brig*
	2. Brendan Behan's *The Quare Fellow*
	3. Jean Genet's *Deathwatch*
Military Training Camps:	1. Arnold Wesker's *Chips With Everything*
	2. David Rabe's *The Basic Training of Pavlo Hummel*
	3. David Rabe's *Streamers*

As different as the plays in each group of three are, the state of impasse and the enduring Structure are still related. In each social setting, the specific yearnings, the "at least" spines, are different. Characters in hospital plays long to get well or to die; characters in asylum plays want to imagine themselves sane or free; characters locked in prison plays plan breaks or power games; and characters called to arms try to subjugate their will to a vision of unity. But just as plays in these different settings focus on different aspects of our spirit, on different private hopes for escape, so, too, do the playwrights of each group of plays empty the characters' impulses towards freedom of any value. And while the settings are not interchangeable, in all these plays of impasse an awesome common denominator does emerge: all these different journeys of the human spirit toward connection with the joy of life end where there is no meaning beyond survival. The movement toward self-fulfillment is thwarted by a relentless Structure characterized either by pain, lunacy, crime, or conformity. Experience is gradually whittled away until the largest action possible in a play of impasse is dwarfed by the enormity, the literal power, of a Structure that turns all symbolic acts into pathetic, ironic sight gags. The final chapter, focusing on Beckett's *Endgame*, suggests a modal picture for plays of impasse.

The mode of impasse is manifest in plays *not* set in institutions, too. This dramatic form has become so central that it is now an underlying assumption of most plays: the givens of a play of impasse are as much taken for granted, I would argue, as were the five-act divisions of French classical drama. The condition of impasse supplies to contemporary drama both a texture of reality and a pivot, a spine. Indeed, in plays by virtually all the major contemporary dramatists, begining with O'Neill's *The Iceman Cometh*, characters are lost, reacting to an overwhelming situation rather than instigating action themselves, reduced to passing the time and telling anecdotes in cul-de-sac worlds like our own but *not* our own. This condition of impasse, entrapment, and despair, sometimes eased and sometimes exacerbated by the memory of desire, is felt, for example, in Pinter's *The Birthday Party* and *No Man's Land*, in Osborne's *The Entertainer* and *Inadmissible Evidence*, in Albee's *The Zoo Story*, *Who's Afraid of Virginia Woolf?*, and *Box/Mao/Box*, in Handke's *Kaspar*, in Bond's *Saved*, in Shepard's *Angel City* and *Seduced*, in Sartre's *No Exit*, of course, and in every play of Beckett's.

There seems, then, to be a formal pattern in almost every play put forth by our most gifted dramatists. This is not for one moment to disparage the integrity of each playwright's singular vision. For this pattern is always altered, invigorated by individual nuance, by insight, and sometimes—as in Beckett's endgames of impasse—by genius. Indeed, the point of my close attention to each script in this study is to go beyond categorization, to evoke the effect of each play *onstage*, to explore precisely the special qualities—the singular voice and vision—each playwright brings to the contemporary mode. As we identify and explore the essence of the Structure of impasse onstage, a modal picture finally emerges, as do recurring themes and images, ideas of a theater.

Why this pattern of impasse in contemporary drama? And why the overwhelming Structure of a total institution looming so large in so many plays in the contemporary mode? Robert Jay Lifton has written that "We live in a world so dominated by holocaust—past, contemporary, and anticipated—that we may look upon ourselves as, in some degree, embodiments of these horrors. This is the vague and yet disturbing 'identity of the doomed' in which we partake."[16] In the chapters that follow, in discussions of plays set in hospitals, insane asylums, prisons, military camps, and finally, in *Endgame,* at the end of the world, I will venture further to consider ideas about the nature of particular social institutions, as they adapt so readily to plays of impasse. Given the ideas expressed concretely as well as verbally in these plays, the world outside is frightening, awful, sometimes in ruins, post-atomic. Inside, even without hope, there is some measure of safety, some chance to survive, to get by, some chance perhaps even to communicate with someone else whose options for movement are equally limited. In these plays, freedom—if it ever comes—does begin on the far side of despair; in this contemporary mode, man must literally be condemned to be free.

For inside the Structure of impasse, there is only now: man is the sum of his present actions alone. And in this frame beyond historicity, there is some freedom to remember, to imagine, to play.

KILLING PAIN IN THE END BEDS

Peter Nichols's *The National Health
(or Nurse Norton's Affair),*
John Arden's *The Happy Haven,*
and Arthur Kopit's *Wings*

In the large women's ward—it was huge, with
more than thirty beds in it—the women never
settled down at the proper time anyway, whether
the light was turned off or not. Many of them had
been there a long time and were thoroughly tired
of the hospital. They slept badly, it was stuffy,
and there were always arguments about whether
the door to the terrace should be kept open or
shut. And there were even a few dedicated en-
thusiasts who talked across the room from one
end to the other, discussing everything from
prices, goods, furniture, children, men, neigh-
bors, right down to the most shameless subjects
imaginable—until midnight or one in the morning.
     Alexander Solzhenitsyn, *Cancer Ward*

ANYONE who has ever been hospitalized will tell you two
things: the illogic of the staff was beyond belief and the
patient who was in the next bed now knows more about
him than his wife does. Solzhenitsyn's *Cancer Ward* will tell
you much more than this, of course, but even this explo-
ration of life at the edge gives emphasis to the heavy sameness of everyday life on the ward. Peopled by those trying
to go on as usual, "discussing everything," as well as by

25

those sick of being sick, "tired of the hospital," sleeping badly, the ward takes on a life, a character all its own.[1] A society of people in pajamas, weak and uncertain, a hospital ward is secret-free, intense, and as uncomfortable as it is close to death.

Popular drama has traditionally reinforced our reverence for men in white as it has played up glamorous diseases and medical miracles. Contemporary playwrights, however, have seized on the hospital setting and the idea of sickness with increasing frequency. The 1979 Broadway season alone saw three such plays, and serious plays at that; among its hits and Tony Award winners were Bernard Pomerance's *The Elephant Man*, Brian Clark's *Whose Life Is It Anyway?*, and Arthur Kopit's *Wings*.

The Elephant Man, based on the true story of John Merrick, a misshapen man in nineteenth-century England, depicts his rescue from the world of freaks by Dr. Frederick Treves, who housed Merrick in the London Hospital, where Merrick became the "pet" of London society. *The Elephant Man* demands much both of its audience and of the actor in the title role, in part because of its episodic structure and difficult subject, but mainly because the audience, once shown Merrick's deformities on slides projected on stage, must then imagine this tormented figure in the uncamouflaged, quite healthy person of the actor playing Merrick. For his part, the actor playing Merrick has to create by means of gait, voice, and posture a physical torment real beyond any he might have suggested with a layer of stage putty.

Whose Life Is It Anyway? concerns the strategies used by a young sculptor, paralyzed from the neck down after a crash, to convince a well-meaning hospital staff to let him die. This pro-euthanasia play stacks its deck. It isolates the immobile sculptor from a world where surely *someone* would want him and would urge him back, and his bedside visitors are all passive bystanders, not a joy-of-life spokesman nor a true love among them. In this way, the play's debates wrench some eerie applause from an audience that ends up rooting for death as preferable to loneliness, *not* for individual freedom—including the right to die—as more valuable than society's enforcement of still life. With its protagonist capable only of talk and head movements, and with its superficially argued thesis, *Whose Life Is It Anyway?* gives a fresh melodramatic turn to the phrase "cerebral drama." Nevertheless, enlivened by acerbic, torrential soul searching, and set completely in a hospital which is rendered with snapshot accuracy, *Whose Life Is It Anyway?* does much with wit and the recognizable side effects of long-term hospitalization to make up for the essential hollowness of the play's pro-euthanasia argument.

Finally, *Wings*, to be considered closely later in this chapter, traces the physical progress and the interior journey of a stroke victim, grappling along the way with disorientation, loss, and navigating anew in a hospital setting. All three of these plays were illuminated on Broadway by the actors who took on essentially tour-de-force roles: Philip Anglim and Kevin Conway in *The Elephant Man*, Tom Conti energizing *Whose Life Is It Anyway?* (as did Mary Tyler Moore, who later on, in a much-publicized casting gender switch, retained much of the toughness and resolve—though she tempered the anger—of Conti's original characterization), and Constance Cummings as the former aviatrix through whose consciousness are filtered the sounds and images of *Wings*. These three plays, now very much in the public eye, along with many other popular successes of recent years, such as Ronald Ribman's *Cold Storage* (a basic two-patient bitter comedy), and Michael Cristofer's *The Shadow Box* (an affecting melodrama set in cottages of a California hospice, a center for the terminally ill), share the hospital setting and the idea of debilitation, not just as plot devices, but as metaphors, as a way to probe human endurance and imagination in an immobilizing world.

Of the many contemporary plays set in hospitals, three stand out for the sophistication of their construction, the clarity of their individual vision of a world stopped cold, and their use of the institution as a model of impingement on a greater scale. Peter Nichols's *The National Health (or Nurse Norton's Affair)*, first produced by the National Theatre at the Old Vic in 1969, and John Arden's *The Happy Haven*, produced at the Royal Court Theatre in 1960, both attack the formidable premises of hospitals and old-age homes with determined irreverence. Both these plays are set in encompassing Structures which, according to Erving Goffman's groupings of total institutions related by intent, are "established to care for persons felt to be both incapable and harmless."[2] In both plays, characters step out of their roles to address the audience, song-and-dance routines interrupt the flow of the action, and surreal fantasies break into everyday scenes. While Nichols and Arden explode the myth of heroic suffering and grapple with an idea of euthanasia, Arthur Kopit's *Wings*, first commissioned as an original radio play for "Earplay" in 1976, and first performed onstage at the Yale Repertory Theater in 1978, uses a comparable setting to an entirely different end. Kopit's play, in contrast to those by Nichols and Arden, seeks to uplift our spirits with an image of singular vitality, with a glimpse of suffering transcended. Nichols's bitter-edged *The National Health* is by far the closest of these plays to documentary; Arden's play, with its sustained level of satirical fantasy, is a metaphysical farce; and Kopit's play experiments with sounds and images to objectify one patient's inner state. Yet different as these plays are in style and theme, they are all rooted in a factual environment; indeed, both Nichols's and Kopit's plays grew out of personal experiences with hospital life.[3] Most important, all three plays communicate a sense of an encroaching world, a haunting space, a Structure of impasse. They are all finally linked, then, by their theatrical mode as well as by their hospital setting.

The National Health (or Nurse Norton's Affair)

Peter Nichols's *The National Health (or Nurse Norton's Affair)* is, as its title suggests, a play with a double focus. Set in a hospital ward, *The National Health* is constructed on two planes of intersecting dramatic action. First, it exposes us to a grim world of disease and death. The hospital ward schedule adhered to by the stereotyped individuals who are the staff and patients of *The National Health* is an almost clinically accurate chronicle of pain tolerance. Second, within the grim ward, Nichols also constructs a play-within-a-play which balances the harsh reality of systematized medicine with a surreal soap-opera version of hospital heroics. In this way, the factual model gradually becomes a microcosm of the world as it is, an ironic reflection of the state of the national health.

The spoof of the TV medical genre flows logically out of the play's authentic premise even though it was originally interpolated into the action by the playwright to lighten the overall effect of his play. *The National Health* was originally drafted as a teleplay, and in its first version it confined the action to a naturalistic reconstruction of hospital ward activities. According to Nichols, "I took the original round to every television company when I wrote it six years ago [in 1964], but none of them wanted to know, so it got shelved. They said it was too depressing." When he revised "End Beds" for staging, Nichols added the parodic *"Nurse Norton's Affair"* to relieve the relentless pain of his play for a theater audience.[4] Ironically, of course, *"Nurse Norton's Affair"* fits right into the hospital ward. Its corny plot and glossy characters are hardly distinguishable from the TV shows it burlesques.[5] And TV watching is quite common in hospitals, where patients in pain often divert their attention with the aid of a bedside TV screen. Indeed, the positive, distracting value of TV watching is recognized in the treatment of chronic patients in the hospital setting. As one commentator explains it, "On many daytime serials, law and medicine are the most populous professions," and "Soap writers love illness, partly because it is so full of dramatic potential for the characters and their friends and families, partly because the audience includes many people in hospitals or at home because they are sick."[6] Even in its escapist interludes, then, *The National Health* is true to its clinical model. When we in the audience are not being beset by the routines and somber circumstances of the bedridden, we are being entertained by the fantasies and projected happy endings of TV doctor shows, an escape in which patients indulge.

The interpenetration of reality and illusion—the precise suggestion of ordinary pain on the ward alternating with stylized vignettes mocking TV's romantic medical melodramas—gives Nichols's play its double edge. This interpenetration is represented by Barnet, the hospital orderly who doubles as the master of ceremonies in the music hall and soap opera sequences. Barnet explains it all in his final speech to the audience: "Wishing for excitement. Still, that's life, isn't it, madam? That's human nature. We're all of us poised on a knife-edge between the urge for security and a craving for excitement. But you haven't come here to listen to philosophical speculation, you want the facts."[7] Setting his hospital ward on that knife-edge between mortality and the music hall, Nichols maintains a delicate balance between an image of actual loss and a parodic dance of death.

The National Health begins, as do many other plays written in the contemporary mode, as an apparently documentary insert of reality into the theater. Entering the theater, the audience finds the stage dimly lit by a blue bulb hanging center. Gradually, we grow accustomed to the stark institutional setting revealed before us by encroaching daylight. Patients are asleep in the ward on stage: they are groaning snoring, uttering incoherent phrases. A West Indian staff nurse, later to be identified for us as Cleo Norton, goes abstractedly about her business, *"giving special attention to the man in Bed 5, who is being drip-fed and drained"* (p. 9). Slowly, the motions of morning activity become more and more noticeable: offstage, the staff nurse joins in a brisk, cheerful reveille with a patient; another nurse crosses back and forth, addressing patients in the institutional baby talk peculiar to her profession; the patients start their daily routine. In these first two scenes of *The National Health*, we are enveloped in the tranquil rhythm of the early morning ritualistic action in the ward onstage. A new day begins in this place of cures and casualties. There is no formal curtain raising: this play, which never actually started, is somehow already going on. The first two scenes, showing work-in-progress, involve us in the even flow and steady pace of hospital care. By the end of these introductory awakening scenes, we are familiarized and concerned with this world where the sickbed is public domain.

The ward fills the empty space between life and death exits. One patient leaves; another arrives; nothing disturbs the tranquility of temperature-taking and bedpan removing. The patients form a nomadic tribe; they come and they go. Indeed, the play begins with a departure and an arrival. We watch Ken, a motorcyclist who has mended after an accident, leave the ward triumphantly. Ready to go, all got up in his gear, Ken takes advantage of his new status as an outsider: he propositions a nurse and jokingly disrupts ward routine. Then, bidding his companions adieu, Kenny calls out to them all, "Get well soon!" (p. 21). Those who stay behind give him a feeble reply. They are still confined to this ward, and by now, so are we. Like Loach, the new patient, we have just been delicately initiated into the system. And through Loach, we have been intoduced to the other patients. Ash, the school teacher with a stomach ulcer who eventually emerges as the choral commentator on the ward, makes Loach at home. Each patient is identified according to his illness, because even though outside the hospital these men have names and occupations, inside the institution men are known for what ails them. In this manner, Nichols incorporates exposition into the everyday routine: each resident of the ward is identified for us as each, in turn, is described ostensibly for the benefit of the new roommate.

Glancing at the bed which now bears the newcomer's nameplate, Ash indulges in a euphemism of ward life. "That bed just happened to fall vacant this morning," he informs Loach (p. 17); earlier he tactfully explained this sudden vacancy to the sound sleeper of the ward:

> ASH. Very enviable. He went in the night.
> FOSTER. In that condition? Never. Transferred?
> ASH (*quietly*). Passed on. First I knew was the screens going round then the resuscitation unit and the heart-machine . . . quite a pantomime but . . . n.b.g. . . . I regret to say. . . .
> FOSTER. I'm blowed.
> ASH. The orderly cleaned him and wheeled him off . . .
> FOSTER. I suppose it was a blessing.
> ASH. A happy release, yes.
>
> (p. 11)

Other patients also affect a detachment from the nearness of death by making private jokes about dying being "a step in the right direction" (p. 12) and by keeping aloof from each other lest they be bereaved.

Like the patients onstage, the audience comes to this setting with an immunity (or perhaps only a resistance) to the pain of others. When we hear of someone dying after a period of prolonged illness, we, too, make commonplace remarks like, "Death must have come as a blessing." Similarly, when we see an appealing character die in a drama, we eagerly suspend our disbelief and indulge in "a good cry." As sociologists see it:

> The truth of the matter is that it is always one single, solitary individual who dies. But society comforts the bereaved and those who are to die themselves by subsuming each death under general categories that appear to assuage its horror. A man dies, and we say "Well, we all have to go someday." This "we all" is an exact rendition of the *Man*—it is everybody and thus nobody, and by putting ourselves under its generality

we hide from ourselves the inevitable fact that we too
shall die, singly and solitarily.[8]

Nichols's play depicts such common behavior, but it depicts
it in death's domain. The shape of the play finally denies
us the means of emotional escape to which we are accustomed.

In the first two scenes of *The National Health*, as we learn
the jargon of patients caught in a parenthesis of their normal activities, we enter the real waiting room of a typical
hospital, and here, we are beyond platitudes. We are introduced to patients on a threshold of pain; and for us, as
for the patients onstage, easy exits are gradually sealed off.
Our first glimpse of ward life opens us to the sense of
isolation in a crowded lonely place. Here, we observe sociological phenomena of ward life objectively presented.
The hospital ward of *The National Health* is true to Goffman's model of "interpersonal contamination" in an institution: the inmate undergoes mortification of the self from
the moment of his admission; he loses control over who
observes him in his predicament and over who on the staff
knows about his past or his prognosis; he is obliged to follow
obscurely explained orders; and he is placed side-by-side
with other sick men, forced into social contact, and sometimes, he must lie near the dying.[9] We see patients keeping
their distance from each other. Defensive mechanisms
(grumpy, quarrelsome behavior, for example) and superficial camaraderie (group-reinforced complaints about food,
service, and other details of the institution) help the patients
avoid an epidemic of human emotion. They talk freely of
symptoms, side-effects, and staff. Ash lists the categories
of activities in which the patients participate: "And this
endless therapy. Electric therapy, physiotherapy, occupational therapy. Chit-chat with the trick cyclist. Marquetry
and basket making" (p. 18). Watching television is another
common activity. In this way the patients separate themselves from the pangs of each other's homesickness: they
occupy themselves and they restrain from inquiries of a

personal nature. This is the real world into which *The National Health* draws us.

Had Nichols confined his play to the private room of a hospital, or indeed, had he focused on the private life of any one patient assigned to this ward, as, for instance, Kopit does in *Wings*, the experiential effect of *The National Health* would have been severely diminished. By confining his audience immediately to a ward in which patients and staff constantly interact, Nichols restructures our response as spectators. He gives us a mere glimpse into the lives of his characters; our knowledge of them is limited to their current knowledge of each other. Our knowledge of Rees, for example, is gathered from Ash's anecdotal sketch of the aged Welsh doctor for the benefit of the audience surrogate, the new patient: "Eighty-two. Stroke. Left him paralysed on one side. Also his brain seems at times as sound as a bell, another time completely in the grip of some delusion about a taxi. He must know he's never going out of here alive, but he won't give in. Spunky old blighter" (pp. 16–17). Physical suffering grips the human spirit in a vise of self-preservation. In psychological solitary confinement, each man on the ward of *The National Health* is struggling alone to endure. Staff members are also restrained from caring for their charges. They treat maladies, not men; and so they, too, maintain emotional distance. This is professionalism on their part. Staff members, typically engaged with inmates in a "cycle of contact and withdrawal" in a total institution, tend to believe that they can perform their duties more efficiently when uncontaminated by personal feelings.[10] Understandably, then, the hospital ward seems frozen with people wary of caring too deeply for others.

The familiar idiosyncrasies accompanying illness and the typical attitudes of nurses initially strike us as comically though faithfully rendered onstage. Old Dr. Rees immediately stands out as a pathethic victim of the institutional tyranny of the healthy over the weak. He is patronized by nurses who call tranquilizers "sleepy-byes," who collect bottles of urine with chiding reminders that "you're the patient

here, not the doctor," and who cajole him to "lie down like
a good boy" (p. 16). Reduced to verbal infancy, Dr. Rees
finds escape from his altered status by means of an insistent
delusion: when a cheerful nurse summons him to a routine
awakening with "Wakey-wakey . . . rise and shine," he looks
at her sternly, certain that a taxi is on its way to take him
home (p. 11). Other patients, however, cannot seal themselves off from their situation in senile reverie. Foster, a
coronary patient, often puts on his earphones as a means
of retreat. Still, the patients must face the ordeal of de-
humanization in an unknown, intrusive institution where
nurses refer to themselves in the third person, and where
they treat ill men like naughty children in a nursery. Half-
aside to the audience, Nurse Lake confesses, "They all look
the same to me" (p. 13).

The situation of *The National Health*, especially in its demonstration of the anxiety and disorientation experienced
upon hospitalization, is true to its societal model. Hospitalization forces a patient into dependency upon professional strangers. He is subjected to mysterious probings and
embarrassing scrutiny; like the inmate of any total institution, he relinquishes his independence; but in the hospital he must also surrender to the physical demands of his
illness. The hospital patient is no longer self-sufficient, and
so he suffers a crucial loss of self-esteem as well as a total
resignation of his will to authority figures. Impotent in his
nightclothes, the patient becomes a case, chronicled on a
clipboard which dangles from the foot of his bed. In a study
of *Patients Are People: A Medical-Social Approach to Prolonged
Illness*, Minna Field tells us what Nichols shows us in the
accurate opening sequences of his play:

> When a patient enters a hospital, he enters a world
> totally different from the one to which he was accus-
> tomed and he has to learn to live in it, to become part
> of it. The large buildings, the long corridors, the sight
> of unfamiliar machinery, the whiteclad doctors and
> nurses, the presence of so many other sick people, all

35

are unfamiliar, bewildering, and all are frightening. To add to this strange, unfamiliar, and frightening feeling, the patient finds that he is no longer master of his own destiny; he has to give up personal control over even the simplest everyday functions. The time to get up, the time to go to sleep, what he will eat and when, with whom he will associate, whether the windows will be open or closed—these and other minutiae of everyday living are no longer determined altogether by his own likes and dislikes or habits built up in the course of a lifetime. Instead, they are now determined by an outside authority and have to be submitted to without question and without regard for personal preferences.

Also, as Field points out, "Each new procedure is . . . a threat because of the unknown it represents. The patient not only fears the pain and discomfort which may be involved but even more he fears what the procedure is likely to reveal."[11]

Our sense of the ordeal of disorientation and dependency is evoked not only by the impersonal, intrusive compassion dispensed by the nurses on their morning rounds, but also by Nichols's comic relief, which shows beyond a doubt, privacy here is nil. An old woman in a flowered dress and white hat systematically makes her way through the ward onstage. She delivers a card and a sermon to every patient in the ward she canvasses. The old woman's text, delivered with unflinching black comedy to a man in a coma, is a simplistic solution for human suffering: "Good day. I have a message for you. It's that God gave His only begotten Son to save us. Us—that's you and me and everyone. So you need only believe and you'll have everlasting life. God bless you and get well soon" (p. 14). Like the old woman who doggedly prescribes a folk remedy for diverse sufferings at regular intervals throughout the play, the nurses in *The National Health* maintain a single message and mien for every patient in their ward.

Depersonalization and isolation are visually suggested in the freeze-frame quality of *The National Health*'s accurately rendered opening scenes. Again Ash, who will emerge as a choral commentator in the course of the play, calls our attention to the symbolic organization of space in the ward onstage. After the new patient, Loach, has donned the pajamas, slippers, and dressing gown which signify his identity as an inmate, Ash observes: "I find, if they keep you in the end beds, you can prepare to meet your Maker. . . . We all start *off* near the end. Under observation. But we slowly work our way along to the furthest window by the balcony" (p. 17). Even in the initiatory sequences of *The National Health*, then, we are made conscious of the symbolic movement across stage space which will signify a patient's progress.

After two scenes of such routines and introspective allusions, Barnet makes his first entrance. The arrival of the orderly at the start of Act One, Scene Three is greeted with laughter and cheers from the patients. When he first appears onstage, Barnet immediately alters our perception of the performance space. His lively entrance heralds a shift in mode as well as in mood. Pushing a wheelchair, Barnet hurries onstage. He *"ogles the audience"* and directs his *"patter"* towards us (pp. 22–23). His energy is contagious; his flamboyance disarms us. Into the drab institution, he brings the welcome off-color variety of a music hall comic. Barnet's stand-up routine is standard, but his sudden transfusion of this familiar form of entertainment into an institutional routine strikes us with its incongruity. Yet Barnet adroitly maneuvers us into a new realm of response. Addressing us with banter and witty remarks, he disregards the imaginary fourth wall. Indeed, Leonard Frey, the actor who played Barnet in the 1974 New York production (Barnet was originally played by Jim Dale with comic *physical* abandon in the London production), improvised frequent comic asides to the audience.

As both a hospital-employed orderly and a music hall master of ceremonies, Barnet operates between two worlds

of performance. Constantly skipping back and forth between two planes of dramatic action, he is both a methodical
attendant to physical needs and a madcap conductor of
psychic release. In his first capacity, he is called upon to
carry out menial chores and to act in emergency situations.
In his second capacity, he provides an alternate show for
the amusement of patient/players, waiting in the authentically drab ward.

Nichols's choice of Barnet as the functional bridge linking his depiction of institutional reality to his institutional
fantasy makes sense. For an orderly plays a subordinate
role in the hierarchy of the health care institution, and with
this subservience to the rest of the staff comes a certain
behavioral freedom, an institutionally sanctioned capacity
for what Goffman terms "role-distancing." As Goffman notes
in his discussion of "The Function of Role Distance for
Surgery," "Subordinates can exercise much role distance,
and not merely through grumbling. By sacrificing the seriousness of their claim to being treated as fullfledged persons, they can exercise liberties not given to social adults."
Further, some of what Goffman terms "the most appealing
data on role distance" comes from situations in an occupational setting where

> a subordinate must take orders or suggestions and must
> go along with the situation as defined by superordi-
> nates. At such times, we often find that although the
> subordinate is careful not to threaten those who are,
> in a sense, in charge of the situation, he may be just
> as careful to inject some expression to show, for any
> who care to see, that he is not capitulating completely
> to the work arrangement in which he finds himself.
> Sullenness, muttering, irony, joking, and sarcasm may
> all allow one to show that something of oneself lies
> outside the constraints of the moment and outside the
> role within whose jurisdiction the moment occurs.[12]

In this way, Barnet's unorthodox behavior suits his status
in the hospital hierarchy faithfully represented onstage.

The maintenance man in *The National Health* manages to distance himself from his demeaning role by clowning and mugging as he completes distasteful chores.

So Barnet's antics have a bona fide premise; his "double stance" as orderly and disorderly stems from a situational fact of role-distancing in an organized activity system. Goffman explains the "simultaneous multiplicity of selves" operating in a situated activity system:

> The person who mutters, jokes, or responds with sarcasm to what is happening in the situation is nevertheless going along with the prevailing definition of the situation—with whatever bad spirit. The current system of activity tells us what situated roles will be in charge of the situation, but these roles at the same time provide a framework in which role distance can be expressed. . . . Face-to-face interaction provides an admirable context for executing a double stance—the individual's task actions unrebelliously adhere to the official definition of the situation, while gestural activity that can be sustained simultaneously and yet noninterferingly shows that he has not agreed to having all of himself defined by what is officially in progress.[13]

Of course, Barnet's disorderly role also has an important theatrical rationale. Because of his double stance as staff member and ward wit, his lively entrance comes as a welcome relief to the theater audience as well as to the ward residents. Once Nichols has graphically initiated us, he must find a way to help us endure the dull pain of the hospital routine. A play like *Home* can hold our attention with its lyricism, its mystery; a play like *The Brig* can rely on its regimentation and precision of movements to engulf us; and a play like *Chips With Everything* has a strong single narrative line. But a hospital's routine is too close to us and too sluggish to engulf us in a mystery of order and rhythm. Like *Marat/Sade*, *The National Health* needs to go beyond a bleak world onstage to sustain our interest—indeed, to get people to come to the theater. Barnet's clowning serves this function: he juggles his job as orderly with his amateur jesting.

Barnet becomes the pivot about which the grim reality of *The National Health* turns into the romantic fiction of "Nurse Norton's Affair." Around the agile figure of Barnet, Nichols's play comes full circle. Barnet reinvents the hospital following the creaky mechanisms of a pulp romance. To bring comic relief to those whose lives are suspended in the ward, Barnet now takes a paperback hospital novel from the stove, moves to a spotlit area downstage, and begins to narrate the first installment of an escapist saga of love and life saving in a hospital (p. 26). This "camp" version of hospital heroism, a parody of the popular genre, is acted with exaggerated gestures in a specific area of the stage reserved for the TV episodes. In the American production directed by Arvin Brown (first at the Long Wharf Theatre in New Haven and then at the Circle in the Square in New York in 1974), the "camp" quality of the TV scenes was also implemented by Barnet's use of a hand mike to narrate the installments: the actor used the microphone to distort his voice metallically and to affect the mellifluous tones of a soap opera voice-over. Indeed, the transformation of the pulp novel into a television soap opera in the American version was a theatrical improvement.

Every episode of Barnet's parodic serial is watched by the theater audience as well as by the patients. At first, we watch the patients watch the TV, but gradually the pain of patients behind the scenes of the absurd "Nurse Norton's Affair" is overshadowed by its hilarious double. In Act One, Scene Four, Barnet narrates the first installment of "Nurse Norton's Affair." As in other plays in the contemporary mode, when actual movement is limited, the flow of imagination builds. By means of a singular consciousness, a communal fantasy is objectified:

> BARNET. Her bedside alarm gave raucous tongue and Staff Nurse Cleo Norton awoke mid-afternoon suddenly, bewilderingly, and some moments passed

40

before she could realise she was in her room at the nurses' residential hostel.

(STAFF *wakes in the bed and mimes to the narrative.*) Her tousled hair and the rumpled sheets were evidence enough of a fitful sleep. If evidence she needed! She flounced over in bed, flung back the sheets petulantly and swung her lithe coffee-coloured legs round till her feet touched the pretty coconut mat she brought from Jamaica all those years ago. Stretching langorously, she reached for her housecoat and wrapped it demurely around her trim figure. . . . Suddenly nauseated, she flung herself on the bed.

STAFF. What's the matter with you anyway, Cleo Norton?

BARNET. —she demanded of herself, half angrily. But the mad ecstatic leap of her heart had already told her.

STAFF. Neil!

BARNET. In the submarine strangeness of the night ward, young Doctor Neil Boyd's fingers had fleetingly touched hers. And his usually stern features had crumpled into a yearning smile. Their eyes had met and ricochetted away.

STAFF. This won't do.

BARNET. —She chastised herself ruefully.

(p. 26)

In its triviality and overwrought tone, this first installment is characteristic of the entire series. It ends, also typically, with a string of unanswered questions accompanied by swelling music. The creaky mechanisms of the trite plot are set in motion, and the patients are hooked by the fadeout teaser:

LAKE. But listen, Joyce, isn't old Mr. Boyd, the young doctor's bluff father, bitterly opposed to mixed marriages?

SWEET. Crikey, yes! He's a terrible diehard.

41

LAKE. But what a surgeon!

SWEET. And just a tick, Beth! Doesn't Sister McPhee
hail from North of the Border?

LAKE. And wait a minute, Joyce, isn't Dr. Neil unu-
sually respectful to his father?

SWEET. And hang on, Beth, isn't Mr. Boyd an eligible
widower?

LAKE. I wonder—

SWEET. You mean—?

BARNET. They stared at each other wordlessly.

(p. 29)

This, of course, is only the beginning. The torrid love scenes
and suspenseful operating sequences in later episodes of
"Nurse Norton's Affair" further mock idealized versions
of staff members who keep their distance from patients on
the ward.

Nichols's play uses supervisory personnel as minor characters in the outer ward-set (accurately reflecting their in-
frequent visits to real wards), but it features them promi-
nently in "Nurse Norton's Affair." Nurse Norton, the star
of Barnet's serial, for example, is a high ranking staff nurse.
And Sister McPhee, who plays the heroine's foil and ends
happily in a May/December union with old Dr. Boyd in
Barnet's serial, ranks immediately below the Matron in a
hospital hierarchy. It makes perfect sense, of course, that
patients project their daydreams about nurses and doctors
into Barnet's syrupy TV concoction. In fact, just as Barnet's
double stance in *The National Health* makes sense, so, too,
his burlesque soap opera is a logical spinoff of ward speculation about nurses and doctors.

With his story-theater, Barnet fulfills his duties as a pa-
tient-aide, helping patients keep death at a distance. For
on the documentary level of action, the TV is a functional
prop in the ward. To satisfy the emotional needs they share
but do not express, incapacitated, dependent, yet estranged
patients often sublimate individual fears while retreating
into the reassuring realm of TV fantasy. Like any audience

42

at a tear-jerking double feature, Nichols's patients momentarily forget their troubles in front of a picture tube. According to Donald M. Kaplan, theorizing on "The Psychopathology of Television Watching," "the rippling of homogeneous slop" shown on TV meets psychological needs which "have to do with disengagement from structured stimuli, and regression to a prestructured, preconflictual state. Television establishes itself in the nervous system with a bare minimum of active negotiation between the subject and the object." Kaplan also notes that "television could be a godsend to those in whom interpretive activity and the self-awareness it leads to produce anxiety—the experience of the imminence of trauma and personal crisis." In short, TV fare is a seductive panacea; Kaplan warns, however, that "television is regarded as no more noxious to the population than opium and morphine were regarded in the cough syrups of nineteenth-century England"; its "emotional toxicity" is a menace to the public.[14] But in the ward, in measured amounts controlled by Barnet, the optimistic stereotypes projected from the TV screen of *The National Health* have a placebo effect on the patients; their qualms are eased by an occasional dose of dime-store fiction. They succumb to the lure of a life-and-death melodrama enacted by caricatures who indulge in meaningful glances, impassioned pleas, heroic sacrifices, and florid clichés.

Our reaction to the television subplot of *The National Health* is much more complex than is the patients' reaction. Both in England and in the United States, *The National Health* disconcerted critics with its heterodox treatment of the sensitive subject of the British (or modern) health state. Ronald Bryden's critique in *The Observer Review*, for example, characterized *The National Health* as "not a play but an extravaganza: a documentary revue, in the manner of 'Forty Years On,' mocking our attitudes to the healing arts by juxtaposing parody with reality."[15] Though *The National Health* won both the London Theatre Critics and the *Evening Standard* awards as best new play in 1969,[16] still, its parodic treatment of British health care left some critics with a discomforting bad taste. Later, in a review of the film version of *The National Health, Variety*, in its distinctive prose, cautioned posssible distributors: "There is an attempt to counterpoint the naturalism of the scruffy ward with a wacky plot-within-the-plot, namely a parody of one of those television medico mellers ('Nurse Norton's Affair'), which affords several players dual roles and a chance to ham it up. The pastiche produces some jolly moments as it strikingly contrasts the chrome-slick fictive hospital with the grim real article, but by and large the device seems too forced and only proves that video pulp as self-parody is hard to top."[17] *The National Health* evoked a similarly disconcerted response in America. Clive Barnes's response was typical. With well-wishing ambivalence, Barnes raved about the production but ended his review by warning, "This is not a play for the sick or the squeamish, and certainly it is not a play for anyone proposing to enter the hospital. But its cruel hilarity does cleanse, and although Mr. Nichols is, at the end, bleakly pessimistic about the human condition, he somehow contrives to send you out feeling cheerful. Until, perhaps, you think about it."[18]

The value of "Nurse Norton's Affair" has to do with its liberating effect. By underscoring the absurdity of the genre he is ridiculing, Nichols forces us to respond to the real situation of *The National Health* less artificially. We laugh at the ersatz suffering and instant cures mimed in mock seriousness in the trite "Nurse Norton's Affair," and so we are less likely to fall for any tear-jerking properties of *The National Health*. With an innocuous diversion realistically drawn from real life, then, Nichols not only entertains us beyond our expectations, he also elevates his outer play to a plane beyond diversion. Its documentary appeal is intensified for us. And once we can no longer feel get-well-card sentiments in the theatrical presence of death, Nichols cuts to the quick.

Barnet is the playwright's scalpel. The entertaining orderly is thrust upon us in cruel bits of comedy and he is always present also to tend to the hospital realm's death-beds. He is chameleon-like: sometimes he is a music hall comic, other times he is a master of ceremonies in the ritual sense, and still other times he is a deadpan narrator. But he is never a straightman, never a silent orderly following orders. In each of his capacities, Barnet plays to us. He exists outside the authentic framework of *The National Health* and behind the scenes of "Nurse Norton's Affair." Barnet is a theatrical bolt; he is a barker.

As a music hall comic with risqué material, Barnet makes us laugh against our wills, for he embodies the pure energy of play let loose in an authentic-looking hospital which is, nevertheless, still a theatrical pretense. We do not want to laugh, for example, at the preparation of a corpse for the morgue, but Barnet performs this task with incongruous gusto; and his verbal patter turns the graphic discussion of mortuary work into a gruesome magic act:

> No, but seriously. . . . I like to see my apparatus laid out like a tea-service, every instrument in its place. With a nice white cloth. . . . (*whips off cloth, shows articles as he names*): Wash bowl, sponges, nail brush and file. Safety razor, scissors, tweezers. Cotton-wool, carbolic soap. Shroud. . . . So anyway I get the call. Ward such-and-such, bed so-and-so. Screens already up, of course. . . . First you strip the patient down, then you wash him spotless with carbolic. Cut the nails—they can scag the shroud. Shave the face and trim the head. Comb what's left. Well, relatives don't want to find themselves mourning a scruff. Now the cotton-wool. Can anyone tell me what I do with that? (*Reacts to . . . WOMAN in audience.*) You're right, madam, absolutely right. Been making that answer all your life and for the first time it's accurate, not just vulgar.   (p. 40)

Addressing his quips and queries to members of the audience, Barnet instructs us in the techniques of a mortician with the panache of a television chef concocting a soufflé. Later in the play, he jokingly shows us the secrets of pre-operative shaving of patients. During these darkly comic

45

sequences which often break into the somber mood of the level of authentically based action, Barnet's humor is often off-color. His music hall routines make us uneasy, for he is not merely showing us something we would rather not see, but he is also treating taboo subjects with disparaging humor.

Barnet's comic patter takes the subject of his monologue out of the serious context we provide for a deathbed; he takes us behind the scene of a pretty funeral. After he has finished closing "the apertures, the points that might evacuate bodily fluids. . . . Lug-holes, cake-holes, nose-holes, any other holes, all right madam thank you very much indeed!" (p. 41), Barnet reassures us in mock seriousness:

> No, I don't wish to give the wrong impression. I'm sure I speak for my colleagues throughout the business when I say that we show every conceivable respect the deceased is due. We may hate the sight of them when they're living but once they've passed on, they get the full going-over. And I don't know about you, but I find that thought consoling. (p. 41)

But we have just seen Barnet in action. He treats a dead man with comic detachment. His verbal desecration of a cadaver shocks us and releases laughter.

On the level of naturalistic authenticity which is maintained throughout the play, the dead man is now an object to be cleaned and removed; and Barnet is a professional at his trade: he circumvents sentiment with irreverence. In his study of "Role Distance," Goffman notes the necessity for distractions and levity to ease the tension in a taxing situation. In the hospital operating room, for example, the anesthetized patient is often the butt of disrespectful humor. According to Goffman:

> During the operation, the body of the patient is the rightful focus of a great deal of respectful sustained consideration, technically based. . . . It is as if the body were a sacred object, regardless of the socioeconomic

character of its possessor, but in this case the consideration given is rational as well as ritual. As might be expected, then, before and after the operation proper there can be observed minor acts of desacralization, whereby the patient is reduced to more nearly profane status.[19]

Still, though Barnet's "non-person treatment" of a corpse is common and, indeed, proper among hospital staff,[20] Barnet does take his role-distancing rather far. The man who has just died in *The National Health* is the aged Dr. Rees; the audience identified with his struggle for a dignified death. The hospital deprived him of that death, and now, his dead body is a stage property. Nichols brings on his magician, who makes the body disappear in a cruel act of everyday magic.

Throughout *The National Health*, Barnet plays tricks with death. By alternating scenes of slow, quiet, real death with fantasy sequences of death-defying stunts set in a *"brilliantly lit"* operating theater (p. 80), Nichols creates a tragic-comic counterpoint to express the theme of his play in formal terms. In Act Two, Scene Two, for example, Mr. Mackie, a seventy-year-old man suffering from stomach cancer, is summarily removed to the terminal ward. Earlier he expressed his death wish, the idea he comes to stand for in this play where each patient is a type, where each is given a particular axe to grind:

> I drift off and nearly sleep and one of these happy days I shan't come back. . . . But someone's always calling me back for a cup of tea or . . . bottle . . . an overdose of the right drug is what I want. . . . I'm too busy coping with the pain . . . they wouldn't kill a pig like this . . . I've no regard for life itself, only the quality of life . . . should be clinics where you could get your death as you get a library book—   (p. 71)

In the next scene, Mr. Mackie's newly vacant bed is regarded triumphantly by the Matron who periodically ploughs

47

through the ward with brusque efficiency, trailed by other staff members in a hierarchical parade. Her inspection of the ward is our ritualistic guide to the power structure and to its echo chamber of commands. The Matron announces that as the beds fall vacant, they are being removed: "The whole ward block is in for a very extensive face-lift. Which I am sure you will agree is long overdue" (p. 79). Theatrically, the effect of this master plan is devastating. By the end of the play, the stage is practically bare, a deserted and almost abandoned space.

Mackie's death is, of course, announced by Barnet. Barnet calls for a spotlight and he delivers his news to us. In graphic, journalistic, almost unbearable detail, he discribes for us what went on behind the screens:

> At the end, Mr.Mackie's heart stopped three times and three times they brought him back. They were fetching the artificial respirator when it stopped again and some daring soul decided to call it a day. . . . I'm sure I speak for all those who knew him in life when I say that he will be remembered as an evil-tempered, physically repulsive old man. The distended lips, the purple ears, those malevolent eyes glaring up at you from the engorged face. But—now the pump's been allowed to pack up, the flesh has receded, that puffiness gone, an altogether younger face has appeared. You can see how—once—someone might even have fancied him. (p. 80)

In the audience, we recall Mr. Mackie's constant pain and his convictions on the question of euthanasia. At the end of Act One, he, like the declining Dr. Rees, bitterly pleaded his case, and his argument expanded a health care facility into a rambling philosophical conceit of a "spiritual cancer" (p. 62):

> This state we're in. This ward. Where men are prevented from death by poverty or curable sickness even the least intelligent . . . least healthy or useful . . . Can't

cure loneliness—boredom—ugliness . . . but at least you can see they're lonely on clean sheets. . . . I'm dying of a stomach cancer and the pain's only bearable with pethedine and morphine. I've asked them to let me die . . . but because of their outdated moral assumptions they have to keep me going. . . . Good *death's* precious too, when the time comes. If you can get it. My heart's stopped once already, which used to be called death . . . now they bring you back . . . I've had it written in my records: don't bring me back again.   (p. 59)

But hearing the details of his dying, we learn that he was brought back again and again and again. Mackie's wish was denied by a dedicated medical team in "this state we're in. This ward."

Throughout *The National Health* such allusions to the ward as a metaphor for "this state we're in" abound. After each such allusion, we are transported back to the eventful, escapist world of "Nurse Norton's Affair." As the head doctor disappears down the corridor at the end of Act One, Scene Eight, for example, Foster, the doomed coronary patient, diagnoses the need of his wardmates. "You . . . need cheering up," he says, "taking out of yourselves. Soon be TV time" (p. 48). TV time, in contrast to real time represented onstage, moves at a rapid pace. In slick soap-operatic sequences, racial prejudice is conquered and a kidney transplant is performed, both with Hollywoodian dexterity. Young Dr. Neil Boyd, mysteriously collapsing and contorting his body in the agonized throes of some stage-worthy illness, is saved by his father's surgical skill in transplanting the kidney donated by Neil's noble West Indian lover. All ends happily in this distortion of romantic love and of hospital procedures.

On the ward, however, all does not end happily. In Act Two, Scene Five, Nichols harshly illuminates the difference between scenes of "real" and fantasized suffering. Simultaneously, we witness two lifesaving attempts: the "real" one fails graphically; in the fantasy, there is a heroic success.

On the ward of *The National Health,* Mr. Foster has suffered a cardiac arrest unnoticed. His critical condition is discovered by the Chaplain, a congenial stereotypical clergyman who pauses at Foster's bedside to deliver a brief pep talk. As the Nurse is called over, Foster falls. He is still wearing his headphones, and he is still clutching the calling card which was thrust between his lifeless hands by the reappearing old woman (who persistently delivers her message even to patients who seem to be sleeping). The patient keels over, and the message of salvation drops from his hands.

Throughout this scene, nurses, medical students, and orderlies try to resuscitate Mr. Foster. First, Nurse Sweet attempts mouth-to-mouth ventilation; then, an Indian student hurries on pushing a Cardiac Arrest Trolley. Together, nurses and the medical student lower Foster onto the floor to facilitate external cardiac compression. The young Dr. Bird, whose tendency to doze off while on extended duty provided a source of comic relief earlier (pp. 45–46), now arrives fatigued again, complaining that she was "just off home for an hour's sleep" (p. 92). But now her ward weariness is not funny. Dr. Bird tells the nurse to administer oxygen, but the nurse searches the trolley to no avail: the spanner for the oxygen cylinder has been misplaced. As the nurse goes off to find one, another orderly arrives; he brings a defibrillator on a trolley. Screens are put up around Foster's bed, but through the screens we see the outlines of clumsy movements. At one point, a screen is accidentally knocked over, exposing Foster's body to the other patients. Finally, the equipment is removed and the staff leave. There is a *"noticeable lack of urgency about these movements"* (p. 94). Mr. Foster is dead.

Meanwhile, a more spectacular operation is in progress. To distract the other patients from the awkward struggle under way for Foster's life, Barnet tells them to "Watch the telly then!" (p. 91). He tries to hide Foster's last medical rites from the other patients by blocking their view with screens and by diverting their attention with a reassuring screen image of hospital heroics. Along with the theater audience, the ward patients "try to concentrate on the Kidney Transplant" performed downstage in a parody of modern medical mythology (p. 92). According to the stage directions, Dr.Boyd and Sister McPhee make a grand entrance into the operating theater of "Nurse Norton's Affair":

> *Their movements are ritualistic but played too much to the gods.*
>
> Boyd *approaches* Cleo's *table, looks at* Anaesthetist, *who nods decisively.* Boyd *turns to* McPhee, *holds out hand for first instrument. The other members of the team close in and hide the operation from view at the very moment when it promises to be interesting.* (p. 91)

The operating theater of "Nurse Norton's Affair" sparkles; the storybook operation (two lovers united by a kidney transplant) is accompanied by the Romeo and Juliet Overture (p. 91). Still, from behind the screens hastily set up around Foster's bed, unadorned dialogue,"*very quiet and natural*" (p. 92), cannot be blocked out. Though we are engaged by the romantic medical climax of "Nurse Norton's Affair," we can still overhear a more natural discussion of death being carried out by shadowy figures behind the screens. Our attention is drawn back to the enclosed area of turmoil around Mr. Foster's bed. The frantic struggle continues, though it is upstaged by its fantastic double.

Barnet crosses back and forth between the two generically opposed scenes, keeping us posted on the progress in each. Moving downstage, he adopts the confidential tone of his soap opera persona. In Barnet's description of Sister McPhee's ecstasy, Nichols carries our society's attitude of reverence for the god-head surgeon to its absurd extreme. As a kidney is lifted in a sterile bag during the transplantation, for example, "above the mask, her eyes met those of the man who, in a rare moment of candour, had freely admitted that he was not God" (p. 93). Meanwhile, back on the ward, as Barnet reports frankly during Foster's death, "All going well as can be expected but not so nice for the other patients. Which is where the telly is a great step forward. Keep their minds off what's going on next door" (pp. 93–94).

Tension mounts in—and between—the two parallel scenes. The kidney transplant ends to the sound of triumphant music, and in ecstasy, the master surgeon and his nurse dance offstage. These partners in *"a pirouette"* have performed successful movieland surgery (pp. 93–94). The distressed student doctors, nurses, and orderlies (all subordinates in the hierarchy) at Foster's bed, on the other hand, have acted out in horrible detail the lonely death of a ward patient. In this double feature, Nichols goes to great lengths to depict medical procedures accurately in the ward sequences. Indeed, the ward sequences of the play are grueling in their length and specificity, leading Walter Kerr to complain of *The National Health* as "an essentially static venture" because there are "only terminal statistics to be recorded."[21] Conversely, "Nurse Norton's Affair" goes to the opposite extreme in its exaggeration and satiric distortion of medical procedures in the operating theater. Indeed, his simplification and sentimentalization of a kidney transplant operation is pointedly inaccurate. And for good reason. After all, all the medical allusions made in the outer play, *The National Health*, clearly have been carefully researched to reflect real medical diagnoses. For the sake of his parody of an operating room romance, Nichols distorts the real risks and ignores medical norms concerning potential donors. That is one of the jokes here.[22] Side by side, then, Nichols presents the facts and a farce of hospital life, and these two autonomous plays merge in a single encompassing setting.

The medical regimen of "Get up, lay down, drink this, swallow that . . . the well-nigh inexplicable rituals of our confinement, friend" (p. 84) ends despondently in an almost empty ward. Deserted by life and by death, Mr. Ash alone remains to reminisce with Ken, a young man now reduced to idiocy by his last motorcycle collision. The two chronic cases are left alone, awaiting transfer out of an outmoded ward. The symbolic nature of the stage space is heightened in this final scene of isolation and despair. The cycle suggested by the endless insistence upon schedules throughout the play is now completed: the play began with Ken's energetic leave taking; it ends upon his involuntary return. With Ken's return, the symbolic nature of stage time is also heightened at the end.

Like the protagonist of Nichols's *Joe Egg*, Ash is a schoolteacher. Understandably, his last lecture, addressed to an idiot, is a lament. Like the lonely men left in David Storey's *Home*, Ash delivers a dirge on the loss of time and of place, on the decline of the British empire and on the deterioration of the English language:

> Simple dignity. Which is what is missing from so much of life today. Grace. Style. We're all the same, we need something fine to which to aspire. We want to rise, not sink in the bog. . . . My hat, the old Queen! She'd come inspecting. We'd spit-and-polish everywhere. . . . D'you know, son, we speak the most beautiful language in the world? That's our heritage. The tongue that Shakespeare spake. Yet most of the people you meet can utter nothing better than a stream of filth.   (pp. 107–108)

In this bleak microcosm of the world as it is, Ash mourns the fragile state of the national health. His monologue in this last entropic movement of the outer play is an ironic commentary on the double entendre of Nichols's title. *The National Health* is both the British hospital system and an irremediable state of being. There is ultimately no help for pain.

Our final glimpse of the disintegration of a way of life and a state of mind is abruptly interrupted by the last scene of "Nurse Norton's Affair." To the sound of a wedding march and the waving of Union Jacks, Dr. Boyd and his quickly cured son (both wearing kilts) marry their respective nurses. Barnet, now an "*acolyte*" in minstrel "*black-face*," sings an epilogue while the entire company, "*quick and dead*," dances a cakewalk and takes bows. With this brutal irony in a tasteless extravaganza, with a minstrel show marriage, Barnet reconciles the two worlds we entered in Nichols's play: "It's a funny old world we live in and you're lucky to get out of it alive," he tells us (pp. 108–109). And so we are. For this "funny old world" of a hospital ward encloses us in a microcosmic model of a medical endgame. And the "funny old world" of "Nurse Norton's Affair" satirically reminds us that building such models is finally just a game itself. Nichols's play vividly illustrates the final irony characteristic of a play of impasse, the bracing realization that endgame models promise no easy ways out of the maze; players may go on indefinitely.

Suddenly, all action onstage ceases. The music and the dancing stop; the patients freeze in their attitudes; the play ends with a silent tableau. And now Barnet sings his last stanza:

> As for the rest there's not a lot to say,
> They're born, they live and then get wheeled away,
> The lucky ones,
> Don't ask me what it means,
> See you again one day behind the screens.[23]

This last music hall turn is appropriately macabre. For the funny man in blackface aims his final warning at us; he includes us among his charges in the "funny old world" onstage. It is a grim, sick joke. Some of us laugh.

The Happy Haven

Like Peter Nichols's *The National Health*, John Arden's *The Happy Haven* catapults us into a disruptive farce. Both plays expose us to a factual routine, the redundant order of which is ritualistic; both plays render health care institutions absurd, giving us a bleak glimpse of our own mortality; and both plays make metaphorical statements about contemporary society. Going further than *The National Health* in its self-conscious theatricalism, Arden's *The Happy Haven* suggests the use of masks, microphones, and slide projectors.

Set in a nursing home, a shelter for the elderly infirm, *The Happy Haven* celebrates in song and pantomime an insurrection in a make-believe institution. The fantastic premise of the play (a doctor's discovery of a youth elixir), the absurd action of the play (a conspiracy among the aged inmates to reclaim control of their lives), and the preposterous denouement of the play (a revengeful dose to their doctor of his own elixir, which reduces him to helpless childhood) are all fairy-tale phenomena. Yet they are made plausible for an adult audience by Arden's powerful characterizations of complementary players in a pervasive "Hospital atmosphere."[24] Here is the difference, then, between Nichols's split-level pessimism and Arden's vision of a world gone mad: whereas truth and lies coexist on the divided stage of *The National Health*, they converge in the mythic space of *The Happy Haven*.

Other contemporary playwrights have also sought to humanize the stereotyped aged onstage. Edward Albee's *The Sandbox*, for example, objectifies the modern tendency to reduce the aged to infancy. This one-act play, written one year before Arden's *The Happy Haven*, simply suggests the *King Lear* syndrome by means of a family configuration on the beach. Mommy and Daddy dump Grandma into a sandbox and then they desert her. Grandma, the only sympathetic member of the family, speaks to her relatives in a voice which is "*a cross between a baby's laugh and cry*," articulating sounds such as "Ahhhhhh! Graaaaa!" To the audience, however, Grandma confides, "Honestly! What a way to treat an old woman! Drag her out of the house . . . stick her in a car . . . bring her out here from the city . . . dump her in a pile of sand . . . and leave her here to set. I'm eighty-six years old!" Albee further develops this theme of the dispossession of the aged in *The American Dream*. Here, Mommy and Daddy discuss having Grandma "put away in a nursing home," while Grandma packs up her

55

boxes and awaits the arrival of the van man. Describing her old age, Grandma says:

> My sacks are empty, the fluid in my eyeballs is all caked on the inside edges, my spine is made of sugar candy, I breathe ice; but you don't hear me complain. Nobody hears old people complain because people think that's all old people do. And *that's* because old people are gnarled and sagged and twisted into the shape of a complaint.

And when asked by the Young Man in *The American Dream*, "Are you old enough to understand?" Grandma replies, "I think so, child; I think I'm nearly old enough."[25] This idea of being "old enough" is also dramatized in such recent plays as D. L. Coburn's *The Gin Game* (1977), John Ford Noonan's *Older People* (1973), Mandel and Sach's musical set in the main room of the Golden Years retirement hotel, *My Old Friends* (1978), and in the vividly evoked nursing-home room setting of Megan Terry's *The Gloaming, Oh My Darling*. Terry writes, "The backbone of the play is the embrace of life, no matter how little of it is left." In her play, two old women "lapse into their oldest age" while they wait together for death. Terry's aged roommates act in a stylized manner; at one point, they chant in a singsong way, "And we're so much older. Nobody would dare to be as old or older. And we're so much older."[26]

What makes Arden's treatment of the old-age home outstanding is his sustained vision of the institution as metaphor, as a Structure which can steal the scene from *any* character, no matter how old, infirm, clever, or charming. From the outset of his play, the title and the theatrical means of masks, pantomime, and direct address combine to sharpen our focus not on old people and their real plight, but on this "almost self-supporting" Structure situated, according to its superintendent, in "pleasant rural surroundings" (p. 195).

The encompassing atmosphere of Arden's play derives from its theatrical setting and form. *The Happy Haven* is prefaced by the "Author's Note" on his intention to create a "formalized presentation" which involves a complex use of masks, an invisible dog (which is not a "delusion"), and a stylized hospital setting, "not too clinical and rectilinear." And here, the playwright also expresses his preference for "the original production at Bristol University, when the play was presented on an open stage, following roughly the Elizabethan model" (p. 193). Arden used the open stage with a small upper platform to suggest a "not localized" hospital space (p. 193) in the Bristol production. As he explained in an interview first published in *Encore* in 1961:

> If you write a play for the open stage, it is by no means a foregone conclusion that it is going to have anything like the same effect when done in a conventional theatre. The scene where the dog grows back in to a puppy worked much better on the open stage—it seemed to belong organically to the play. At Bristol there was no set in the accepted sense of the word—the stage background was built to follow the architecture of the studio theatre anyway. We had a sort of back wall with doors, but the colour scheme followed straight through from that of the auditorium, so that to somebody who didn't know the building at all, you couldn't see where the stage set left off, and where the theatre began. There are a number of purely technical devices, which I introduced simply to see if they would work on the open stage. There are certain "experiments" in this sense: they don't affect the story or plot in any way. The dog is one. Another is—a thing which didn't quite work in London—the doctor's lectures. In Bristol these were very funny because he was in what was practically a lecture-theatre anyway. On the Court stage [in the later London production directed by William Gaskill] they were too withdrawn from the audience and therefore rather tiresome.[27]

In its original concept and form, then, *The Happy Haven* uses spatial continuity to envelop its audience in an absurd distortion of a total institution established, according to Doctor Copperthwaite (Superintendent of the Happy Haven), "for the amelioration of the lot of the aged" (p. 195). Masks, songs, direct addresses to the audience, and moral dialectics are thrust out towards the entire theater in Arden's expansive staging of a grotesque endgame.

THE PLAY BEGINS with a device used by many other plays in this contemporary mode. At the very start of *The Happy Haven* the conventional fourth wall is ignored. According to the opening stage directions, "DOCTOR COPPERTHWAITE *enters on upper stage and addresses the audience directly*" (p. 195). In his opening remarks, the doctor looks down on us and cordially welcomes us to the Happy Haven:

> Ah-hum. Good evening, ladies and gentlemen. First, let me say how glad I am to see you here. . . . We are, as you know, as yet only a small institution and our grant from the revenues of the National Health Service is alas not as generous as it might be—but, well, I dare say you'll know the old proverb—Time mends all. (p. 195)

Having introduced himself haltingly both as a master of ceremonies and as the director of a social service, Doctor Copperthwaite leads us on a guided tour through his establishment. Treating spectators at a theater as if we were influential visitors at an old age home, Arden's enterprising doctor instantly casts us in his encompassing play. First, we listen to the Superintendent's salespitch being delivered from the upper platform, and then we watch an elaborate performance being put on for our benefit by a select group of patients.

A birthday party in honor of the now ninety-year-old Mrs. Phineus has been scheduled to coincide with our visit. Looking down at his small group of what Goffman would term "pet inmates," the doctor narrates for us the institutional display in which they participate. This "open house" display of "pet inmates" is characteristic of real total insti-

tutions. According to Goffman, "Institutional display may
... be directed to visitors in general, giving them an 'appropriate' image of the establishment—this image being calculated to allay their vague dread. . . . In the guise of being shown all, the visitors are of course likely to be shown only the more prepossessing, cooperative inmates and the more prepossessing parts of the establishment."[28] As the Happy Haven display goes on for us visitors, every movement of the celebrants is pointed out by the proud doctor:

> Well, she's going to cut the cake and they'll congratulate her. She's our oldest, Mrs Phineus her name is, and she's been a widow for twenty years. (*Enter* NURSE BROWN *with cake. She carries it to Mrs Phineus, and puts the knife into her hand.*) Now here's the cake, and here's the knife to cut it: and Mrs Phineus is just about to cut it; and she's *cut* it! (p. 196)

The doctor's rousing narration of the party in progress before us seems more suited to the broadcast of a sports event. By no means does the pantomimed party warrant such play-by-play enthusiasm.

Under the doctor's condescending direction, the patients are on their best behavior when the play opens. Performing like well-behaved playmates in his presence, these five unintentional "specimens" for Doctor Copperthwaite's research project are quite capable of putting on company manners. And we, of course, are the company. As in *The National Health*, in the performance of *The Happy Haven*, institutional personnel acknowledge our presence, recognizing us as an audience at a social function. But unlike the disabled patients on Nichols's ward who are *not* aware of the audience, the geriatric inmates of Arden's home *are* also conscious of our presence. They, too, occasionally address us directly. And unlike Nichols, who uses a double plot to link theatricalized life to pretty fiction, Arden uses a single plot to fill in that gap. *The Happy Haven* integrates genuine details of hospital routine and patient/staff interactions into the framework of a science fiction parable. So while *The National Health* alternates between pathos and parody, *The Happy Haven* is consistently farcical in its treatment of an ironic state of being.

Even the title of Arden's play is patently ironic. If it does not take us long to register the doubleness in the title of *The National Health*, the title of *The Happy Haven* takes us no time at all. At the very outset of the play, we recognize a euphemism when we hear one. After all, in the world of real nursing homes, as one sociologist notes, "Particularly from the point of view of their residents, a name with more attractive connotations may seem preferable" to the term "nursing home."[29] Doctor Copperthwaite's catch phrases such as "Time mends all" and old people in "the evening of their lives" (p. 195) are also immediately recognizable as facile clichés for the real state of the aged. At the other equally unpleasant extreme, of course, is the textbook terminology concerning the physical decline of the aged who need nursing home care, "The predominant patient disability relates to cerebral arteriosclerosis with organic brain syndrome of varying degrees and other organ involvement and vascular disease as the basis, as in heart, kidney, and peripheral arterial disease. Typical of the geriatric patient is the concurrent involvement of multiple organ systems such as chronic pulmonary edema, arthropathies, urologic disease, and neoplasms of various organs."[30] This physical state is what Doctor Copperthwaite means when he rhapsodizes hypocritically about the "evening of life," an age he secretly hopes to end. So his patronizing baby talk grates, yet it is not much of an exaggeration of what happens in real nursing homes. His voice-over commentary on a displaced birthday party reflects the tendency—especially pronounced in an institutional setting—to mistake physical degeneration for mental regression and to treat old people like withered, misshapen, aging children. Reduced to undignified infancy and goaded into premature senility, the residents of Arden's societal model are the weary victims of their own physical tenacity.

The dehumanizing nature of Doctor Copperthwaite's research is made clear in the first scene. After he lets us peek in at the birthday party, he refers to a sheaf of notes: "While they're all enjoying themselves, it would perhaps be apropriate if I were to give a brief resumé of their names, ages, and case histories" (p. 196). His tone now shifts from paternal bemusement to pragmatic concern. Suddenly, the Superintendent of the Happy Haven sounds like a foreman in a factory. He speaks in the colloquialisms of mechanical double talk as he displays the "specimens" he has assembled before us:

> We'll start with Mrs Phineus. . . . Some obstruction recorded in the condensers, sandbox apertures require occasional overhaul. . . . Now then: number two. On Mrs Phineus's right we have Mr Golightly. . . . Fitted six years ago with improved Walschaerts valve-gear replacing original Stephenson's link motion, and injectors also recently renewed. Latent procreative impulses require damping down on the firebox, but less so then formerly. Next one, number three . . . Mrs Letouzel. Aged seventy, all moving parts in good condition . . . occasional trouble from over-heated bearings when financial gain is in question. . . . Now next to her we have Mr Hardrader, number four, our best running specimen. . . . Finally, on the extreme left, you will see Mr Crape. There has been here an unfortunate case history of overall deterioration, but last year was given a complete refit, including elongated smokebox, revised cylinder-head design, and replacement of obsolete perforated splashers. (pp. 196–197)

The contemporary technical idiom is being used here the way Pinter uses absurd and scary factory language in such plays as *Trouble in the Works* (1959), *The Caretaker* (1960), and *The Tea Party* (1965). In *The National Health*, too, Barnet talks this way whenever death seems near. Doctor Copperthwaite, with his master plan on his mind now, methodically moves along an assembled lineup of aged patients. As his mechanical commentary clearly indicates, he sees these subjects as over the hill.

Doctor Copperthwaite's funny description of his patients as if they were antiquated steam locomotives is also chilling, because an immediate theatrical tension—an eeriness of time and place, an askew reality—has been established upon the first appearance of the old people. For while they act their age, they are all wearing what the playwright terms "character masks of the *commedia dell'arte* type, covering the upper part of their faces only" (p. 193). Of course, the old people's masks serve a practical purpose: Arden's old people are stylized and disfigured by means of masks, so the age of the actor playing the role is inconsequential. Arden has clarified his use of masks here from the pragmatic angle:

> When I began to work on *The Happy Haven*, I found it was developing into a grotesque comedy about an old folks' home—the original idea was for a much more naturalistic play, which would have employed actors about the right age for the characters—and then when the theme seemed to be demanding more stylized treatment, it seemed a good idea to use masks on young actors and actresses. You can't have actors, like, say, Edith Evans and Sybil Thorndike in that sort of play, because they are too near the real age, and it becomes cruel in the wrong sense. And also, on a purely technical level, the older the actors the slower they go. If you are writing a comedy, this imposes problems.[31]

Most significantly, like the open stage, the masks are at once a theatrical projection of a social institution and an objectification of an internal state. To project a social institution, the masks distort human features, signifying in a stylized manner the dehumanized state forced upon the aged in our society. Projecting an inner state, the masks objectify the struggle between the mask and the self, organically integrating this theme into the action of the play.

Of all the characters onstage, only the doctor is without

a mask. Ironically, though, thanks to the absurd jargon he spouts, Doctor Copperthwaite emerges (except when alone with the joy of his experiment, and when he becomes his own victim) as the closest to a grotesque in this play. An exaggerated cross between an administrator and a science-fiction mad scientist, he is mainly interested in the charts and checkups of his patients. He never stops to consider the possibility that they might not *want* to chance rejuvenation. Later in the play, he again examines each specimen with mechanized efficiency. "How are you generally, I mean, walking, talking, reading the papers? Waterworks?" he asks each in turn (p. 242). The clinical single-mindedness of the doctor is also demonstrated in his attitude toward the audience: he sees the spectators as potential supporters of his experiment, so he favors us with a clinical rundown of his raw materials.

Paradoxically, those five patients on whom the doctor has designs—though they consistently wear masks—are individualized even in Copperthwaite's opening remarks. The dialectic of the play, objectified in the conflict between the doctor's false face and the patients' credible masks, is suggested even in the opening scene. When he eavesdrops on (or later examines) his patients, the doctor sees only one facet of characters who have learned to conceal complex emotions in public, but who belie their masks in private. In that first scene, for example, we see evidence that the patients are more agile as well as more lifelike than they seem under their doctor's scrutiny. For when Doctor Copperthwaite turns his attention away from the party he has staged, and he begins to list for us the qualifications of each candidate for rejuvenation, the old people's party grows noticeably more lively. Overhearing the ribald refrain of a song they now sing in unison, the doctor decides it is past their bedtime. "Off to bed, boys and girls, you're half an hour late as it is, burning the candle at both ends, y'know," he serenades them (p. 197). Sent off to bed like naughty children, the old people are underestimated by their cajoling and plotting caretaker.

Once they discover his secret plan, Doctor Copper-thwaite's declining patients prove to be formidable opponents in a game of ideas. Behind their masks are human faces, and the thesis upon which this farce is premised eventually surfaces. As Mrs. Letouzel tells Mr. Crape in a lively discussion: "Here we are, look at us, dried up in this Institution, the only things we know how to do are the worst things we ever learned—plotting and planning, avarice and spite" (p. 220). Later, Mrs. Letouzel again expresses her divided self behind the complacent mask as she addresses her companions in an angry outburst: "Here we are, worms. Old ones. We don't want to die, but we none of us dare state that we want any more life. Let's look around us! Now then, who cares? . . . Nobody, not even the Doctor" (p. 254). In this manner, then, Arden organizes our response to his institutional players: stereotypes of senility are presented to us on absurd premises, and these stereotypes, like the proverbial worm to which Mrs. Letouzel refers, are finally, emphatically overturned.

Instrumental in their final coup is the patients' quite believable proficiency in games of strategy. Left to their own devices, these old people engage in typical intrigues, flirtations, and sophisticated games of self-exposure. Mrs. Letouzel often produces questionable documents for Mrs. Phineus to sign, and in the second scene of the play, she sings to the audience of her villainy (pp. 205–206). In the third scene, Mr. Golightly tells us of his "yearning heart" and rehearses his confession of love for Mrs. Phineus (p. 207). The predominant pastime here, however, is simpler game playing. Many of the mundane recreational activities available to nursing home inhabitants are incorporated into the framework of *The Happy Haven*. Arden's patients play darts, dominoes, and spillikins in the restful spot where they wait to die (p. 207). At one point, Mrs. Phineus initiates a spirited game of hopscotch governed by fluid rules which insure her own victory. Allowing herself extra "rests" and unabashedly putting the gold cigarette-case marker on the final square, she ecstatically declares herself the winner:

"*Home! I* won. *I* won. *I* won. *I* won. Yes. *I* won. *I* won. *I* won. Yes. *I* won. *I* won. *I* won. Yes. *I* won. *I* won. *I* won" (p. 212). So despite the mask which fixes her role in this farce of ideas, Mrs. Phineus is also a lifelike character, capable of rejoicing over her power to alter the rules of a game.

The lethal game of truth, introduced to us by Mrs. Letouzel, is played to the finish in Arden's theatrical vision of an institution. In the mild rhythms of a nursery rhyme, the patients occasionally call time-out from role playing with a codified refrain:

Let's play the Truth game—we're old enough, aren't we?

> Truth or Lie, till the day I die
> Strike you dead if you tell me a lie.
> (p. 208)

Playing according to the rules of this most treacherous game devised by her fellow patients, Mrs. Phineus metaphorically removes her mask in the second act. Mr. Crape has asked her why she does not want "to have to die" (p. 250). Her response is candid, unflinching:

> I'm an old old lady
> And I don't have long to live.
> I am only strong enough to take
> Not to give. No time left to give.
> I want to drink, I want to eat,
> I want my shoes taken off my feet.
> I want to talk but not to walk
> Because if I walk, I have to know
> Where it is I want to go.
> I want to sleep but not to dream
> I want to play and win every game
> To live with love but not to love
> The world to move but me not move
> I want I want for ever and ever.
> The world to work, the world to be clever.

Leave me be, but don't leave me alone.
That's what I want. I'm a big round stone
Sitting in the middle of a thunderstorm.
(pp. 250–251)

An unsentimental old woman, selfish by necessity, Mrs. Phineus is well aware of the inferior position into which old age and dependency have thrust her. As she articulates her mode of endurance in a state of impasse, her poetic monologue resonates. It is a movingly direct personal confession, metrically stylized; and it expresses in simple terms a universal yearning for a yoking of opposites within the self. Mrs. Phineus longs simultaneously for stasis and for the semblance of movement. Her monologue affords us a poetically heightened awareness of the self behind the artificial mask.

In this farcical play of ideas, the dramatic elements of plot, character, speech, and setting are *all* stylized. Still, throughout *The Happy Haven* as in Mrs. Phineus's monologue, Arden forces us to see the face behind the mask, to grapple with the actuality beneath exaggerated gestures, to think about the individualized characters who embody conflicting ideas about the energies of youth and age. We become conscious of the play as a metaphor for the paradox of progress not only in society, but also in the self.

Our double vision of the patient/staff farce of social *and* psychic progress is achieved by means of characters' misunderstandings, imitations, and pantomimes. Watching such behavior, we get the joke, but we also get a powerful sense of each group's fear of the other. Among the old people, Mrs. Letouzel, for example, satirically dubs Doctor Copperthwaite "our Lord, Priest, and Superintendent, great Guardian of the Mysteries—" and she continues her ironic nicknaming in a song:

Take off your hats, bow down:
The High King wears the crown,
He lays out his land with a long directing hand
And the measurements all written down.
(pp. 254–255)

Earlier in the play, the patients ridicule Doctor Copperthwaite's professional dialect: "Bah wah wah wah-wah, Nurse Brown, Nurse Jones, swabs, basins, towels, liniment, ointment—" (p. 216). The patients' expressed fear and resentment of this "undisputed custodian of everything that's good for us," warranted or not, is common among individuals who must adjust to the unfamiliar setting of an old-age home. In fact, according to sociologists, "There is every reason to feel insecure and frightened as we face the final stage of life, recognizing that . . . from this point on our daily lives will be controlled by others." Surrendering his life to strangers, the older person "does not know to what extent he can trust these others to know his wants. He is not even sure that they care what happens to him."[32] Indeed, throughout the play, Arden's older people react, as might their real-life counterparts, with wariness to the man in charge of their well-being. Playing their real-life parts, the patients see only the "role sector"[33] which relates to them.

Now, the inmates of *The Happy Haven* have good reason to be suspicious. But Doctor Copperthwaite, too, is much more complex than his opponents suspect. His machinations are part of an absurd quest. Like the patients, even the zealous Superintendent shows us his true colors, and like the patients, he, too, embodies both truth and lies, following his own rules to win prestige and personal gratification. His villainy may, in fact, be seen as humane research gone haywire, beyond ethics in a burst of hubris. For Doctor Copperthwaite, the egocentric scientist of the Happy Haven, is also a psychologically realized character: he plays football poorly on weekends (p. 225), he is coaxed by his mother to meet marriageable girls (pp. 234–235), and he is appealingly enthusiastic about his experiment. When he tests his elixir on Mr. Hardrader's invisible (but real) dog in his lab in Act Three, Scene Two, for example, Doctor Copperthwaite's unrestrained joy is contagious. Excited at the prospect of completing his experiment, the young doctor indulges in some playful hocus-pocus. "Ladies and gentlemen," he announces, "Twenty-four hours

. . . and hey presto, open sesame, abracadabra—I'll tell you confidentially, it is going to turn green" (p. 258). Later, as he awaits the magical change of color, he gazes at his retort and he cheers it on with the chorus of a popular song (p. 260). And finally, having turned a dog into a tiny puppy, Copperthwaite congratulates himself ("*Yes!* It's worked! It *really* has worked! Oh my God, I'm a famous man," he exclaims in a funny instance of dramatic prolepsis), he cuddles and coos over his rejuvenated pet, and he expresses sympathy for "poor Mr. Hardrader," the old man whose dog he usurped for transformation (p. 262). In this scene of discovery, the doctor, who elsewhere in the play comes closest to being a grotesque if callow villain, comes across for a moment as three-dimensional. The momentary appeal of the doctor here is also helped by his bare face. Remember, until his transformation occurs, Doctor Copperthwaite does not wear a mask. This self-proclaimed "Doctor Faustus of the present generation" (p. 198) succumbs to feelings of pride and power in his scientific feat. Alone in his lab, his presumptuous outbursts are barefaced expressions of a self-satisfied researcher.

With this glimpse of the human side of him in mind, we can see that the doctor's detachment from his "specimens" for experimentation is an exaggerated attitude, but it is also rooted in reality, where patients can seem nameless to researchers and one-dimensional to doctors. So this stereotyping of the other works both ways in *The Happy Haven*: just as Doctor Copperthwaite dehumanizes his patients, so, too, the old people envision their doctor as a satanic figurehead, devoid of human qualities. The two factions of *The Happy Haven* miss what we in the audience find out: they stay oblivious to each other's dreams.

Finally, then, Arden's parable on the perils of scientific research is ambivalent. The conflict ultimately emerges as ontological as well as social and psychological; it is irresolvable, an expression of dramatic tension.

The scene of Doctor Copperthwaite's dog trick, his

breakthrough discovery, is ultimately heavily symbolic. For even as the doctor is being humanized, he is being frozen into an image of power in a total institution from which there is no escape. According to Arden's introductory note, nurses and orderlies don hospital antiseptic masks during "clinical" scenes (p. 193). Now, Doctor Copperthwaite offers cigarettes to the three orderlies who aided him in his experiments. Politely invited by their superior to smoke, the orderlies comply in pantomime:

> *They stand side by side. The* ORDERLIES *remove their masks and all three take a few formal puffs at cigarettes. Then they drop their butts, grind them into the floor, and turn back to the work.* ORDERLIES *replace masks.* (p. 260)

This ritualized version of staff hierarchy crystallizes an idea of power, order, and terrible control. The doctor, the personification of the will of the Structure, is himself finally subdued, limited by the Structure he represents. He again participates in a ceremony, later, in the paradoxical climax of the play, but there his omnipotence dissolves as he shrinks in physical stature.

The paradox of the climax extends into the audience, too, for once again we are recognized by the players, but even though we are acknowledged as participants in a final ceremony within the Structure, we are powerless to change the outcome of the play. Like other plays in the contemporary mode set in institutions, *The Happy Haven* encompasses us in its form, but finally confronts us with the illusion of performance. In the final scene, mime is used satirically to convey an idea of the aged and of the nature of an audience: *"The coffee, etc., is handed to the* VISITORS. *When the* OLD PEOPLE *make conversation with them, the* VISITORS *reply in wordless goggling noises which sound both patronizing and genial"* (p. 266). Again, according to the playwright, the Distinguished Visitors "wear masks similar to those of the Old People, but less individualized" (p. 193). With masks, movement, and garbled sounds, Arden plays metaphysical charades.

Anticipating the garish ending of Nichols's *The National Health*, we find the ending of *The Happy Haven* is musical and menacing. But Arden's fable, too, ends in black humor, in a predictable reversal: the patients' rebellion and revenge are remarkably successful. They pin the Visitors against the edge of the stage and then inject the doctor with his own elixir. When the doctor reenters, he has changed: A little boy sucking a lollipop *"in a formal fashion"* and wearing a *"round, chubby, and childish"* mask which *"resembles the actor's own features closely"* emerges as a new addition to the population of the Happy Haven (p. 271). Contentedly rocking the little boy who formerly played doctor, Mrs. Phineus sings a lullaby (p. 272). A lullaby seems a suitable finale for a fairy-tale farce, but the forcibly rejuvenated doctor is pathetically out of place in this institutional travesty. Having wreaked havoc on the Happy Haven, the old people encircle the foundling now in their care.

The aged members of the new regime form a momentary tableau. Together they face us, and collectively they issue a formal statement:

> Everybody, listen! Take warning from us. Be cheerful in your old age. Find some useful hobby. Fretwork. Rugmaking. Basketry. Make yourselves *needed*. Remember: a busy pair of hands are worth ten thousand times the Crown of a Queen. Go home, and remember: your lives too, will have their termination.   (p. 272)

This prophetic curse, recited in unison by the old people, is a *memento mori* aimed directly at us. Like Barnet's standing invitation to "See you again one day behind the screens" in *The National Health*, the old people's warning is an eerie reminder of our own appointment in an entropic state of modern society. Earlier in this final scene of *The Happy Haven*, Doctor Copperthwaite marvelled that "The Institution is greater than the Man" (p. 264). And so, as this pageant of extended life in impasse ends, the now miniature doctor is wheeled offstage in a regal procession of his world-weary former subjects.

Like *The National Health*, then, *The Happy Haven* sidesteps our theatrical expectations; it makes us laugh when we do not want to laugh. In comparably bleak social settings, both plays manage to balance a stark situation with musical and slapstick interludes. Both use characters to embody ideas, and both engross us in graphic images that are overdetermined so that a health care facility also becomes a metaphor. Both *The National Health* and *The Happy Haven* defile the immaculate image of white-garbed men and occupy the theater with an absurd reflection of death's grimace.

Undoubtedly, the factual circumstances in the naturalistically designed ward of *The National Health* are a painful reminder of the atrophy of the human spirit in a health care facility. But the romance, purple prose, and provocative coming attractions of "Nurse Norton's Affair" prove addictive. We, too, become avid fans, relieved to tune in to Barnet's sequels. In Arden's travesty of an old-age Eden, on the other hand, the shape of the total institution is consistently distorted. The metaphysical farce renders a familiar institution new and unpredictable. With its ambitious though uneven *commedia dell'arte* style and its equivocal ending, *The Happy Haven* is jarring.

In the rebellion at *The Happy Haven*, we see that institutionalization and passivity are not synonymous. Characters are not necessarily always passive in a state of impasse onstage. Indeed, sometimes a play of impasse derives its strength—its ability to jar us—precisely from the tension between a stilled situation and the energy locked within it. Like the theatricality of Behan's *Quare Fellow* (expressing overt disregard for prison rules), the rebellion in *The Happy Haven* brings its participants comfort and joy but no release from their actual situation. Like the play within the play of Weiss's *Marat/Sade* (inspiring revolution in the madhouse), the rebellion in *The Happy Haven* unleashes in the characters an impulse and energy to play despite the unbeatable odds against their making a permanent change in the way things are. Such plays of impasse hold precious little hope for the characters of getting out, but the jarring memory of hope and the desire to play endure and surface. Such emotions can lead to an equivocal ending that will leave us in turmoil.

Wings

Arthur Kopit's *Wings* begins in turmoil. In contrast to Nichols's *The National Health*, *Wings* is sparse, hazy in its setting; in contrast to Arden's *The Happy Haven*, it focuses on one sympathetic individual suddenly hurled into a bewildering Structure. Extreme naturalism characterizes *The National Health*; paradoxes, moral issues, and Brechtian techniques characterize *The Happy Haven*; the individual will to break free is at the heart of *Wings*. This play complements the other two in its expressionistic use of the institution in the contemporary mode.

Wings explores the struggle of a stroke victim to speak, to connect her inner world with the confusing one outside. The play follows Emily Stilson, a middle-aged former aviatrix and wingwalker, from the moment of her stroke through her hospitalization and therapy for aphasia. Using the metaphor of flight, of finding one's way back over snowbound land when low on fuel, *Wings* achieves a lyricism that is surprising, considering it is a play about the loss of words, about the broken circuits between feeling and expression.

The hospital and the recreation room of a rehabilitation center are suggested rather than precisely copied onstage. Sounds and images are filtered through the central character's exploded mind. Sometimes garbled, sometimes lucid, these sounds and images convey to the audience an essence, an echo of setting, which sharpens as the play progresses through its four stages of "Prelude," "Catastrophe," "Awakening," and "Explorations."

The "Prelude" segment of *Wings* objectifies the stroke by means of a ticking alarm clock which inexplicably ticks "*a trifle louder than normal*," then "*skips a beat*," and then stops. Mrs. Stilson, reading a book in "*a cozy armchair visible downstage in a pool of light, darkness surrounding it*," is at first perplexed, then alarmed, and finally, "*she stares out in ter-*

72

ror."[34] The "Prelude" blackout then immediately gives way to the "*noise*" of the "Catastrophe" section of the play (p. 8).

With "Prelude's" gripping opening sequence of normalcy shattered, using the ticking clock as an expressionistic objectification of an inner state, Kopit draws his audience from the start into a world askew, where everyday objects seem distant, sometimes unrecognizable, and dangerous. An ordinary object by day *can* take on a shadowy night energy, as in Pinter's *Homecoming*, where Lenny explores one of his hypotheses about the night-side of life:

> Eh listen, I wonder if you can advise me. I've been having a bit of a rough time with this clock. The tick's been keeping me up. The trouble is I'm not all that convinced it was the clock. I mean there are lots of things which tick in the night, don't you find that? All sorts of objects, which, in the day, you wouldn't call anything else but commonplace. They give you no trouble. But in the night any given one of a number of them is liable to start letting out a bit of a tick.[35]

In context, this speech is a verbal strut, one of Lenny's aggressive speculations meant to intimidate his kin. Out of its immediate context, this speech makes sense of much of contemporary drama's attention to heightened detail, to ordinary objects enlarged, to photographic reality blown up, to life as an *objet trouvé*. In *Wings*, the tick of an ordinary object stops, signifying with blank, silent lucidity the onset of a stroke. Inside Mrs. Stilson's mind from the start, we in the audience come to recognize how everyday objects, bathed even in sweet white light, can be twisted by subjective perception.

The second section of *Wings*, "Catastrophe," renders a hospital setting as experienced by a patient. Here the hospital staff is ordinary, but it takes on eerie, intrusive qualities when presented to a disoriented patient. Images, Mrs. Stilson's voice, and sounds outside herself combine as the "Catastrophe" builds to a crescendo. Images of sudden hos-

pitalization, the *"visual images Mrs. Stilson perceives"* (p. 9),
rush by us:

Mostly, it is whiteness. Dazzling, blinding.

*The mirrors, of course, reflect infinitely. Sense of endless space,
endless corridors.*

*In this vast whiteness, like apparitions, partial glimpses of
doctors and nurses can be seen. They appear and disappear
like a pulse. They are never in one place for long. The mirrors
multiply their incomprehensibility.*

*Fragments of hospital equipment appear out of nowhere and
disappear just as suddenly. Glimpse always too brief to enable
us to identify what this equipment is, or what its purpose.*
(pp. 14, 16)

At the same time, the audience hears sounds that are
ordinary bits of life, like wind, but these are overwhelmed
by sounds that signal emergencies. Among these garbled,
interloping sounds *"emanating outside herself"* we hear those:

Of someone breathing with effort, unevenly.

Of something ripping, like a sheet.

Of a woman's scream (though this sound should be
altered by filters so it resembles other things, such as
sirens).

Of random noises recorded in a busy city hospital, then
altered so as to be only minimally recognizable.

A hospital paging system heard.

Equipment being moved through stone corridors, vast
vaulting space. Endless echoing.
(pp. 14–18)

The third group of sense data contributing to the "Ca-
tastrophe" section's jolting effect on the audience are Mrs.
Stilson's words, *"the words she thinks and the words she speaks.
Since we are perceiving the world through Mrs. Stilson's senses,"*

writes Kopit, *"there is no sure way for us to know whether she is actually saying any of these words aloud"* (pp. 9–10). Strongest of all we hear her say

> —all around faces of which
> nothing known no sense
> ever all wiped out blank like
> ice I think saw it once flying
>
> (p. 17)

In performance this section of *Wings* achieves an effect of disjunction, of, as Kopit puts it, a feeling that *"some real event is occurring; that real information is being received by the victim, but that it is coming in too scrambled and too fast to be properly decoded. Systems overload"* (p. 9). Indeed, by the end of the "Catastrophe" section, the audience identifies completely with Mrs. Stilson: we perceive everything only as she does; our vision and hearing of action are governed by her subjective experience. So, because of the " *'musical' sense of this section as a whole"*—"it must *pulse and build"* (p. 10)— we are imprisoned in Mrs. Stilson's incoherent head as completely as she is; through garbled sound and dizzying motion, we fall, too.

The *"journey"* (p. 10), the *"adventure"* (p. 25) has begun. Once we feel the confusion, the loss, the want of words, we enter the next phase of *Wings*, "Awakening." This phase moves at a slower pace, and whereas "Catastrophe" hurled us inward in space and time, "Awakening" begins to reach outward to connect words to things, to clarify spots of time. Still, Mrs. Stilson's point of view is at the heart of the play. Because of the rush and intensity of "Catastrophe," we have accepted this given of *Wings*: we are inside Mrs. Stilson's mind. Now, accepting that given, we can hear her voice expressing in "Awakening" what are probably unspoken reactions to her room (*"The room that I am in is large, square. What does large mean?"*), to her doctor's questions, and to her struggle to respond (*"Oh my God, this is grotesque!"*) (p. 28).

The hospital life, disturbing and new to any patient, is

particularly troubling to the stroke victim; she is not just in a hospital, but her own perceptions seem to occur in a cave. This double sense of disorientation is brought home to the audience using "*a dazzling bouquet of flowers*" (p. 31), as the clock was used in the first segment. Their presence in the sterile-looking hospital room, the intensity of their color in this white, gauzy world, is overwhelming. According to the stage directions:

> *It is as if she has never experienced color before. And the experience is so overwhelming, both physiologically and psychologically, that her brain cannot process all the information. Her circuitry is overloaded.* (p. 32)

Like being born, "Awakening" is traumatic for Mrs. Stilson. We see her feeling suffocated, invaded when she sees a bouquet of flowers. We hear her inner thoughts and her jargonaphasia, the particular kind of speech, as Kopit points out in his Preface, that is "typical of a certain form of aphasia" and "characterized by neologisms, and sounds very much like double talk or gibberish" (p. ix). The words all stay inside, while sad double talk comes out. As Mrs. Stilson explains to her therapist, Amy, "The words, they go in somelimes then out they go, I can't stop them here inside or make maybe globbidge to the tubberway or—" (p. 44).

From "Awakening" through "Explorations," the final sections of the play, the therapist, Amy, serves as the bridge between the inner and outer worlds of *Wings*, two worlds that grow closer as Mrs. Stilson progresses. Amy is an encouraging, enlivening force onstage. Also, now that the action is set in a rehabilitation center, the play's focus gradually widens to include a range of other characters as well as more objective sense data. At the start of "Awakening," for example, we are still primarily locked in Mrs. Stilson's consciousness, but sounds and images independent of her consciousness seep through to her and to us. These sounds and images are quite different from those we experienced in the chaotic jumbled din of "Catastrophe." Rather, as the stage directions indicate, "*This is not a hospital anymore, and a kind of normalcy prevails"* (p. 52). We hear sounds of *"some-one fooling around on the keyboard,"* playing snatches of half-remembered tunes, we glimpse a TV, a group of people including *"doctors, therapists, nurses, attendants, patients, visi-tors,"* and we hear another twist of language: the sound of Ella Fitzgerald singing scat (p. 51).

The overriding effect of the "Explorations" section of *Wings* is *"of mystery and adventure"* (p. 56). This effect is achieved both imagistically and aurally. Like the stopped clock in "Prelude," like the pandemonium and darkness of "Catastrophe," and like the vibrant colored bouquet in "Awakening," the props and echoes of "Explorations" loom large, rivet our attention, and objectify the thoughts and feelings of a now strengthened inner voice—still not always lucid, but now conscious of its separation from the physical voice.

Most important to the development of Mrs. Stilson as a character is that in "Explorations" she is not afraid. Ac-cording to the stage directions, *"she begins to wander through a maze of passageways. The mirrors multiply her image, create a sense of endlessness."* Nevertheless, she wanders through this maze accompanied by what the playwright calls *"blocks of sound,"* that is, she goes past sounds of different voices in different rooms of the rehabilitation center, past voices and images theorizing, doing therapy, singing, laughing, lec-turing. And the trip becomes *"an adventure. With terrifying aspects to be sure"* (pp. 55–56), but Mrs. Stilson does not give in to the terror. She goes through the labyrinth of dark panels onstage, "flying blind," and she emerges to the sound of wind or bells, to blue light, to wonder, and to airiness (p. 58).

At this point the exterior world comes into focus onstage; the play, with its touching scenes of several patients in speech class, moves to include dialogue—a change from the ri-cochetting, parallel exchanges of earlier sections. For the most poignant example, we hear Mrs. Stilson, outdoors in winter, ask her speech therapist what to name the snow, the white stuff "falling from the sky":

MRS. STILSON. Where do you get names from?
AMY. I? From in here, same as you.
MRS. STILSON. Do you know how you do it?
AMY. No.
MRS. STILSON. Then how am I supposed . . . to learn?
AMY (*softly*). I don't really know.
MRS. STILSON *stares at Amy. Then she points at her and laughs.*

(p. 70)

The "Explorations" section is filled with this kind of delight in rediscovery among other people who now come into sharp focus.

Mrs. Stilson's joy and resolve give a high-spirited edge even to the final moments of *Wings*, moments which seem almost completely hallucinatory. For the last time Mrs. Stilson has that feeling of soaring, of being lost in the clouds, adrift. In her mind, she begins to circle, trying to find a place to land, trying not to crash. Then there is a "*sudden, sharp, terrifying flapping sound*" and she gasps, she has a sensation that she is wingwalking, and, according to the final enigmatic stage directions:

No trace of terror.
Music. Hint of bells.
Lights to black.
Silence. (pp. 77–78)

The play ends as mysteriously as it began, probably with another, perhaps final stroke.

The power of *Wings* derives primarily from its noble central figure, a woman who emerges from a wreckage to find her thoughts scattered like pieces of a jigsaw puzzle. The effort she expends to connect thoughts to language, her desire to make sense, to remember, to communicate, and ultimately, to make metaphors, to make a poem out of a life, is what energizes the play. There is considerable power in *Wings'* controlling metaphor of flight, in its image of a mind imprisoned for want of words, and in the determined, lovely figure about whom all its sounds and visions swirl.

UNLIKE Beckett's *Happy Days* (1961), a hallmark contemporary play in which dirt engulfs the lyrical ever-hopeful Winnie as if life itself were quicksand, however, Kopit's *Wings* is finally limited by the clinical nature of Mrs. Stilson's anguish and longing. Many people see how Winnie's situation metaphorically can imply hospitalization, aging, and death even as *Happy Days* includes and finally transcends such a vision of isolation and determined brightness in the unrelenting heat of the sun. But *Wings'* literalness holds it down. For the staging of his play, originally conceived as a radio drama, Kopit added a visual element, what he describes as "a special setting, in order to show the audience what the woman's world looked like—with all its uncertainty and alteration of space and time relationships. There would be a screen that turned opaque or transparent, mirrors that distorted, space could either represent airiness or a black void of isolation and paranoia."[36] But even with its core of meaning about language as a daredevil stunt and even with its evocative mood, the play never achieves the kind of poetry of the theater—the concrete physical lyricism—that Beckett achieves with his arid landscape and with his cheerful, fussing Winnie in *Happy Days*. The social setting of *Wings* remains overwhelmingly literal, perhaps because of the play's steady, unflinching focus on the very real task faced by the stroke victim. Mrs. Stilson's problems remain a function of her physical condition rather than of something larger. Further, although *Wings* is built on the metaphor of aphasia as a fall, a grounding from flight, as one reviewer put it, "Unlike a Beckett, however, or even a Pinter, Kopit is not really interested in such fundamental questions, though it must be said for him that he has created a dramatic situation that does at least imply the existence of serious ideas of this kind."[37] Kopit's central idea of language as a connection—of the loss of language as a kind of solitary confinement—remains embedded in the actual situation of a stroke victim.

Wings is of special note in a study of plays of impasse because its shortcomings as a work of art are largely due to its lack of one of the mode's central characteristics: the poetic transformation of a social system into a microcosm. Grounded so firmly in authentic events and tasks, and focused on an infirmity quite tangible to its audience, *Wings* never fully achieves a transition from the particular to the general. Ironically, with this shortcoming—and indeed, we do miss something, we do feel vaguely that the play is unfinished even as we are deeply moved by it in performance—*Wings* reminds us of a fundamental urge present in plays in the contemporary mode. Plays of impasse have in common a basic urge towards transforming societal facts into conceits, towards reacting to grueling, patterned life as if it were a song; they attempt to reckon with randomness and loss and deal with orders and disarray by infusing contemporary life—particularly its overwhelming social Structures brimming over with pain and anger—with the functions of art. *Wings* never fully realizes this dream of art and order; really only *Endgame* comes to the very edge, even having Clov articulate outright this urge to confound entropy. "I love order. It's my dream. A world where all would be silent and still and each thing in its last place, under the last dust," he says as he straightens up Hamm's place; "I'm doing my best to create a little order."[38] A dream of order by one imprisoned in this world is the kernel of plays of impasse, such as the paradigmatic *Endgame*. But *Wings*' achievement is that it evokes a parallel dream, a parallel longing in its audience.

The wide appeal of *Wings*—it was performed on the radio show, "Earplay," at the Yale Repertory Theater, at the New York Shakespeare Festival Public Theater, and on Broadway—probably has something to do, then, not only with Constance Cummings's luminous, spirited performance and with the sound show, but also with the public's fear and curiosity about what it is like to have a stroke, and with our need to see sense and order made of such random pain and loss of self. The medical event and its aftermath, turned into an inner monologue, a voyager's log, is depicted on-stage and given metaphorical resonance.

SUSAN SONTAG writes:

> Illnesses have always been used as metaphors to enliven charges that a society was corrupt or unjust. Traditional disease metaphors are principally a way of being vehement; they are, compared with the modern metaphors, relatively contentless. . . . For purposes of invective, diseases are of only two types: the painful but curable, and the possibly fatal.
>
> But the modern disease metaphors [Sontag refers specifically here to TB and cancer] are all cheap shots. . . . Only in the most limited sense is any historical event or problem like an illness.

Nevertheless, in her piercing study of the impulse towards the metaphor of illness in modern literature, Sontag recognizes the mythicized side of illness, the mysterious aspect of this "night-side of life," and she explores the process by which a dark fact of life becomes a metaphor. "Any important disease whose causality is murky, and for which treatment is ineffectual, tends to be awash in significance," she writes. "First, the subjects of deepest dread (corruption, decay, pollution, anomie, weakness) are identified with the disease. The disease itself becomes a metaphor. Then, in the name of the disease (that is, using it as a metaphor), that horror is imposed on other things. The disease becomes adjectival."[39] Sontag argues that a serious illness such as cancer, seen by contemporary society as an "all-encompassing . . . disaster," lends itself to metaphor because "the interest of the metaphor is precisely that it refers to a disease so overlaid with mystification, so charged with the fantasy of inescapable fatality."[40] Sontag's point is that people who have the real disease are better off without the added burden of mystifying symbolism, without the weight of metaphor. She is, of course, right. But the metaphor endures, probably because we need it to comfort us in the face of death, the "inescapable fatality." As John Leonard put it in his review of *Illness As Metaphor*, "Death in itself isn't evil; it is normal. But as surely as we will die, we are machines for making metaphors about it. Metaphors are our way of thinking about death, as well as our way of pretending not to think about it. From the beginning, in all art and all religions, these are the nets we cast to snare the terror, to pull back the loneliness."[41]

In plays of impasse in contemporary drama, what Sontag identifies as "the fantasy of inescapable fatality" is central. This net of metaphor frequently extends across a vividly depicted institutional abyss to "snare the terror." Metaphors are vehicles to "snare the terror," and not just the terror for death, but the terror for contemporary life, too, for what Sontag calls "the large insufficiencies of this culture, for our shallow attitude toward death, for our anxieties about feeling, . . . for our inability to construct an advanced industrial society which properly regulates consumption, and for our justified fears of the increasingly violent course of history."[42] If we can bear to look, we find this "net of metaphor" in powerful scenic images and evocations of the "night-side" of contemporary life: in the end beds of *The National Health*, the magic elixir of *The Happy Haven*, and the acrobatics-in-flight of *Wings*.

IMAGINING FREEDOM AT THE ASYLUM

Peter Weiss's *Marat/Sade*,
Friedrich Dürrenmatt's *The Physicists*,
and David Storey's *Home*

The new man stands looking a minute, to get the set-up of the day room. . . .
Across the room from the Acutes are the culls of the Combine's product, the Chronics. Not in the hospital, these, to get fixed, but just to keep them from walking around the street giving the product a bad name. Chronics are in for good, the staff concedes. Chronics are divided into Walkers like me, can still get around if you keep them fed, and Wheelers and Vegetables. What the Chronics are—or most of us—are machines with flaws inside that can't be repaired, flaws born in, or flaws beat in over so many years of the guy running head-on into solid things that by the time the hospital found him he was bleeding rust in some vacant lot.
Ken Kesey, *One Flew Over the Cuckoo's Nest*

THIS METHODICAL PIGEON-HOLING of his wardmates, according to Chief Bromden's vision of a vast Combine's circuitry, initiates us into his mad world in *One Flew Over the Cuckoo's Nest*. Through that character's clouded eyes, Ken Kesey's novel depicts in broad strokes an institution for the insane, sketched "like a cartoon world, where the figures are flat and outlined in black, jerking through some kind of goofy story that might be real funny if it weren't for the

83

cartoon figures being real guys." A "real guy," one Randall P. McMurphy, who challenges the "Therapeutic Community" of *One Flew Over the Cuckoo's Nest*, is first dubbed a "Ward Manipulator" and is finally driven to violence and broken by those caricatured people in charge of this "little world Inside that is a made-to-scale prototype of the big world Outside."[1] In the course of Kesey's picaresque novel tracing the adventures of a newly committed mental patient, McMurphy discovers a nightmare truth. He finds that, as one social critic notes, mental asylums "rarely offer asylum" to those experiencing a "descent into 'unreality.' " Rather, psychiatric hospitalization is "more destructive of self than criminal incarceration."[2] Admitted to an asylum for the insane, a mental patient finds himself trapped in a far corner of his mind.

The illogic facing a patient committed to a modern mental hospital, burlesqued in Kesey's novel, is founded on reality. The modern American concept of voluntary admission, for example, involves legal semantics reminiscent of the illogic governing the underworld of Lewis Carroll's *Alice in Wonderland*. According to the American Civil Liberties Union handbook on *The Rights of Mental Patients*, "If a prospective patient says, 'no, I do not want to be hospitalized,' the hospital will disregard that decision and call it irrational. But if the same man recants, under pressure, and signs in as a 'voluntary' patient, the hospital will accept that decision and call it rational."[3] Like Lewis Carroll's Alice, then, the perplexed newcomer to a mental asylum has fallen "down, down, down," and when his descent is suddenly stopped, he finds himself lost in a strange hall of dark passages and locked doors. With madness converging on him from every direction, he cannot know which way to turn.[4] His fall is broken, but so is he. Thrust into another world where the gravity of logic does not hold, he must struggle against enormous odds to regain his own equilibrium, for he, like poor Alice, must wander among mad people.

The stigma of madness is as old as is its diagnosis. Sociologists tell us in this case what we already know: we avert our eyes when they light upon "abnormal" behavior in public; we shun contact with those demonstrating signs of deviant behavior. Mental patients are painfully aware of the stigma accompanying their illness in our society, for as Goffman repeatedly observes in his studies both of mental patients and of the American culture to which they want to return, we all tend to "read" peculiarities or "non-performance" of courtesies in public as "alarming" or "threatening" signs.[5] Yet in a darkened theater, we do not avert our eyes from madness. On the contrary, like Pentheus, who quickly succumbs when Dionysus tempts him to break a taboo to spy on secret rites in Euripides' *The Bacchae*, we, too, want to witness from a safe distance the mysteries of a world apart. We do not want to enter the madhouse; we merely want to see it.

In the theater, of course, as one social worker has ironically phrased it, "We have come a long way since the world of Bedlam when, on Sunday afternoons, the public would watch the 'lunatics' as objects of amusement."[6] Still, drama has traditionally emphasized the sensational aspects of mental asylums and exploited madness for its shock value onstage. The appeal of such plays is analogous, at bottom, to the appeal of that old social pastime associated with the London madhouse. It is deeply rooted in modern western culture; it derives from our fascination with madness, our fear of it, and our social taboos. Peter Weiss's *The Persecution and Assassination of Jean-Paul Marat as Performed by the Inmates of the Asylum of Charenton Under the Direction of the Marquis de Sade* (first presented in London under the direction of Peter Brook in 1964), Friedrich Dürrenmatt's *The Physicists* (originally produced in 1962 in Germany), and David Storey's *Home* (first presented in 1970), however, are madhouse plays which take us beyond curiosity, beyond voyeurism, to a poetic vision of an insane society akin to our own. All three of these plays of impasse in extreme reconstruct an asylum, a total institution, onstage; all three take a societal model of an asylum and treat it as a microcosm;

85

and all three end at the edge of play, that is, they show us how pale is the line we imagine separating insane and sane behavior, the madhouse and the playhouse, an idea of acting and a drama of ideas. These plays also show us contrasting aspects of the contemporary dramatic mode from which all three spring: Weiss's *Marat/Sade* is a historical pageant about lunacy, revolution, and theatrical force; Dürrenmatt's *The Physicists* is a satirical thesis play about energy confined by social power; and Storey's *Home* is an imagistic landscape of world-weary minds.

Weiss, Dürrenmatt, and Storey all use the theater as an intellectual forum, and all use asylums as physical metaphors for social decline, emptiness, profound forlornness, and despair, by inhabiting their plays of impasse with vacant-eyed spirits weary of desire. In their evocations of atmospheres of oppression, these three plays show the range of responses by plays of impasse to a world stopped, trapped, tied up in knots by the tension between dictatorial control and chaotic freedom, the two ostensibly therapeutic forces at odds in a terrifying Structure sheltering psychic decay.

Marat/Sade

Peter Weiss's *Marat/Sade* is an extreme instance of the contemporary dramatic mode, fusing social commentary with a sense of psychic isolation in a densely authentic and oppressive environment. Here, perhaps more than in any other play of impasse, the audience is controlled, shocked, and shattered by the secret society which invades its consciousness. *Marat/Sade* more than exposes the physical and philosophical savagery of a metaphorical madhouse; it finally commits us to an idea and a searing image of asylum at Charenton.

Our response to *Marat/Sade* is shaped first and foremost by the imposing Structure of the asylum. We are engulfed at first by the play's extreme naturalism, by its detailed rendering of the bizarre and random behavior of madmen

86

milling about their bath hall in an eighteenth-century asylum. Indeed, the documentary-like intensity of the extras onstage, imposing the minutiae of the institutional experience on the audience, startled theatergoers when the playwright's concept was indelibly translated into stage terms in 1964 by Peter Brook, the director of the renowned Royal Shakespeare Company production of this play in London. Like Joan Littlewood in her relationship to Brendan Behan's *The Quare Fellow* and *The Hostage* and like Judith Malina in her relationship to Kenneth H. Brown's *The Brig*, Peter Brook deserves considerable credit here for bringing his theatrical imagination to bear on a script of incredible plasticity, and, most important, for the credibility of the institution taking the stage. In an interview following the New York opening of *Marat/Sade*, Brook acknowledged his collaboratory role as director:

> The author had an extraordinarily complex and daring vision, and one that was very hard for him to put down on paper. The nearest he could get was the title, which reflects a complex stage machine we had to recapture. And I think that what we do on the stage, for better or worse, is exactly what the author himself was seeing on the stage of his mind, seeing in his vision. This is why I am very jealous of any attempt to divide his work from mine. I feel that any criticism of the production is a criticism of his play and that any praise of the production is a praise of his vision.[7]

From the start, then, *Marat/Sade* involves the audience in an accurately depicted Structure barely able to contain madness onstage. And according to Peter Brook, "for better or worse," that formidable, graphic, engulfing Structure and the life teeming in it represent a coupling—common in the contemporary mode—of directorial control with dramaturgy.

In the Royal Shakespeare Company production, especially, the director's expansive design energized the playwright's intellectual concept. In his introduction to the published version of the script in English, Brook himself alludes to the shape of the play as *he* saw it. Here, he refers admiringly to the "prismatic structure" of *Marat/Sade*, and he defends the heterodox theatrical vision associated with its definitive production. This is Brook's signature on Weiss's play:

> Brecht's use of "distance" has long been considered in opposition to Artaud's conception of theatre as immediate and violent subjective experience. I have never believed this to be true. I believe that theatre, like life, is made up of the unbroken conflict between impressions and judgments—illusion and disillusion cohabit painfully and are inseparable. . . .
>
> One of the London critics attacked the play on the ground that it was a fashionable mixture of all the best theatrical ingredients around—Brechtian—didactic—absurdist—Theatre of Cruelty. He said this to disparage but I repeat this as praise. Weiss saw the use of every one of these idioms and he saw that he needed them all. His assimilation was complete.[8]

This assimilation of multiple approaches to contemporary drama is characteristic even more of Brook than it is of Weiss. In his production of *Marat/Sade*, spectacle dominated the stage. Explosive ideas were carried across the footlights in visual flashes of Artaudian cruelty.

Luckily, Brook's Royal Shakespeare Company version of *Marat/Sade* has been preserved on film. Released by United Artists in 1967, it was directed and adapted for the screen by Brook. Some changes in design accompanied the film version, in which the asylum setting is more graphically depicted. The bare setting of the Broadway show, described by Howard Taubman in *The New York Times* as a "wide, lofty uncurtained stage, furnished with a few planks, benches and several pits,"[9] is replaced on the screen by tubs and tiles.

The film attempts to achieve an effect congruent to that achieved onstage by actors playing bit parts as lunatics, who were responsible to a great extent for the disturbing impact of the play on its original New York theater audience. One member of that audience, Walter Kerr, found their extremely naturalistic representation of insanity not only disturbing but also distracting. Awaiting the resolution of an ideological debate, he castigated the cast and director for changing the rules of the drama of ideas. Marat and Sade are indeed dialectical characters, but their podium is a mad show, and their contest is between mind and matter. Kerr complained about this revamping of a standard dramatic mode:

> Whenever Marat, or de Sade, prepared to make a statement of philosophical position, all creative hell broke loose around him. Actors, purporting to be lunatics, drooled spittle, masturbated, rattled chains in buckets, violated the promised sound of words by the sight and sound of spectacle.[10]

Other members of the theater audience, not sharing Kerr's complaint of missing language because of movements, were nevertheless deeply affected by the *physical* presence of lunatics who seemed to be each in a world of his own, always at the brink of breaking through the play to notice and then to assault the audience. Theatergoers seated in the front rows even tried occasionally to change their seats, to gain distance from the harrowing action directly before them. To evoke a congruent atmosphere of danger in the screen version, Brook used asylum bars to suggest a concrete separation necessary between the show and its audience. According to Bosley Crowther, Brook's film "makes us feel that we, too, are captured inside a giant and teeming cage. . . . And, three or four times, we are permitted to see the great steam-room from the outside, with a profiled audience in the foreground watching what goes on behind bars. It is this . . . illusion of being in the room—of being momentarily blinded by a whitewash of light . . .—that give[s] the viewer a feeling of being immediately involved."[11] In the film version, then, a metal framework separates us from the white-tiled walls of the asylum bath hall. In Brook's stage version, no such separation existed; because of the intensity of the actors, no physical barrier was needed to suggest danger. The danger seemed real.

To achieve this effect Brook encouraged each of his actors to create his own cocoon of madness every night. In contrast to Judith Malina's direction of *The Brig* in 1963 and Joan Littlewood's *The Quare Fellow* in 1956, where the actors were drilled in rehearsal as if they were truly inmates in a prison, Brook's approach in rehearsal was more inner-directed. As one commentator observed:

> Brook himself had visited a few asylums around London and Paris, but he wanted the actors to forgo that kind of instruction and dig out the madness in themselves. His method worked with fairly terrifying results, but not without some attrition on the cast. . . . In the U. S., the show goes on six nights a week with two matinees and produces a lot of cases of melancholia, misanthropy and persisting miserableness of the spirit. Few of the twitching muscles or lunatic glares recur after working hours, but the forced tension needed to feign madness is not easily dissolved. An immediate and deeply felt, or deeply feigned, hate for the audience helps the players get into the spirit of *Marat/Sade*.[12]

The result of such an approach to playing at madness, then, was a not entirely unfounded sense of danger and tension for the actors as well as for their audience.

To further intensify what Artaud calls the "excruciating, magical relation to reality and danger" that is the "only value" of theater,[13] Brook eliminated from both his stage and his film versions of *Marat/Sade* the curtain called for in Weiss's published text. In order to draw the audience into an encompassing illusion of real madness contained in an asylum onstage, to suggest immediacy, and to evoke that Artaudian "excruciating, magical relation to reality and danger," Brook not only cut the curtain, but he also expanded the opening segment of naturalistic action. In both the stage and film versions of Brook's production, then, there is no proper start of the action. The audience entering the theater or watching the film's first moments may observe, for many minutes more than the script indicates, the "offstage" activities of the inmates, who wander aimlessly about their stage business until the clanging of the asylum bell signals the start of the official performance.

As THE PLAY, set fifteen years after Marat's murder, gradually opens, the patients are milling about onstage. In white uniforms sometimes aproned by colorful, homemade costumes for their play within ours, they sit, stand, and lie down. According to Weiss's stage directions, the patients' presence "*must set the atmosphere behind the acting area. They make habitual movements, turn in circles, hop, mutter to themselves, wail, scream and so on*" (p. x). These extras dominate the stage during the curtain-raising sequence; thereafter, they function as a grotesque backdrop of humanity for Sade's play within the play. Another naturalistic detail is furnished by "athletic-looking" male nurses (p. x) who attend the more dangerous inmates and who are completing "*a few routine operations of bathing and massage*" (p. 3) as the play begins. Accompanied by the tolling of the asylum bell, a "*ceremonious procession*" of inmates, who have parts to play in Sade's historical drama, is led to the acting area by Coulmier, the director of the clinic of Charenton, and his bejeweled family. The actors take their positions, the tolling of the bell ceases, and there is a fanfare. Coulmier welcomes us as visitors to his institution.

With its crowd of singular madmen, with its insistent ringing of an asylum bell instead of a traditional raising of a curtain, and with Coulmier's opening speech addressed to us, *Marat/Sade* immediately exceeds conventional expectations. By our curious attention to the madmen peopling the stage, by our quieting down at the sound of the bell, and by our collective silent agreement to play the part Coulmier assigns us in his opening address, we consent to follow the rules of a dangerous theater game. As Henry Hewes noted in his review of *Marat/Sade*, "We are to represent the bourgeois French curiosity seekers who used to amuse themselves by visiting mental institutions."[14] The stage is a panorama of mental illness. We face distorted figures of despair and derangement. They are staring at us.

In his prologue to Sade's play, entitled, "The Persecution and Assassination of Jean-Paul Marat," Coulmier welcomes us to his clinic, and he officially sanctions the inmate "therapy" about to occur:

> We're modern enlightened and we don't agree
> with locking up patients We prefer therapy
> through education and especially art
> so that our hospital may play its part
> faithfully following according to our lights
> the Declaration of Human Rights
> (p. 4)

Coulmier further assures us that Sade has written this play for our "delectation and for our patients' rehabilitation" (p. 4). We see that Sade had even sought official approval for the subject of his amateur theatrical.

Hearing Coulmier's prologue, we in the audience feel compelled to concede at the outset that the director of the asylum at Charenton does seem to be enlightened, recognizing as he does the modern notion of art-as-therapy. Today, of course, such "removal activities" (or "kicks") are widely recognized as providing for asylum inmates according to Goffman, "something for the individual to lose himself in, temporarily blotting out all sense of the environment which, and in which, he must abide." Discussing a specific contemporary American asylum, Goffman further observes that "for a handful of patients, the semi-annual theatrical production was an extremely effective removal activity: tryouts, rehearsals, costuming, scenery-making, staging, writing and rewriting, performing—all these seemed as successful as on the outside in building a world apart for the participants."[15] In his study of "Role Distance," too,

Goffman stresses the therapeutic value of institution-sponsored theatricals:

> There is the fact that in prisons and mental hospitals, where some inmates may constantly sustain a heroic edifice of withdrawal, uncooperativeness, insolence, and combativeness, the same inmates may be quite ready to engage in theatricals in which they enact excellent portraits of civil, sane, and compliant characters. But this very remarkable turnabout is understandable too. Since the staged circumstances of the portrayed character are not the inmate's real ones, he has no need (in the character's name) to exhibit distance from them, unless, of course, the script calls for it.[16]

The therapeutic value of performance in mental hospitals is now so widely recognized, in fact, that it has also been applied in other rehabilitative total institutions. One of the most notable of these was New York's drug addiction center, "Daytop Village," where former inmates polished their psychodramatic therapy sessions into a well-received play called *The Concept*, described by one moved critic as an encounter group "synthesis of dramaturgy, documentary and psychosocial therapy."[17] Miguel Pinero's *Short Eyes*, a contemporary melodrama set in a house of detention, is similarly an outgrowth of a theater workshop founded at the men's division of Bedford Hills Correctional Facility in Westchester County, New York in 1972. Upon their release, the prisoners involved in the project banded together as an ensemble acting company called "The Family." That group, sometimes including Miguel Pinero who is described by many theater critics as a gifted yet still troubled ex-convict playwright,[18] continues to work together, occasionally at Joseph Papp's New York Shakespeare Festival at the Public Theater; it is most widely known, however, because of the film adaptation of *Short Eyes*. More and more, the well-founded institutional concept of theater-as-therapy is leading some inmates out of institutions and to the public theaters. Unfortunately, it can also lead to an unfounded and disquieting romantic notion of any therapy-as-theater.

A recognizable convention such as theater-as-therapy may comfort *Marat/Sade*'s audiences only for a moment, however. After all, the madmen onstage before us make up a jolting cross-section of mental anguish. They act very differently from their twentieth-century sedated institutionalized counterparts. Despite this fleeting moment of comfort when we first perceive Coulmier to be a forward-looking asylum director, we soon discover that his innovations and his notions of progressive treatment are simple-minded. Approval for Sade's play, for example, had been given, ironically enough, on the basis of the suitability of the bath house setting for a play about the murder of Marat. Coulmier assures us, deadpan:

> I agree with our author Monsieur de Sade
> that his play set in our modern bath house
>   won't be marred
> by all these instruments for mental and physical
>   hygiene
> Quite on the contrary they set the scene
> For in Monsieur de Sade's play he has tried
> to show how Jean-Paul Marat died
> and how he waited in his bath before
> Charlotte Corday came knocking at his door
> (pp. 4–5)

From this first fatuous speech of the asylum director, then, even before his resident playwright has said a single word, we discover that Coulmier is no match for Sade. He is so gullible in the presence of this model patient that he has missed the obvious danger of staging a play on a revolutionary topic on the anniversary of the act *and* in an institution where workers such as those muscular male nurses we see hovering about spend much of their time quieting rebellious madmen.

From Coulmier's opening words onward, the action of *Marat/Sade* becomes double-edged. Its historical point of departure is the early use of amateur performances for therapeutic value at the asylum at Charenton under the direction of Sade, who was an inmate there from 1801 until his death in 1814. As Weiss explains in the "Author's Note on the Historical Background to the Play," appended to the published text of *Marat/Sade*:

> In exclusive Paris circles it was considered a rare pleasure to attend Sade's theatrical performances in the "hiding-place for the moral rejects of civilised society." It is of course probable that these amateur performances consisted in the main of declamatory pieces in the prevailing style. (p. 105)

Ostensibly, then, the action of this play is both historically based (Sade did stage plays at the asylum at Charenton) and naturalistically credible (such activity among inmates is therapeutic). But although the director of the Clinic commends Sade at first for the naturalistic appropriateness of staging a play about the tub-imprisoned Marat in an asylum bath house, he—along with the audience—eventually discovers just how symbolically and didactically appropriate are Sade's choice of the setting and the subject of his play. The bath house setting seems, in Coulmier's official view, to be an economic and clever use of the playing space at Sade's disposal. Sade, however, recognizes the area's more complex potential. By means of Sade, the play's pivotal character, Weiss's drama departs both from history and from naturalism.

Marat/Sade is set on the 13th of July, 1808, fifteen years after the fact of Marat's murder; and Sade's play, commissioned as a therapeutic measure but carried out as a subversive plot, breaks through the time barrier imposed by its subject matter. Not only does Sade insist on bringing Marat up to date on the events which have followed his death, he also decides to confront Marat with his own ideology. Weiss writes in his appendix to the published text of *Marat/Sade* that although "Sade's encounter with Marat, which is the subject of this play, is entirely imaginary, based only on the single fact that it was Sade who spoke the memorial address at Marat's funeral," what interests Weiss in bringing together Sade and Marat in this play is the potential for a dialectical drama based on "the conflict between an individualism carried to extreme lengths and the idea of a political and social upheaval" (p. 106).

But the action of *Marat/Sade* grows increasingly frenetic, moving beyond an intellectual confrontation between Sade and Marat towards a climactic physical confrontation between madmen and their keepers. In an interview with A. Alvarez, Weiss articulated his own ambivalence about the philosophical debate between Sade and his imagined Marat; he acknowledged his intentional use of the asylum as a microcosm; and he pointed out the aesthetic side of his political dialectic. Weiss told his interviewer:

> But the whole play for me, of course, is very personal. On one side, I'm the individual who thinks it's hopeless to change anything in society, that we can't do anything and it's just like hell anyhow; whatever we do is just doomed to be a disaster. That's the point of Sade. . . . And then there is the other point of view: we are in between other people and we want to change something, our lives and perhaps the lives of others too; that's the point of the Socialist and of Marat. And those two absolutely different points of view, they always get together and try to find some solution.[19]

Weiss has rigged the ending of his play to reflect his own torn opinion of who wins the debate in the play-within-the-play. Also, Weiss has used alternative endings to the play. The ending used during the New York run of the Peter Brook production, for example, differs significantly from the one preserved both in the published text and on film. According to the final stage directions in the published text, Roux "*springs forward and places himself before the marchers, his back to them, still with fettered arms.*" He calls out, "When

will you learn to see / when will you learn to take sides."
Then,

> *He tries to force them back, but is drawn in and vanishes*
> *from sight in the still advancing ranks.*
> *The* PATIENTS *are fully at the mercy of their mad marchlike*
> *dance. Many of them hop and spin in ecstasy.*
> COULMIER *incites the* NURSES *to extreme violence.*
> PATIENTS *are struck down.*
> *The* HERALD *is now in front of the orchestra, leaping about*
> *in time to the music.*
> SADE *stands upright on his chair, laughing triumphantly.*
> *In desperation* COULMIER *gives the signal to close the curtain.*
> *CURTAIN* (p. 102)

According to Margaret Croyden, a chronicler of Peter
Brook's work, the New York production ended with an
even deeper irony, with an actors' revolt. Croyden writes:

> In a savage but phantasmagoric nightmare, the luna-
> tics, whose fury had been rising, shout for freedom
> and liberty; they take over the asylum, turn over the
> furniture, and attempt to rape the nuns and kill the
> guards. But the guards, encouraged by Coulmier, wield
> their clubs and sticks; a fierce battle breaks out: a real
> revolution is on. Now the inmates march down to the
> apron of the stage, menacing the audience. Suddenly
> a whistle is heard; everybody stops short; a stage man-
> ager runs up on the stage to control the company; the
> audience is saved. Relieved that it is really only the end
> of the play, the audience applauds the actors. But the
> actors (or inmates) parody the applause. A steady,
> rhythmic, ironic clapping breaks out. Standing there
> at the edge of the apron, virtually impinging upon the
> spectators, smirking sardonically, even viciously, the
> inmates continue to clap. Some of the audience, sens-
> ing the actors' mockery, leave quickly; some sit and
> wonder about the identity of the sane and the insane,

and about the meaning of revolution. Sade looks on, triumphant.[20]

To further convolute the philosophical implications of his play, Weiss has mentioned using alternative endings for different productions, for different nations:

> The play, at least in its first version, leaves it up to the audience to decide for itself [between the arguments of Marat and Sade]. Later I added an epilogue, which has been played only in Rostock (E. Germany), which makes it clear that from the playwright's point of view Marat is right. Sade's doubts are valid—we know the difficulties that have arisen in some of the socialist countries—but the epilogue makes it clear that some societies, then as now, require radical change. One recognizes the necessity for radical changes in society, and yet cannot avoid noting that they are often accompanied by unexpected effects. . . .
>
> I have continued to change the printed version between productions. It is now in a fourth edition, and there are substantial differences between that and the play which was initially performed. Along the way, I also eliminated more and more of the stage instructions as I began to realize that directors work more imaginatively when the playwright is not guiding their hand all the time.[21]

Probably the most significant verbal variable in the ending of *Marat/Sade* is the following exchange between the Herald and Sade immediately following the murder of Marat in Episode 32, present in Brook's screen version but absent from the published text:

HERALD.   Tell us Monsieur de Sade for our instruction
just what you have achieved with your production.
Who won? Who lost? We'd like to know
the meaning of your bath-house show

SADE.   Our play's chief aim has been—to take to bits
         great propositions and their opposites,
         see how they work, then let them fight it out.
         The point? Some light on our eternal doubt.
         I have twisted and turned them every way
         and find no ending to our play.
         Marat and I both advocated force
         but in debate each took a different course.
         Each wanted changes, but his views and mine
         on using power never can combine.
         On the one side he who thinks our lives
         can be improved with axes and knives.
         Or—the one who'd submerge in his imagi-
            nation
         seeking a personal annihilation.
         So for me the last word cannot ever be spoken.
         I am left with a question that's always open.[22]

All Weiss's revisions and alternative endings aside, the
central reason why the winner of the debate in the play-
within-the-play remains debatable (no matter whether Marat
or Sade gets the last laugh in any given production) is that
Weiss has put their debate *in* a play *in* an asylum *in* a
theater—in short, in an ontological conundrum. In the context of the action, the debate becomes a subtle, cruel joke
on those members of the audience who, like Walter Kerr,
are sometimes straining to heed the intellectual debate, for
finally, as Weiss suggests by his laissez-faire attitude towards
directors, the confrontation between the playwright, Sade,
and his dramatic persona, Marat, is ironically overshadowed by the Structure suggested by the madhouse which
encloses and inevitably negates them both.

So Sade's experimental theatrical therapy for mental patients serves Weiss on two levels: an asylum show is a valid
plot device in the naturalistic framework of *Marat/Sade*, and
Sade's script is a theatricalization of the playwright's conflicting ideas. The inmate production is both mimetic and
schematic, for Sade's unconventional scenario transcends

its purportedly therapeutic function. Charenton's resident celebrity has resourcefully suited his rhetoric, ideas, and actors to the present situation. His histrionic display calls forth revolt from the roots of psychic experience, and it reinforces rather than corrects situational improprieties, symptoms of derangement. Charenton's experiment in group therapy is finally a fiasco, but Sade's directorial debut in the asylum's "modern bath house," surrounded by "instruments for mental and physical hygiene" (pp. 4–5), is a literal *coup de théâtre*. His play calls for the acting out of repressed desires among the most disturbed members of the inmate population. Here, in familiar, despised surroundings, the distinctions between reality and illusion may become blurred by passion.

Sade insures the overlapping of play into stage reality by typecasting his actors. He chooses a somnambulist to play the role of Corday; she is led through her part like a sleepwalker in a half-remembered dream of death. He chooses an erotomaniac to play the role of Duperret; he *"takes advantage of his role as Corday's lover at every suitable opportunity"* (p. ix). He chooses an obsessive, withdrawn patient to play the role of Simonne Evrard; she *"seizes every opportunity"* in her capacity as Marat's mistress to change his bandage with her unsteady hands (p. viii). He chooses a straightjacketed inmate to play the role of Jacques Roux; his physical restraint objectifies the censor's control over his rabble-rousing remarks (p. 7). And for the title role of the bathing, rotting Marat, Sade chooses: "a lucky paranoic one of those / who've made unprecedented strides since we / introduced them to hydrotherapy" (p. 6).

Other patients, extras in Sade's incendiary play, also confuse their supporting roles with their real situation at Charenton. In crowd scenes, especially, some patients become possessed by the spirit of their performance as they connect their present conditions to the events of the recent past which they resurrect. A "regrettable incident" occurs, for example, when a patient with a clergyman's collar around his neck breaks loose from the group and hops forward on his knees. The blasphemous prayer of this former abbot of a monastery is abruptly halted as "MALE NURSES *throw themselves on the* PATIENT, *overpower him, put him under a shower, then bind him and drag him to the back*" (pp. 30–31). Later, the patient who plays Jacques Roux becomes incensed by his own rhetoric and must be forcibly restrained by Nurses who drag him off the dais and strap him to a bench (p. 46).

Although most of the patients exhibit some form of this role confusion, the Four Singers in Sade's play are instead involved in alternate "removal activities" of asylum life. Their separate "escape-world" of gambling and drinking exists side-by-side with the primary removal activity, the play now in progress. The Four Singers—stretched out on the floor playing cards (pp. 15–16), filling in time with pranks, dice, and card tricks (p. 38), passing around a bottle (p. 44), and scratching themselves and yawning (p. 84)— are also engaged in remedial play. Unlike the other participants in Sade's functional performance, however, the Singers stay on the sidelines of the acting arena. Even as Roux is being forcibly restrained, the Singers "*listen to the disturbance, but soon lose interest*" (p. 44). Consistently, the detached antics of the Four Singers remind us of the real function of Sade's play as a diversion from the tedium of a total institution. The Singers also function as a framing device linking Weiss's outer play to Sade's inner play. By keeping his Singers occupied in a natural manner, Weiss frees them from the contagious chaos of Sade's play, from which they stand apart as choral commentators.

Eventually, however, all the actors abandon themselves to their parts which are, in fact, extensions of themselves. Sade's play betrays its supposedly therapeutic intention. Under normal circumstances, one of the values of inmate-organized entertainments is the acknowledgment, channeling, and purgation of rebellious feelings through playful expression of such feelings. Goffman observes the benefits of exchanging "conspiracy for expression":

There is often a hint or a splash of rebellion in the role that inmates take in these ceremonies. Whether through a sly article, a satirical sketch, or overfamiliarity during a dance, the subordinate in some ways profanes the superordinate. . . . The very toleration of this skittishness is a sign of the strength of the establishment state. . . . To act out one's rebellion before the authorities at a time when this is legitimate is to exchange conspiracy for expression.[23]

Transcending an asylum's normal limit of rebellious acting-out, however, Sade's play incites rather than alleviates the rebellious urges of the inmates. For Sade's play, like one of Mme. Irma's little pageants in Genet's *The Balcony*, is "a true image, born of a false spectacle."[24] His creation of a luminous double for their present state of suspended animation causes a sensation among the asylum inmates. They, too, long to escape from a cell of passivity. Like Sade and his allegorical figures culled from an episode of history, they, too, would welcome a violent affirmation of their own existence *now*.

During the play proper, Sade's psychodrama upstages Weiss's use of a madhouse as a microcosm. Encouraging improvisation among his mad method actors, Sade turns a historical play into a theatrical happening. This Dionysian instigator goads his cast into complete identification with their mimetic action; the ensemble players of Charenton apply Sade's lessons from history to their own restless community, and consequently they infuse their play with a subtext concerning their own subjugation to an imposing power. As Sade's drama of ideas exposes the asylum by veiled analogy, unrest mounts among the inmates. Whispering Corday's name as an incantation to revolt (p. 13), for example, the patients also recite chants of "Freedom Freedom Freedom," while beating out the rhythm emphatically: "Who keeps us prisoner / Who locks us in / We're all normal and we want our freedom" (p. 12). Overtly harmless revels become frenzied rites; like Bacchic celebrants, the unfettered members of the cast of Sade's play finally lose control and unleash fury. A shadowbox interlude threatens to become a full-scale riot.

The Herald is the border guard between Sade's inflammatory entertainment and the controlling reality of the encompassing institution. His position in Sade's production is precarious. He introduces, explicates, and often apologizes for episodes of Sade's conception. Like Barnet in Peter Nichols's *The National Health*, the Herald steps out of the engulfing action, and he speaks to us for his author. At irregular intervals, the Herald, having donned a harlequin smock over his hospital shirt, must stop Sade's show to defend an especially disturbing passage on the basis of historical accuracy, to remind a possibly offended audience that the action of Sade's play all happened once upon a time (p. 30), or to apologize for the revolutionary rhetoric of what he assures us are outdated diatribes (pp. 43–44). The Herald placates an increasingly agitated Coulmier with justifications for Sade's restoration of passages which were to be cut from the performance. Politely overriding the censor, the Herald guides us into a labyrinth of paroxysmal action.

Drawing us into the inmates' theatricale with a shrill whistle and a sharp tap of his staff, the Herald is Sade's ironic spokesman. His job is to interrupt frequently with reassurances scripted by Sade:

> We only show these people massacred
> because this indisputably occurred
> Please calmly watch these barbarous displays
> which could not happen nowadays
> The men of that time mostly now demised
> were primitive we are more civilised
>
> (p. 22)

Such constant reassurances are cold comfort, recited as they are against the cold, stark background of the mental asylum. These conciliatory platitudes mouthed by the Herald are also Sade's—and Weiss's—transparent condemnations of massacres which could and *have* happened "nowadays." Sade has interpolated the Herald's disclaimers, his ironic asides and protestations, which are meant to deceive the asylum officials and the invited guests (represented by us). But we are still ourselves after all, members of the post-World War II audience, and we sense that the Herald's coded speeches are Artaudian "signaling through the flames"; they follow Artaud's dictum for the theater "to break through language in order to touch life."[25]

THE CHARACTER of Marat is a psychodramatic extension of the character of Sade; he is his double, his attempt to "break through language in order to touch life." Together, Sade and Marat reflect the paradox confronting a revolutionary playwright. Marat, the advocate of mass freedom in Sade's subjective drama, is a prisoner of his own diseased body. Sade, the advocate of individual freedom in the encompassing drama, is himself a prisoner in an asylum. Marat withdraws to the cooling water of his tub; Sade withdraws to the turbulent waves of his imagination.

In Episode 12, "Conversation Concerning Life and Death," Sade engages his projected double in a two-sided polemic, a discussion of nature which is, in the play's larger framework, an unresolvable debate about the political and psychic power of art. At this point in the play-within-the-play, however, the theatrical essence of the conflict is overshadowed by its statement of ideas in comparative stasis. For Episode 12 follows a particularly grotesque mime of the brutal justice of Marat's regime. After the excited patients are quieted, Sade laments the decline of bloodthirsty throngs; he is nostalgic for the good old days of slow, torturous murders like those we have just seen in dumb show (pp. 23–26). Sade claims to see death as the "basis of all of life":

Every death even the cruellest death
drowns in the total indifference of Nature
Nature herself would watch unmoved
if we destroyed the entire human race

(*rising*)
I hate Nature
this passionless spectator this unbreakable iceberg-face
that can bear everything
this goads us to greater and greater acts
(p. 24)

Marat, Sade's rationalist counterpart, replies, "What you
call the indifference of Nature / is your own lack of compassion" (p. 26); then he offers an alternative to Sade's
Artaudian aesthetic of cruelty to test nature. From his tub
in the asylum's rehearsal hall for revolution, Marat suggests
commitment to an idea as a means of surviving in absurd
circumstances:

If I am extreme I am not extreme in the same way as you
Against Nature's silence I use action
In the vast indifference I invent a meaning
I don't watch unmoved I intervene
and say that this and this are wrong
and I work to alter them and improve them
The important thing
is to pull yourself up by your own hair
to turn yourself inside out
and see the whole world with fresh eyes
(pp. 26–27)

Sade himself remains detached, unengaged, until, in what
is perhaps the most striking example of Brook's incorpo-
ration of symbolic action into a naturalistic setting, Sade
later slowly enters the acting arena to expose himself—
mind and body—to the pain of his revolutionary vision. As
Sade stands naked before us, baring his back to the whip
he hands to the somnambulistic Corday (who is herself an
invention of Sade's dark mind), he recounts his psychic
experiment in the Bastille. He confesses:

In prison I created in my mind
monstrous representatives of a dying class

who could only exercise their power
in spectacularly staged orgies
I recorded the mechanics of their atrocities
in the minutest detail
and brought out everything wicked and brutal
that lay inside me
In a criminal society
I dug the criminal out of myself
so I could understand him and so understand
the times we live in
(p. 47)

Sade reminds his audience of "desecrations and tortures" committed by "giants" harbored within his imagination (p. 47). As Sade describes the brutality with which he saw his own prophecies coming true, he submits to a rhythmic flogging by Corday. Under Brook's direction, this episode, "Monsieur de Sade is Whipped," exemplified the play's intrinsic theatrical poetry. For Corday struck Sade with a defiant toss of her head, not with a whip in her hand. In synchronization as Corday made these hypnotic lashing motions, patients imitated the hissing sound of a whip rhythmically striking flesh. According to one New York critic, this "whipping of Sade by Charlotte Corday with her long hair, though not literally painful, stings."[26] Placing a real whip in an inmate's clenched fist would, of course, seriously jeopardize the impression we have of naturalistic accuracy. Aware that Corday's blows could inflict no real pain given the premise of the play, Brook substituted a symbolic motion of scorn for an overt assault. Such a substitution reminded the audience that "The Assassination of Marat" is just an insane asylum diversion, with a murderess who is not at all dangerous or armed with a weapon in a real sense; moreover, it intensified for the audience the symbolic thrust of Sade's words, agonizingly brought forth while he is being flogged.

When "Monsieur de Sade is Whipped" in the Brook production, we suddenly get a visceral sense of what Artaud means when he writes that "everything that acts is a cruelty," and that the stage demands a "concrete physical language" to express thoughts "beyond the reach of the spoken language," to express *metaphysics-in-action.*"[27] Artaud proposes a theater in which "violent physical images crush and hypnotize the sensibility of the spectator seized by the theater as by a whirlwind of higher forces."[28] This elusive, ecstatic vision has inspired virtually all playwrights and directors working in the contemporary mode. Indeed, the engorged Structure of plays of impasse is the fulfillment of Artaud's demand for all acts to be felt as a concrete language of impingement, for all physical objects to be felt as crushing, hypnotic forces.

But rarely have the lucidity and power of the moment when "Monsieur de Sade is Whipped" in the Brook production been equalled. Sade's anachronistically charged words are verbal bricks hurled at the audience with Artaudian accuracy. When Corday is dragged away from Sade's crumpled body, the asylum's playwright-in-residence breathlessly warns the audience that the revolution is leading

> To the withering of the individual man
> and a slow merging into uniformity
> to the death of choice
> to self denial
> to deadly weakness
> in a state
> which has no contact with individuals
> but which is impregnable
> (p. 49)

The considerable power of this soliloquy is intensified by the rhythmic flogging that underscores Sade's words. As Sade submits himself to those symbolically self-inflicted lashes of Corday's whip, he seems eerily close to us and vulnerable. For in this soliloquy, Sade, Weiss's embodiment of historical inquiry and psychic probing, describes a political state of mind all too familiar to a 1965 audience.

Sade's testimony is multifaceted: it is at once the un-
guarded confession of an inmate's practical means of survival, the set-speech defense of a manipulative playwright,
and the voice-over disavowal of a modern man out of time.
Sade concedes defeat, and he defines himself on this cruel,
modern ground of individual despair:

> I am one of those who has to be defeated
> and from this defeat I want to seize
> all I can get with my own strength
> I step out of my place
> and watch what happens
> without joining in
> observing
> noting down my observations
> and all around me
> stillness
> (p. 50)

Like an inmate in an asylum, Sade has become a disciplined
being, concealing evidence of what sociologists vividly dub
"spiritual leave-taking" beneath a passive demeanor, behind a misleading appearance of cooperation. At the same
time, Sade's adoption of a placid mask as a method of
survival (his means of "making out," in the sociological
vernacular) in a massive Structure mirrors our contemporary en masse resignation to external control. The character of Sade exhibits a familiar personal distancing, a special kind of moral "absenteeism," a detachment identified
by sociologists as "a defaulting not from prescribed activity
but from prescribed being." He displays a superficial adoption of sanctioned behavior especially found in mental hospitals where any deviation from "normal" behavior, any
"signs of disaffiliation," even the "common expressions
through which people hold off the embrace of organiza-
tions—insolence, silence, *sotto voce* remarks, uncooperative-
ness, malicious destruction of interior decorations, and so
forth," are read as symptoms, as "evidence that the patient
properly belongs where he now finds himself."[29]

Sade is careful to mask such "signs of disaffiliation" in himself, and to pin them instead on others, on the actors performing his play of opposing ideas in which the struggle with the institution is integrated into a relentless struggle within the split self. In Episode 26, "The Faces of Marat," for example, Sade's second self projects his own distorted self-image onto the accusing faces which appear from his past (pp. 62–71). Similarly, the political figures who polarize the stage in the episode of "The National Assembly" may be seen as grotesque objectifications of a split internal state. As the Herald tells us in his prologue to this episode, "Marat is still in his bathtub confined / but politicians crowd into his mind" (p. 73). As he works through his own visions of cruelty, Sade caters to the decadent whims of his keepers and their guests who have come here to be amused by gyrating, gesticulating madmen; meanwhile, he plans to sabotage their asylum from within its walls. Like the members of his modern audience, Weiss's historical clairvoyant seems to be a passive observer. But this impression is deceptive: Sade encourages his fellow inmates to storm the insurmountable barricades of totalitarian control while he himself slips with verbal agility across a chronological chasm.

Throughout *Marat/Sade*, Weiss's fictive playwright manipulates the response of his twentieth-century audience with allusions to modern warfare and genocide in an eighteenth-century asylum. The patients in his production judge man to be a "mad animal" (p. 32) who can "talk of people as gardeners talk of leaves for burning" (p. 88). Marat warns us of wars "whose weapons rapidly developed / by servile scientists / will become more and more deadly / until they can with a flick of a finger / tear a million of you to pieces" (p. 56). And Sade himself, hinting at horrors recognizable as our own, asserts "Nature herself would watch unmoved / if we destroyed the entire human race" for we have already "experimented in our laboratories / before applying the final solution" (p. 24). All these words are freighted with the weight of recent history, that last phrase in particular being a hollow reminder of the rationalization of concentration camps. Such familiar phrases are strewn throughout the action of the play. Sometimes we in the audience do not even hear them; they go by in the din, sounding vaguely familiar. Other times, they come through loud and clear, hitting us at odd moments, implying vague yet lethal analogies between the world as it is and the jarring world onstage.

Both Sade and the Herald are Weiss's theatrical impostors. Both seem to take us into their confidence (Sade with his anachronistic references to twentieth-century atrocities, and the Herald with his denials of malice of forethought in rhymed doggerel), yet both turn on us at the end of Sade's show. Throughout *Marat/Sade*, these two characters link us to the rules of Weiss's game: both face us directly, hinting broadly that despite the peculiarity of its cast and setting, this is actually a play of ideas; these madmen and this formidable asylum are metaphors for modern man and his crazy world.

By putting the catch phrases of post-atomic society into the mouths of eighteenth-century madmen, Weiss expands the dimensions of the contemporary theater. *Marat/Sade* uses its historical premise and naturalistic phenomena to engulf us in an asylum setting; it uses its primary characters and their formal recitations to engage us in a contrapuntal interplay of ideas; it uses a stylized reenactment of revolutionary deeds to lead us to logical analogies; and it uses these same dramatic inventions to expose us to an archetypal battle raging within a divided self. But it never stops reminding us of *now*.

The multiple levels of *Marat/Sade* are made ironic by its self-conscious twentieth-century theatricality, for Weiss finally traps us in a Pirandellian construct. We are constantly reminded of our communal role at this ceremonial event not only by Sade's references to a ruined world where total institutions serve as laboratories for absurd experiments seeking a "final solution" in which to dissolve the human spirit, but also by the devastating end of this play which may touch us directly. The debate seems at first to be between Sade and Marat, spokesmen respectively for personal and political freedom. But the Marat of this play is, after all, an invention of Sade's; the two roles are finally complementary models of a singular man, elements of a single consciousness which emerges in the final movement towards synthesis in *Marat/Sade*. After the play-within-the-play has demonstrated the apparently antithetical positions of Marat and Sade, it then fuses these two positions in an assault upon the enveloping institution. When the somber game of Sade's design erupts, however, chaos rules not only the institution, but also our stage. Only then—when the players go berserk and start to advance towards *us* in a "mad, marchlike dance" (p. 102), when the cruel theorist and his existential scapegoat both become reasonable voices echoing in the chaotic din of passion, and when play threatens to spill over into reality—can we in the audience comprehend Weiss's poetic dialectic, the tension between the naturalistic and symbolic functions of theatrical signs, the tension possible when contemporary drama localizes an apocalyptic vision.

Chaos finally breaks out in the epilogue of Sade's play about the passion of his Marat. After repeated postponements during which Sade disrupts Corday's deliberate slow motions resembling "*a ritual act*" (p. 14) with discussion, exhortation, and pageantry, the central action of the play is completed. During her third visit, Corday once more approaches her prey, raises the dagger from beneath her bodice, and is poised to strike. Suddenly, however, the Herald blows shrilly on his whistle, and all the players freeze in their positions. In the last minute of their increasingly urgent game, the Herald must once again call time out. He explains Sade's strategy in terms which suggest the didactic aims of Brecht's epic theater:

Now it's part of Sade's dramatic plan
to interrupt the climax so this man
Marat can hear and gasp with his last breath
at how the world will go after his death

111

With a musical history we'll bring him up to date
From seventeen-ninety-three to eighteen-eight
(pp. 95–96)

Poor old Marat is now serenaded by the Four Singers who *"perform grotesquely in time to the music"* of a *"very quick military march."* The Herald *"displays banners showing the date of the events as they are described"* (p. 96). Parading past Marat with derisive pomp come fifteen "glorious years"; a medley of war rings in our ears. Only after the final refrain, a rhythmic cheer for revolution, can Corday fulfill her historical role and her dramatic task. She kills Marat with a ceremonial gesture, and the Patients *"let out one single scream"* (p. 99). This communal shriek punctuates their performance. According to Weiss's stage directions, Corday crumples on the stage, Sade stands contemplating the scene, and Marat topples over in his tub *"as in David's classical picture, with his right hand over the edge of the bath. In his right hand he still holds his pen, in his left his papers"* (p. 99). Sade's play is over; it ends with a familiar image recreated in a stage tableau. A picture of history seems to frame the play.

But Weiss's play is not yet over. His epilogue takes that representational image out of its frame, and hurls it at the audience. Accompanied by *"soft ceremonious music,"* Coulmier officially closes the show with political platitudes expressed in rhymed doggerel which suggests that he, too, delivers set speeches:

Enlightened ladies pious gentlemen
Let's close the history book and then
return to eighteen-eight the present day
of which though not unclouded we may say
it promises that mankind soon will cease
to fear the storms of wars the squalls of peace
(p. 99)

Of course, the modern audience recognizes the bleak irony of Coulmier's conciliatory remarks. More significant, however, is the dramatic fact of which his address reminds us:

Weiss's Structure, his model onstage of unending oppression, impinges on us, too.

We may see Sade's futile dilemma from a historical distance, but the players see *us* on a more immediate plane. We have been assigned a part in this bedlam; we tacitly accepted this role at the start, and now we must play to the finish. As Johan Huizinga states in *Homo Ludens: A Study of the Play Element in Culture*:

> This intensity of, and absorption in, play finds no explanation in biological analysis. Yet in this intensity, this absorption, this power of maddening, lies the very essence, the primordial quality of play. . . .
>
> Since the reality of play extends beyond the sphere of human life it cannot have its foundations in any rational nexus, because this would limit it to mankind. The incidence of play is not associated with any particular stage of civilization or view of the universe. . . . Play cannot be denied. You can deny, if you like, nearly all abstractions: justice, beauty, truth, goodness, mind, God. You can deny seriousness, but not play.
>
> But in acknowledging play you acknowledge mind, for whatever else play is, it is not matter. Even in the animal world it bursts the bounds of the physically existent. From the point of view of a world wholly determined by the operation of blind forces, play would be altogether superfluous. Play only becomes possible, thinkable and understandable when an influx of *mind* breaks down the absolute determinism of the cosmos. The very existence of play continually confirms the supra-logical nature of the human situation. Animals play, so they must be more than merely mechanical things. We play and know that we play, so we must be more than merely rational beings, for play is irrational.[30]

Marat/Sade is founded upon this principle of play: play releases man from his rational bonds. It exists in a world apart; it immerses us in another experience, yet it never challenges the "supra-logic" of everyday life. This unique reality of play is the saving grace for those condemned to Weiss's resilient Structure. As in other plays of impasse, where the Structure's defeated population may find its only joy in play, *Marat/Sade* asserts the autonomy of play; it demonstrates how

> Play *interrupts* the continuity and purposive structure of our lives; it remains at a distance from our usual mode of existence. But while seeming to be unrelated to our normal life, it relates to it in a very meaningful way, namely in its mode of representation. If we define play in the usual way by contrasting it with work, reality, seriousness and authenticity, we falsely juxtapose it with other existential phenomena. Play is a basic existential phenomenon, just as primordial and autonomous as death, love, work and struggle for power, but it is *not* bound to these phenomena in a common ultimate purpose. Play, so to speak, confronts them all—it absorbs them by representing them. We play at being serious, we play truth, we play reality, we play work and struggle, we play love and death—and we even play play itself.[31]

Weiss has called *Marat/Sade* a "disciplined happening,"[32] and this suggestive term suits the play well. The substance of Weiss's play is not to be found in the ideological confrontation between Sade and Marat; rather, this level of conflict knots with that of the psychological conflict, and both are inextricably bound by the form of *Marat/Sade*, in which Weiss intertwines mutiple strands of reality. His play-within-the-play releases the inmates from the bonds of their maladies; the parable they enact incites them to revolt; and in a mad frenzy they turn therapeutic play into psycho-dramatic aggression. Weiss's play, like Sade's within, is an experiment. Like Sade, Weiss writes a drama concretely expressing irrational forces which defy rational theorists of revolution. Like Sade, Weiss endows his actors with a stage reality as vivid and as secret as their own. And like Sade,

Weiss attacks his audience regardless of their social or moral stance. For *Marat/Sade* is a play in movement, not in stasis. Its climax involves us in the paradox of uncontrolled freedom by abandoning the etiquette of the playhouse, the logic of debate, and the discipline of the self all at once. In the final moments of *Marat/Sade*, the outer and the inner realities of both the asylum and the stage collide. Strands of reality unravel before us, and the result in the theater—and by extension, in the world—is anarchy.

So after building layer upon layer of theatrical consciousness, Weiss's play ends where it began. All those levels of microcosm, embodied dialectics, and psychodramatic projections are suddenly stripped away when Sade's show ends. What remains before us is a vivid reconstruction of an asylum, and madness is everywhere. Sade's amateur troupe, aroused by the passion of the songs they learned by rote, confuse themselves with their make-believe roles and begin to revolt. Coulmier's propaganda is drowned out by the prophetic sound of the patients' stamping feet. Even the Herald, formerly the most contained actor, loses his hold on the difference between illusion and reality, playing and being. He begins throwing "*buckets etc.*" around, starts the contagious brawl with the male nurses, and is last seen in front of the orchestra, "*leaping about in time to the music*" (pp. 101–102). When the Herald falls into the pit, he precipitates a general commotion. All the inmates—Sade's method actors in a primordial improvisation—refuse to relinquish the power of play.

The inmates of Charenton advance toward us, "*fully at the mercy of their mad marchlike dance. Many of them hop and spin in ecstasy*" (p. 102). They are responding to their unfamiliar psychic state of freedom according to the tenets of Jerzy Grotowski's Poor Theater: "At a moment of psychic shock, a moment of terror, of mortal danger or tremendous joy, a man does not behave 'naturally.' A man in an elevated spiritual state uses rhythmically articulated signs, begins to dance, to sing."[33] The stage is filled with violent acts. An angry mob of madmen threatens our safety. They seem ready to storm over the footlights across more than a century and a half to force their way into a modern audience. As their ecstatic revolt gains momentum, Sade *"watches with a faint smile, almost indulgent"* (p. 101), and finally, he *"stands upright on his chair, laughing triumphantly"* (p. 102). The representational insurrection which he masterminded has taken on a life of its own.

No matter which ending of *Marat/Sade* we experience, then—the Brook-directed ending in which the Royal Shakespeare Company actors finally seemed to drop their roles in the play and to exude their own genuine hatred of us, or Weiss's published version of the ending in which actors maintain their play-identity as madmen—still, the effect of the end of the play is double: it is a relief and it is troubling. If the production follows the published text, chanting and rhythmic cries reach a crescendo when the curtain hastily descends on the antics of the asylum. *"Music, shouting and tramping increase to a tempest"* (p. 101). The inmates are engaged in a temporary takeover of their asylum which is also our stage. As the curtain falls, we get a glimpse of the brutal force which will bring the inmates back to their senses. Yet we are relieved when that curtain drops, for it means that *our* play is really over: we are no longer jeopardized by the onslaught of terror; once again we are safe in our theater seats.

We cannot applaud, however, when this version of *Marat/Sade* ends, for we can still hear the screams of the inmates as they are struck down behind a satin curtain. If the production follows the Brook curtainless model, on the other hand, all action freezes when the sound of the whistle signals the end of the play. Stopped are both the revolution of madmen and the brutal force called forth to quell it. An image of chaos yields to the rules of a game, a play on a stage. In relief, we applaud, for that whistle, that freeze-framed action, and that "stage manager" running onstage to end the play are relatively conventional cues for us that this fictive reality is containable, controllable, fixed. But Brook's production involves us one step further. His actors, no longer eighteenth-century madmen, look long and hard into the audience, and they mock our applause. What these actors see in our faces we cannot know, but we do wonder, and we will not forget that wonder.

A SPECTACULAR MAD SHOW of revolution, *Marat/Sade* is shocking in its authenticity, and it is cruel in the Artaudian sense. From within the encompassing framework of an eighteenth-century asylum, Weiss's play bombards us with stark ceremonies and furious, anguished sounds. In the Brook production in particular, *Marat/Sade* finally storms the fourth wall of the conventional modern theater, and it looses temporary bedlam on the contemporary stage. Dürrenmatt's *The Physicists* and Storey's *Home*—two other contemporary plays exploring the edges of insanity and the want of asylum—share with *Marat/Sade* its questioning of just who belongs in the madhouse and who dares decide. All three of these plays are historical conceits: *Marat/Sade* is a revolution confined to the straitjacket of history; *The Physicists* is an atomic age warning; and *Home* mourns the decline of the British empire.

Yet *The Physicists* and *Home*—both of which, despite formal power, are surely lesser plays than the astonishing *Marat/Sade*—contrast with *Marat/Sade* when it comes to pace and tone: unlike the inmates crowded in the bath hall at Charenton who emit a strident battle cry, the geniuses taking refuge in *The Physicists* and the guests chatting on the lawn of *Home* pour forth a muted lament. Bedlam is never unleashed in these two plays, not even for an instant, for Dürrenmatt's and Storey's inmates are shrewder than the people of Charenton. They know that there are no escape routes. They harbor no hopes of breaking the impasse. In *The Physicists* and *Home*, the sense of insanity that reaches a feverish pitch in *Marat/Sade* is tempered by a recognition of the contemporary condition of despair and inquietude, when life itself demands a show of strength, when insanity emerges as a sovereign state of mind.

The Physicists

Friedrich Dürrenmatt's *The Physicists* is a play of ideas. Talking about the intention of his play, the playwright has said, "It is not so much a play about the hydrogen bomb as about science itself, and the impossibility of escaping the consequences of one's thinking. Once a scientist has followed a certain trend of thought he simply cannot run away from its consequences, its practical results. That is an act of cowardice." Although Dürrenmatt's play has political overtones, he insists, "What prompted me to write *The Physicists* was not politics at all. I was interested in working out a situation, a situation that takes the worst possible turn; and also the workings of chance, which always fascinate me. In this case everything turns on the physicist who wants to escape into a lunatic asylum, having chosen the worst possible lunatic asylum to hide in; and on that choice, which is pure chance, the fate of the world may depend."[34]

Using the asylum setting for a case study of "the workings of chance" and the "consequences of one's thinking," *The Physicists* complements *Marat/Sade*, a play in whose asylum setting chance is worked out in a historical framework and thought is drowned in a cacophony. Ironically, when *The Physicists* was directed in London in 1963 by Peter Brook, Dürrenmatt found the approach to his idea and asylum setting curious. "I had imagined the English actors would underplay much more than the Germans or the Swiss. But not at all," he told an interviewer. "In one of the best of the German productions, for example, the mad lady doctor made her revelations at the end sitting quietly on the sofa, using very little voice and emphasis. That gave it a marvellously mad effect. In Peter Brook's production there is a great deal of movement and vociferation. The London production is also the first I have seen that does not strictly adhere to the set as I described it in the stage directions. In Zurich, Berlin, Munich, and Hamburg they all followed my idea of a circular room with three doors leading to the physicists' rooms at the back. Here [in London] there is only one door."[35] Clearly Brook's production of *The Physicists* heightened that play's core of agitated "movement and vociferation" as it heightened—to a much greater degree, of course—the core of agitation, lunacy, and revolution in *Marat/Sade*.

With their comparable settings and comparable frenetic movement toward a final impasse, *The Physicists* and *Marat/Sade* are still stylistically dissimilar. Weiss's play, without Brook's direction, is dead serious. *The Physicists*, however, is a comedy. In his often-quoted essay of 1955, "Problems of the Theatre" ("Theaterprobleme"), Dürrenmatt discusses what he sees as the problem of contemporary dramatists, the impossibility of expressing the tragic sense in a world gone awry:

> Tragedy presupposes guilt, despair, moderation, lucidity, vision, a sense of responsibility. In the Punch-and-Judy show of our century . . . there are no more guilty and also, no responsible men. It is always, "We couldn't help it" and "We didn't really want that to happen." And indeed, things happen without anyone in particular being responsible for them. Everything is dragged along and everyone gets caught somewhere in the sweep of events. We are all collectively guilty, collectively bogged down in the sins of our fathers and our forefathers. We are the offspring of children. That is our misfortune, but not our guilt: guilt can exist only as a personal achievement, as a religious deed. Comedy alone is suitable for us.

For Dürrenmatt, whose theory sheds light on many contemporary plays of impasse, the Punch-and-Judy show of our age belies the tragic impulse. "Our world has led to the grotesque as well as to the atom bomb, and so it is a world like that of Hieronymus Bosch whose apocalyptic paintings are also grotesque," he writes. "But the grotesque is only a way of expressing in a tangible manner, of making us perceive physically the paradoxical, the form of the unformed, the face of a world without face; and just as in our

119

thinking today we seem to be unable to do without the concept of the paradox, so also in art, and in our world which at times seems still to exist only because the atom bomb exists: out of fear of the bomb." In *The Physicists*, a play of what Dürrenmatt might call "immaterializing" stages, "the tragic is still possible even if pure tragedy is not. We can achieve the tragic out of comedy. . . . Actions of state today have become *post-hoc* satyric dramas which follow the tragedies executed in secret earlier."[36] In Dürrenmatt's poetics, expressed in his theoretical writings and in the opening stage directions to *The Physicists*, "the satire precedes the tragedy."[37]

Like Tom Stoppard's *Every Good Boy Deserves Favour* (1978), a play set in a Soviet mental hospital cell shared by a political dissident and a madman who thinks he has a symphony orchestra handy (the play's title is the mnemonic phrase for "EGBDF," the notes on the lines of the treble clef), *The Physicists* focuses on the asylum as a social phenomenon, on madness as socially or politically diagnosed. Like Stoppard's play, which brings a full orchestra in black tie to the stage so that we in the audience hear the madman's imagined music and we see it performed, *The Physicists* makes the madman's vision seem sane and lucid. Describing his use of the rather extravagant concrete metaphor of the full orchestra transported to an asylum cell in *Every Good Boy Deserves Favour*, Stoppard has said, "The subject matter seemed appropriate to the form: the dissident is a discordant note in a highly orchestrated society."[38] Similarly, *The Physicists* uses science, music, and a satirically rendered asylum to express a serious thesis.

A man of reason in a world gone mad, caught between his morality of logic and his impulse towards survival—a man alone, arguing with himself, debating issues while around him rational order collapses—this is a recurring image in Friedrich Dürrenmatt's plays. Dürrenmatt's focus on the struggle for integrity by an individual surrounded by an irrational, relentless force is surely related to his nationality and to his age. The Swiss playwright, born in

1921 near Berne, the son of a Protestant pastor, studied theology and philosophy at the Universities of Berne and Zurich, and began his career as a writer during World War II. Like his compatriot, Max Frisch, whose *The Firebugs* (1958) may be seen as a political allegory about passive compliance with the demands of stockpiling invaders, Dürrenmatt tends to set his plays at the edge of modern civilization; his plays are complicated mechanisms in which suspenseful situations and philosophical discussions interlock, cutting characters off from conventional means of escape onstage. The most famous of these plays in America are probably Dürrenmatt's third play, *Romulus the Great* (1949), a farcical history play about a ruler who embraces the end of his empire; a mellowed version of his *Visit of the Old Woman* (1956), a revenge play of ideas about lovers' debts and the price of a life; and his *Play Strindberg* (1969), a broad transformation of *The Dance of Death* into a choreographed boxing match of marriage.

DÜRRENMATT'S *The Physicists*, first presented in 1962, is an atomic-age play: its setting is a madhouse, one of the most popular concrete metaphors in plays of impasse, and its premise is civilization perched atop a powder keg. A play of this kind finally calls into question several assumptions: What is sanity? Where are the boundaries of the asylum? How is a lunatic to be distinguished from a scientist, or from a sage, or from an actor? In a sanatorium that doubles as an image of shelter from engagement in an unstable world *and* as a stylized reflection of that unstable world, paradoxes abound. As Möbius, the pivotal character of this play, observes, "Only in the madhouse can we be free. Only in the madhouse can we think our own thoughts. Outside they would be dynamite" (p. 82).

Inside the madhouse, too, however, Möbius's ideas are dynamite, for his philosophical last resort is really an elaborate trap set for him by forces from the world outside. "*Les Cerisiers,*" an exclusive "*villa*" of a sanatorium, is described in the opening stage directions as a secluded establishment serving *"the mentally disturbed elite of half the Western world."* Though we see only the physicists' quarters on stage (the stated policy is " *'birds of a feather' should 'flock together'* " here), we hear of other clientele being treated offstage— *"decayed aristocrats, arteriosclerotic politicians (unless still in office), debilitated millionaires, schizophrenic writers, manic-depressive industrial barons and so on"* (pp. 10–11). The guest list mocks psychiatric jargon and the status symbols of neuroses. Its tone typifies that of the first movement of *The Physicists*, from the mock murder mystery opening with the nurse's corpse on the floor and the madman fiddling offstage to the arrival of Frau Möbius to visit her deluded husband.

By the time Frau Möbius's visit is over, however, the mood of brittle comedy has darkened considerably. What at first seemed to be a quick-paced parody of therapy, logic, and suspense thrillers gradually becomes a play of ideas built about an eerily cold center, Möbius's "Song of Solomon to be sung to the Cosmonauts," a poem which ends with an apocalyptic image of life petrified in a space capsule:

> Outcasts we cast out, up into the deep
> Toward a few white stars
> That we never reached anyhow
>
> Long since mummied in our spacecraft
> Caked with filth
>
> In our deathsheads no more memories
> Of breathing earth.
> (pp. 43–44)

Like this psalm of decay and inertia that he recites in the shadow of an overturned table, and like the play on pointless revolution in *Marat/Sade*, Möbius's life is stalemated.

Möbius's situation, like that of his imagined astronauts and like that of the inmates in *Marat/Sade*, is also freighted with the weight of recent history. A scientist certain that society could not bear the consequences of his research into a Unitary Theory of Elementary Particles and its corollary Principle of Universal Discovery, Möbius chose, fifteen years before the play begins, to elude the grasp of mankind by opting for madness, or dropping out into madness. Claiming to communicate with King Solomon, Möbius managed to continue his inquiries in peace, secretly and alone.

Until now: by the end of Act One, Möbius has bid farewell to his wife and three sons in a false fit of madness, and just as Einstein and Newton strangled their nurses before the play began, at the end of Act One Möbius must kill *his* nurse, a woman who loves him, who believes in his sanity and intelligence, and who has arranged for him to be released from the sanatorium into her care. But this cannot be. "If you're in a madhouse already, the only way to get rid of the past is to behave like a madman," reasons Möbius (p. 46). Finally, after his nurse fails to heed his warning that "It is fatal to believe in King Solomon" (p. 49), he strangles her, in the shadows where *"only their silhouettes are visible"* (p. 56). With this act of will, Möbius renounces the life outside.

Act Two is filled with revelations like that of Möbius's feigned madness. It turns out that all three physicists are living in the sanatorium incognito. Einstein and Newton are really agents Eisler and Kilton, scientists and members of Intelligence Services (p. 69). Each had to kill his nurse when she grew too suspicious. Now that the three men discover one another anew, scientists and murderers all, Möbius sums up the position of three colleagues engaged in a cat-and-mouse game of espionage, false identity, and murder:

We must endeavor to find a rational solution. We cannot afford to make mistakes in our thinking, because a false conclusion would lead to catastrophe. The basic facts are clear. All three of us have the same end in view, but our tactics differ. Our aim is the advancement of physics. You, Kilton, want to preserve the freedom of that science, and argue that it has no responsibility but to itself. On the other hand you, Eisler, see physics as responsible to the power politics of one particular country. What is the real position now? That's what I must know if I have to make a decision. (pp. 78–79)

After weighing the arguments put forth by Einstein and Newton, Möbius rejects their urging to come out with his findings and to fulfill his "duty to open the doors for us, the non-geniuses" (p. 74). He decides not to choose between the two political systems his fellow inmates represent. Instead, Möbius elects to stay where he is.

Like Pirandello's Henry IV, a man petrified in an image he forged for himself, Möbius also manages to persuade others to join him in a perpetual charade of insanity. He convinces Einstein and Newton that their mission—to reclaim him—must be abandoned in the light of their actions, the murders of their nurses. "Are those murders we committed to stand for nothing?" he asks. "Either they were sacrificial killings, or just plain murders. Either we stay in this madhouse or the world becomes one. Either we wipe ourselves out of the memory of mankind or mankind wipes out itself." A pact is made. Integrity does have a place in this world, then. Its place is in the asylum. "For us physicists," Möbius reasons, "there is nothing left but to surrender to reality. It has not kept up with us. It disintegrates on touching us. We have to take back our knowledge and I have taken it back. There is no other way out, and that goes for you as well" (pp. 81–82).

The Physicists could easily end with the ritual libation among the three guardians of the secrets of power. They toast the strangled, sacrificed nurses, and each pronounces an irony of life in a parenthesis:

NEWTON.   Let us be mad, but wise.
EINSTEIN.   Prisoners but free.
MÖBIUS.   Physicists but innocent.

(p. 84)

A final balance has been struck. A tug of war, a tension remains between the twin poles of reason and madness,

belief and skepticism, hope and despair, escape and entrapment, gain and loss, the self and the other.

But the play does *not* end here. Instead the play opens
up. After the trio's joint decision to stay away from the rest
of us, each returns to his own room, identified by Fräulein
Doktor Mathilde von Zahnd as a lair, a cocoon of his imagination. Now, the sudden appearance of the doctor, at-
tended by troopers, has a chilling effect, taking the play
beyond that neat double edge of capitulation and revolt.

The start of the final phase of action is punctuated by a
moment of silence, the clearing of the table (the wine glasses
with which the victory of personal sovereignty was toasted
are removed), and the appearance of the doctor, hunch-
backed and crisp as usual in her white surgical coat. She is
now followed, however, by black-uniformed men who address her as "Boss," and who hang a new picture on the
wall. This time it is a portrait of General von Zahnd, a
military ancestor of the deformed doctor onstage. Over-
shadowing portraits of politicians, privy councillors, and
other family members, the military image on the wall combines with the black uniforms, the brisk commands, the
guns, barred windows, and searchlights to alter our perception of the nature of the sanatorium.

The doctor's confession, a matter-of-fact progress report,
reduces the debates and strategies we have followed, the
myteries of hidden identity we have kept track of, to folly.
Her delusion is that "Solomon, the golden king" has appeared before her as well as before Möbius. Madder than
her patients, Fräulein Doktor von Zahnd raves on that Möbius has betrayed the sacred trust of Solomon by trying "to
keep secret what could not be kept secret. For what was
revealed to him was no secret. Because it could be thought.
Everything that can be thought is thought at some time or
another. Now or in the future." Barring escape from her
asylum, the doctor reveals that, inspired by visions of King
Solomon, she has siphoned off Möbius's discoveries "to
rake in the necessary capital." She has created a "giant
cartel" after having "Year in, year out . . . fogged [Möbius's]
brain and made photocopies of the golden king's procla-

mations, down to the last page." Now, she tells her captive think-tank, she is ready to set her big plans in motion. She announces, "I shall exploit to the full, gentlemen, the Principle of Universal Discovery," and she explains how the institution is being redefined in the light of her new megalomaniacal ambitions:

> What you see around you are no longer the walls of an asylum. This is the strong room of my trust. It contains three physicists, the only human beings apart from myself to know the truth. Those who keep watch over you are not medical attendants. Sievers is the head of my works police. You have taken refuge in a prison you built for yourselves. Solomon thought through you. He acted through you. And now he destroys you, through me. (pp. 89–91)

This overwhelming delusion of the doctor, that King Solomon will destroy the others through her, dominates, because it is backed by real power: a philosophical shelter is finally revealed as a totalitarian state of mind. "It is all over," Newton says (p. 92).

Some critics have argued with the enigmatic ending of *The Physicists*, calling it a gear shift, and asking, "Why should opting out put the genius so mysteriously and irrevocably in the hands of power maniacs?"[39] The answer lies in the force of that inexplicable ending onstage, and in Dürrenmatt's own commitment to a dramaturgy akin to Brecht's. Dürrenmatt conceives of his stage as an instrument to play on, as a space for "disillusionment." This idea, related to Brecht's *Verfremdungseffekt*, demands of the drama an incongruity, a friction between the shapes, the signification, and the sequences of action. Moreover, like the jolting reversal that ends *Marat/Sade*, and even more like the tables turned at the end of *The Happy Haven* (a play quite close to *The Physicists* in tone, theme, and comic rhythm), the ending of *The Physicists*, with its sinister yet ridiculous suggestion of a fascist takeover, is dislocating. This kind of final dislocation is characteristic of plays in the contemporary mode. Locked into their institution, imprisoned in one of society's escape hatches, Möbius and his cronies are finally left immobile, at an impasse of logic.

With the doctor's victory speech and the disillusioning, dislocating action that follows it, Dürrenmatt turns his madhouse/theater metaphor around: first, with the doctor's mad triumph, a quest for asylum, for self-imposed exile has led to defeat by a single, stronger, more lunatic will. And still, the engine of the play does not stop. Finally, the physicists step out of their play and address us directly. Dürrenmatt's opening stage directions include a comment on his decision to "*adhere strictly to the Aristotelian unities of place, time, and action.*" According to the playwright, "*The action takes place among madmen and therefore requires a classical framework to keep it in shape*" (p. 10). More important, by adhering to that classical shape throughout most of the play, Dürrenmatt manages to counterpoint form with farcical action *and* to underline the checkmate of cerebral freedom in a spot of modern time. When that frame is finally broken—when the physicists step forward and address us directly in turn— then its value is found. For now, as Kilton, Eisler, and Möbius formally introduce themselves to us as Newton, Einstein, and Solomon, the boundaries between acting and being are broken. The effect is like that of removing a representational image from its frame and hurling it at the audience. For there is a bleak irony in the play's winding down, a coldness, a forced separation from the play proper. The physicists' biographies, formerly a game—all illusions—are now matters of fact, documentary entries delivered in the cold, noncommittal tones of obituary columns or encyclopedias.

Möbius has the last word in *The Physicists*. "I am Solomon. I am Solomon. I am Solomon. I am poor King Solomon," he says (p. 94). And somehow, his final self-identification with another differs essentially from those intoned by his colleagues. For his transformation is born of an entropic image. His Solomon's wisdom is cruel and hollow; his Solomon's domain is a wasteland, "the radioactive earth" (p. 94), the last asylum.

Beyond language, there is one last sound: according to the stage directions, "*Now the drawing room is empty. Only* EINSTEIN's *fiddle is heard*" (p. 94). The effect here is one of counteraction, as a void is infiltrated by music; in the contradiction between spatial stasis and temporal movement— a military takeover and violin playing—is the doubleness of Dürrenmatt's vision of impasse. As he notes in his "21 Points to *The Physicists*," appended to the printed text, "Within the paradoxical appears reality," "He who confronts the paradoxical exposes himself to reality," and "Drama can dupe the spectator into exposing himself to reality, but cannot compel him to withstand it or even to master it" (p. 96).

Ideas defy confinement, and so this tragic satire ends with an unresolvable paradox: Möbius/Solomon's final, formal address to us outside the frame of the play proper is a terrifying testimony of the captive self, but his last remark *within* the frame of the play proper—"What was once thought can never be unthought" (p. 92)—affirms an inner freedom to remember and to imagine.

Home

An inner freedom to remember and to imagine checked by an outer world of restrictions also describes the situation of David Storey's *Home*. Yet this play, another instance of the contemporary mode, is calm and subdued in its depiction of sanatorium life. In contrast to the pounding *Marat/Sade* and to *The Physicists* (whose plot one critic aptly dubbed "slalom-like"),[40] *Home* is an evocative play about people confined to rest. By no stretch of the imagination is *Home* political; but like *Marat/Sade* and *The Physicists* it is, in the final analysis, a powerful dramatic analogue for our age of waiting and watching the sky.

When David Storey's *Home* first opened in London and New York in 1970, some critics were quick to categorize it as "a kind of Briticized *Waiting for Godot*" or as "a revue-sketch parody of Pinter."[41] Such associations are easily made. Like Beckett's plays, *Home* is characterized by static surface action and lack of an elaborate plot. And like Pinter's *The Birthday Party*, *Home* never actually confirms just who or where its characters are. But a much more profound connection is to be made: in *Home*, as in the plays of Beckett and Pinter, anxiety makes characters pause, repetition makes fear and pain a couple of jokes, and two people talking to each other does not insure a single conversation. Like plays by Beckett and Pinter, Storey's *Home* depicts an order which is destructive, a winding down that threatens the individual. Nevertheless, *Home* itself, an evocative "Chekhovian mood piece,"[42] a much more enduring, lyrical play than its detractors perceived, stands on its own now even as it did when it was a Broadway success, sparked by the complementary performances of Sir John Gielgud and Sir Ralph Richardson. *Home* works metaphorically as a model of modern life, and it works concretely as a close-up of the private world of five mental patients. It is a symbolic play built on a firm foundation of new naturalism.

This "new naturalism" of Storey's[43] results in the creation onstage of a heightened, pervasive reality. In his famous comment on *The Wood Demon*, the first version of *Uncle Vanya*, Chekhov argues for his kind of naturalistic drama:

The demand is made that the hero and the heroine (of a play) should be dramatically effective. But in life people do not shoot themselves, or hang themselves or fall in love, or deliver themselves of clever sayings every minute. They spend most of their time eating, drinking, running after women or men, talking nonsense. It is therefore necessary that this should be shown on the stage. A play ought to be written in which the people should come and go, dine, talk of the weather, or play cards, not because the author wants it but because that is what happens in real life. Life on the stage should be as it really is and the people, too, should be as they are and not stilted.[44]

Storey's kind of naturalism, however, goes beyond Chekhov's insistence on the illusion of every day. Storey's plays attempt to reconstruct with an almost documentary accuracy the world of clocks and calendars, schedules and routines in a circumscribed world. Characters are subordinated to an environment which defines as well as supports their action. In Storey's *The Contractor*, for example, a tent for a lawn party is erected, and then, after an unseen marriage ceremony, it is dismantled. *The Changing Room* also focuses on traditionally peripheral action in a traditionally backstage setting: in this play, the stage space is converted into the locker room of a rugby stadium in the north of England before, during, and after an offstage game. Again in *Life Class*, Storey limits the action of his play to a single, defining, regulating environment, in this instance an art class. And the title of *The Farm*, too, identifies its setting as its subject. In *Home*, however, Storey's between-the-acts mode extends itself into a way of life. Here, Storey builds a heightened situation around just four metal garden chairs, the sturdy outdoor furnishings of an institutional estate.

Storey's simplest setting becomes a most elaborate Structure, for in *Home* the backdrop takes center stage. Purposeful action is completely circumvented by the inhabitants of *Home*; time passes slowly; aimless shapes amble in listless fellowship. Finally, *Home*'s naturalism is markedly symbolic, for the world-weary mental patients who shrug, sigh, and stroll around the minimal set of *Home* seem to chat in an everyday, offhand, random manner; but the cumulative effect of their dialogue, like that of Pinter's people, is to turn naturalistic speech into symbolic vocal gestures. What one critic has called the "poetic polyvalence" of Storey's plays[45] is most pronounced in *Home*. Action reverberates on multiple levels here. The minimal setting of this play houses a naturalistic reconstruction of contemporary asylum life, a paradigm of thwarted yearnings, a dramatic idea of petrified action, *and* a self-conscious sense of the stage as the world in a parenthesis. Such are the dimensions of Storey's apparently shapeless setting. At once an image and an idea of total desertion, *Home* is a play about killing time.

THE PLAY BEGINS as a naturalistic riddle. We see two middle-aged gentlemen approach separately. According to the stage directions, Harry's attire is casually conservative; Jack is dressed in a similar fashion, but *"with a slightly more dandyish flavor."*[46] Harry carries a newspaper; Jack carries an elegant cane. Both are deliberate in their dress and their movements. Both are quite proper as they seat themselves at a round, metal table. There is nothing else on stage. The table could be anywhere. The men make themselves at home.

A tedious conversation ensues. We in the audience try to follow its circuitous route; we listen for clues to the relationship of these two men. We want to identify them and to place them in their social setting. If it were not for the hopscotch of their patter, they might be identified as guests at a holiday resort.[47] But their formal and polite conversation defies placement. Their disclosures seem most like those bartered by recent acquaintances: guarded and innocuous, punctuated by perfunctory phrases such as "Ah, yes," "Oh, no," and "Really?" The hesitant conversation we overhear at the start of *Home* has the familiar ring of a modern conversational ritual, the pattern of gradual self-revelation to a stranger in a public place. This mirror-game of language is by common code ambiguous, guarded, and vague. Our inability to pinpoint the locale of *Home* seems, at first, then, to be due more to the universality of such Pinteresque exchanges than to the particularly disturbing sense of displacement which *Home* will cumulatively generate. At first, the two men take turns reciting conventional platitudes:

(JACK *picks up the paper and gazes at it without unfolding it*)
JACK. Damn bad news.

HARRY. Yes.
JACK. Not surprising.
HARRY. Gets worse before it gets better.
JACK. S'right . . . Still . . . Not to grumble.
HARRY. No. No.
JACK. Put on a bold front. (*He turns the paper over*)
HARRY. That's right.

(pp. 4–5)

Almost from the start of this match, we can tell that the players are out of practice. Their chatter is nervous, occasionally incoherent; this conversational ping-pong has become a struggle.

Eventually, this amorphous conversation takes on a poetic reality of its own. For the players, still straining to follow the rules of a half-remembered social game, strive for rhythm and content:

HARRY. Clouds . . . Watch their different shapes.
JACK. Yes?
    (*He looks up at the sky, at which* HARRY *is gazing*)
HARRY. See how they drift over?
JACK. By jove.
HARRY. First sight . . . nothing. Then . . . just watch
    the edges . . . See?
JACK. Amazing.
HARRY. Never notice when you're just walking.

(p. 5)

This drifting conversation itself resembles the clouds which hover above *Home*. Jack most often looks up, searching the sky for clouds and shadows. Another character says that Jack fears an atomic bomb overhead. But Jack informs the others that he served in the Royal Air Force; he knows about overcast skies; and he has heard it rumored that "When the next catastrophe occurs . . . the island itself might very well be flooded. . . . While we're sitting here waiting to be buried" (p. 30). Jack's speculation, like his sky and his surroundings, is empty. Like the clouds, the conversation drifts without direction from topic to topic, subtly changing its shape in the process:

JACK. I had an uncle once who bred horses.
HARRY. Really?
JACK. Used to go down there when I was a boy.
HARRY. The country.
JACK. Nothing like it. What? Fresh air.
HARRY. Clouds.
    (*He gestures up*)
JACK. I'd say so.
HARRY. *My* wife was coming up this morning.
JACK. Really?

(pp. 8–9)

Sometimes the shift is less subtle. Sometimes one verbal segment is abruptly broken off as a new one is pieced together, for Harry and Jack dread silence more than they fear clouds. Gradually, we in the audience stop gathering clues about other times and other places; the rambling dialogue, which seemed to us at first to be a discursive variation of the familiar expository opening characteristic of naturalistic drama, continues beyond its usual time limit. Storey's new naturalism attenuates exposition until it clouds over the entire play.

The silent past is a huge cloud hovering above the present talk; the past is vague, amorphous, menacing:

HARRY. The past. It conjures up some images.
JACK. It does. You're right.
HARRY. You wonder how there was ever time for it all.
JACK. Time . . . Oh . . . don't mention it.

(p. 13)

As they sidestep their past, Harry and Jack try never to miss a beat. Every scrap of dusty information is material for a conversation. Ideas are stretched until they snap. When one topic is exhausted, a new one is quickly introduced. Then, after an awkward transition to the next verbal segment, momentary tension is relieved by laconic counterpoint. There is an almost vaudevillian fluidity in their one-liners as these two tired straight men glide from one safe topic to another, careful not to go beneath the surface of their isolation.

On this naturalistic level of *Home*, Harry and Jack conjure up hazy images of the past. Later in the play each will cry silently for something he cannot say. But first, with broken utterances and non sequiturs, Harry and Jack exchange some facts about their former lives. Harry is a heating engineer; he served in the army; in his youth he fancied becoming a dancer or a flutist; he is separated from his wife; they have no children. Jack is a distributor of foodstuffs in a wholesale store; he served in the Royal Air Force; in his youth he hoped to become a priest; he and his wife have two grown children. We have no way of knowing if they are telling the truth, but neither do they. *Home* is removed from the facts of families and professions. It is a private place.

When Harry and Jack go off for a stroll before lunch, their places at the table are taken by a pair of coarse, lower-class women. The dialogue between Kathleen and Marjorie clarifies the nature of *Home* on several levels: it makes plain the location of *Home* on the naturalistic level; it serves as a lower-class contrast to the preceding small talk between Harry and Jack, thereby suggesting the microcosmic element of this sparse play which reduces a dramatic pattern to a series of mutations of social groupings around a garden table; it counterpoints the male dirge for the fall of modern man with a medley of female complaints, turning *Home* into a futile discussion play; and when the dialogues between the fallen men and women have been played out in all possible variations, the dialectic is exposed as just a grown-up game of musical chairs, a way to consume the time between meals on the archetypal grounds of a modern resting place for the mind. Nothing happens in *Home*; this is a play which self-consciously avoids action, for it confines itself to a theatrical vacuum. A sanatorium is an insulated society. In its tranquilized atmosphere, inmates—or residents—try to act like "normal" people. They roam freely, but within the boundaries of the institution; and they converse freely, but they are careful to avoid confrontations. To the outsider, this could be a health resort; but to its desperate guests, this is the last resort.

Home, then, is a theatrical dead end: it is a play about listless people who no longer want things to happen. They lack energy; they lack vitality. Resigned to their retreat, they sit and they sigh. Towards the end of the play, one of the characters remarks, "One of the strange things, of course, about this place . . . is its size. . . . Never meet the same people two days running," and he then takes inventory of his barren surroundings, counting "one metalwork table, two metalwork chairs; two thousand people" (p. 104). Two thousand people! So there are others living here. But this "little island" (p. 103), this colony of British misfits, can barely support life. Its residents are stationary; its garden chairs are hardly moved; and its table remains the centerpiece in this slice of still-life. "One thing you can say about this place," another inmate observes, "S'not like home" (p. 95).

What, then, is it like? Most directly, it is a naturalistic study of psychic hibernation. Kathleen and Marjorie immediately confirm our suspicions about the locale of *Home*. Kathleen blames her sore feet on institutional strap shoes: "Took me laced ones, haven't they? Only ones that fitted. Thought I'd hang myself, didn't they? Only five inches long" (p. 42). She surmises that the tight shoes were issued to slow her down—to thwart escape as well as suicide. Later repeating this lament to Harry and Jack, she adds: "Took me belt as well. Who they think I'm going to strangle? Improved my figure, it did—the belt. Drew it in a bit" (pp. 72–73). Marjorie also supplies us with clues by means of which we verify our guesses about the institutional frame of *Home*. Her complaints help to identify the nondescript setting and recurrent speech patterns for the audience. For example, she compares this institution to "the last one" she was in; that was a place of progressive notions where they: "Let you paint on the walls, they did. Do anyfing [*sic*]. Just muck around . . . Here . . . I won't tell you what some of them did" (p. 42).

Gradually, then, we realize that just as Peter Weiss's eighteenth-century asylum in *Marat/Sade* is a spectacular microcosm constraining the timeless symptoms of revolution, Storey's more modest, more insinuating asylum treats the individual withdrawal specifically symptomatic of our times when a fine line separates sane from mad behavior. Indeed, the ambiguity of its whereabouts is *Home*'s purest element of naturalism. The doubleness of Storey's method is evidenced by this calculated displacement: on the one hand, Storey normalizes action into an everyday haze to universalize it; on the other hand, Storey's neutralizing of mad behavior to make it congruent with our own serves not only to make it symbolic, but also, ironically, to make it even more particular. In a modern sanitorium, in fact, such typical behavior would be commonly observed.[48] So while the theatrical element dominates *Marat/Sade*, it is finely drawn in the shadows of *Home*. Storey's sanatorium is a sort of half-way house between a rest home and an insane asylum. It is an almost invisible institution: voluntary inmates are unrestrained; psychiatric supervision is hardly noticeable. Indeed, at first glance, it resembles a spa more than it does a madhouse.

The women proceed to compare their symptoms of unstable behavior. They speak in cold, detached tones. Recounting the facts of despair, they seem oddly removed from their own breakdowns. Marjorie recalls a crying jag triggered by the birth of her daughter (pp. 43–45), and Kathleen in turn remembers a more violent collapse. She began by trying to catch some serious disease. When that did not work—when the doctor said, "Nothing the matter with you, my girl," and sent her home—then she "got home; smashed everything in sight. . . . Winders. Cooker . . . Nearly broke me back . . . Thought I'd save the telly. Still owed eighteen months. Thought: Everything or nothing, girl" (p. 44).

After Act One, Scene Two, the audience is oriented to the naturalistic frame in which Storey's *Home* places us. The naturalistic riddle posed by the laconic gentlemen is solved for us by the broad hints of their coarse compatriots. On this basic level in the performance of *Home*, the playwright substitutes audience speculation for stage action. Act One is static, yet it holds the stage, for *Home* invites audience participation throughout. And this mental participation is most apparent in Act One. We sense the mystery being set before us on a stage almost devoid of clues. Throughout Act One, we attend the voices and gestures of four moving figures like detectives at the scene of some unknown crime. Thus, *Home* restores a sense of wonder to a modern audience: we see and hear ordinary things, but we instill them with significance because they are bracketed before us onstage. In this way, Storey uses his most ambiguous setting thus far to stretch his audience's sense of place, time, and identity in drama. The where, when, and who of the characters meandering before us—the givens in plays with clearly defined boundaries such as Storey's *The Contractor, The Changing Room, Life Class,* or *The Farm*—are unknowns for quite awhile here. Storey uses this ambiguity of setting to explore the symbolic potential of extreme naturalism in *Home*. Rather than immediately introducing us to a recognizable asylum situation in which we would perceive and categorize all actions, indeed, rather than allowing his audience to visit *Home* with even the vague preconceptions that a nonpunning title would call forth, Storey chooses to initiate us gradually—primarily by means of empty spaces and conversational lulls—into a seemingly neutral environment that is, finally, a void.

Storey's reductive naturalism soon takes on symbolic overtones. The uncluttered landscape and redoubled figures combine to suggest an abstraction of a dramatic idea. The thesis of petrified conflict is physically presented by means of a formal configuration. During the women's woeful jabber in Act One, Scene Two, for example, Harry and Jack pass back and forth across the stage. Occasionally, they cast a glance at the ladies. The effect of their recurrent return to the scene is both pathetic and comic. The men seem to have restricted their stroll to an area adjacent to the table. Wary of wandering far, they linger; and they walk together the way they talk together—in circles. Immediately, we recognize that the juxtaposition onstage of the sedentary shrews and the strolling gents is incongruous. In clothes, manners, and sensibilities, these two middle-class men are diametrically opposed to these two lower-class women. The men are terse; the women are garrulous. The men try to ignore their distress; the women gab about their complaints. The men gingerly avoid implications and improprieties in their dialogue; the women, however, delight in innuendoes, screeching gleefully at the mildest double entendre. The men are sentimental; the women are puerile. Basically, this is a difference of class: Harry and Jack are refined; Kathleen and Marjorie are vulgar. These two couples have next to nothing in common.

But Harry, a "specialist in house-warming," and Jack, a "retailer in preserves" (p. 48), do have one thing in common with Kathleen, the wife of a "corporation employee" who "cleans up muck" (p. 73), and Marjorie, the wife of a bus driver (p. 73). They are all at home here. In this separate society which erases class distinctions, Harry and Jack join the ladies for a chat. In the course of their first meeting, these four antithetical characters recognize the others as extensions of themselves, and this seemingly incongruous quartet makes small talk until lunchtime. There are introductions all around, rumors about the other inmates, and remarks about the lack of facilities. Harry articulates the code of the institutionalized: "We all have our little foibles, our little failings. . . . Hardly be human without. . . . The essence of true friendship, in my view, is to make allowances for one another's little lapses" (p. 57). And Jack cries briefly. The four agree to meet here again after lunch for "A little chat . . . Time passes very slowly" (p. 61). Linking arms, they all go off to lunch together. This gesture signifies the close of Act One on multiple levels of Storey's mimetic and symbolic stage: on the naturalistic level, camaraderie is affirmed and intermission conveniently coincides with a sanatorium lunch break; on the metaphorical level, antithetical dramatic character types group together on a common ground; yet these characters suggesting sociological and psychological types remain individuals, left in a world without comfort, which they must share.

Act Two of *Home* begins after lunch and ends before teatime. It, too, adheres to an institutional pattern of "free time" to be filled between the structured activities of the day. And now, again, a debate among distinct voices dwindles down to a single dramatic idea of lost causes. At once a model of a sinking society and an analogue of personal displacement, Act Two of *Home* further reduces Storey's idea of the theater to its essential element of individual performance.

Thus, Act Two starts with a pantomime. According to the stage directions, Alfred, a *"well-built young man of about thirty,"* struggles with the garden table *"as if it had a life of its own"* (p. 65). After successfully wrestling with the table, Alfred has a bout with the chairs, overcoming them as well. He performs these feats of weightlifting sporadically throughout Act Two. Later, we learn that Alfred was an apprentice painter and decorator (p. 90), but he has been lobotomized.[49] The other inmates watch the antics of the feebleminded wrestler:

MARJORIE. Sit down.
JACK. Yes.
   (He sits)
ALFRED. Wanna fight?
JACK. No . . .
ALFRED. You?
MARJORIE. No, thanks.
ALFRED. Got sixpence?
JACK. No.

MARJORIE. Here. You seen my friend?
ALFRED. No.
MARJORIE. What you in for?
ALFRED. In what?
MARJORIE. Thinks he's at home, he does. Doesn't know
  his own strength—do you?
ALFRED. No.
MARJORIE. Took a bit of his brain, haven't they?
ALFRED. Yeh.
MARJORIE. Feel better?
ALFRED. Yeh.

(pp. 88–89)

Alfred's methodical actions ritualize the conventions of the other inmates. His performance serves as a play-within-the-play, clarifying the redundant verbal patterns of the others by means of mute gestures. Alfred's dumb show of strength is a balance of reality and metaphor. His wordless struggle with the chairs is a casual sanatorium occurrence reconstructed onstage. But it also objectifies the inner struggles of the other inmates. For just as Alfred grapples with metalwork, Harry, Jack, Kathleen, and Marjorie contend with language. Like the rest of the action of *Home*, Alfred's sluggish movements are both mimetic and symbolic.

Indeed, all of *Home* is symbolically as well as naturalistically ordered. In Act Two, the playwright rearranges his two-character groupings for variations on the theme of Act One. Storey's approach to staging calls forth an analytic response from the audience: we become involved with the play as an idea of form. Storey demonstrates this idea in the shell-game progression of Act Two. First, Kathleen and Harry talk, and then Marjorie and Jack pair off for a chat. In each of these two duets, the psychotic candor of the woman counterpoints the capricious evasions of the man. Just as Kathleen indiscreetly probes Harry's past (pp. 68–69), when those two go off for a stroll before tea, Marjorie pries relentlessly into Jack's life:

140

JACK. Life . . . mystery . . .
  (*He gazes up.* MARJORIE *watches him*)
MARJORIE. What you put away for, then?
JACK. Oh . . . what?
MARJORIE. In here.
JACK. Oh . . . Little . . .
MARJORIE. Girl?
JACK. Girl?
MARJORIE. Girls.
JACK. Girls?
MARJORIE. In the street.
JACK. Really?
  (*He looks around*)
MARJORIE. Here . . . What you in for?
JACK. A wholly voluntary basis, I assure you.
MARJORIE. Wife put you away?
JACK. Oh, no. No, no. Just a moment . . . needed . . .
  Thought I might . . .

(pp. 83–84)

Jack confides that he is going "Home tomorrow!" but he
and Kathleen agree that it is "Hardly worth the trouble"
(p. 86). For the cadences of this home are also those of the
larger world outside. As in Act One, in Act Two of *Home*
the four inmates finally form a quartet. And as in Act One,
in Act Two the men search the sky for clouds and they cry
quietly. When Kathleen and Marjorie hurry off to tea, Harry
and Jack are once again left alone onstage together.

So this accurate depiction of life suspended in a sanatorium seems to come full circle and thus to end almost as
it began. Like Act One, Act Two of *Home* naturalistically
records the daily pastimes of the four mental patients. After
lunch, there is a very polite game of musical chairs played
by Harry and Jack, who take turns sitting in the unoccupied
chair. Meanwhile, Kathleen and Marjorie go through a familiar routine of tattling on each other's misdemeanors.
Later, Harry and Jack play an elegiac game of word associations, starting with "Empire the like of which no one

has ever seen," and progressing through "Penicillin," "Darwin," "Newton," "Milton," and "Sir Walter Raleigh" to end with "This little island" and "The sun has set" (pp. 102–103). Clearly now, Storey's sanatorium is barely maintaining survivors of a civilization in an institutional shell. But as one resident phrases it, "If one can't enjoy life as it takes one, what's the point of living it at all? One can't, after all, spend the whole of one's life inside a shell" (p. 58). In an interview published in *Life*, Storey characterized the controlled naturalistic technique of *Home*. "Oh, there are scenes," he admitted, "that verge on the dramatic, but they usually stop short of it. . . . The actors invite the audience into the play, without insisting."[50] Monosyllabically mourning the decline of the British empire as Act Two winds down, Harry and Jack invite us, without insisting, into their shell, the home which is both an encompassing public institution and a world like our own.

The word games of Act Two not only illuminate the microcosmic dimension of *Home*, but they also heighten our awareness of the spiraling effect of the play. The word games are finally clear sounds in a widening gyre of desolation. In *Home* there are only chance encounters, card tricks, and conversations. A dialectical drama is doomed here, for in Storey's representative shelter, life has been drained of conflict. Human tensions and polarities—flirtations, discussions, debates—are diminished to an inconsequential stature.

Only time endures as a genuine antagonist. In Act One, for example, Harry remarks upon "the amount of dust that collects in so short a space of time" (p. 20), and Jack talks about filling the voids in the sanatorium schedule. "One works. One looks around. One meets people. But very little communication actually takes place," he says (p. 22). Both these observations alert us early in the play to the polyvalence of commonplace remarks in Storey's subtle play of impasse. And in Act Two, Jack once again calls attention to the time span waiting to be filled. "One of the advantages of a late lunch, of course, is that it leaves a shorter space

to tea," he says (p. 83). In this play, then, as in the sanatorium, time is measured by the intervals between meals.
For this reason, Act One ends very quietly according to the
timetable of sanatorium life. There is no climax. There is
no ostensible change. Likewise, Act Two ends in apparent
quietude. As at the opening of Act One, Harry and Jack
stand on opposite sides of a deserted stage at the close of
Act Two. Two silent, spent, bleary-eyed men stand apart
and gaze out at nothing. This final tableau of *Home* is at
once a snapshot of mental decline and an image of human
despair. With naturalistic fidelity, Storey's play measures
out madness in the sedating doses of modern custodial care.

Unlike Peter Weiss's *Marat/Sade*, which looses bedlam on
the stage, *Home* infiltrates rather than assaults our consciousness. It leads its rapt audience circuitously astray,
depositing us in a vague outdoor spot which gradually signifies both an asylum doorstep and a mental construct. At
first, we recognize the two distracted figures onstage as
familiar profiles engaged in social face-saving. In the course
of the playing, however, the nuances of naturalistic staging
belie the neutral appearance of the people and their place
in the world. What seems at first to be a series of ordinary
interchanges is exposed at last as a pattern of disturbing
symptoms. By reducing dramatic conflict to its purest form
(that of life against the deadly weight of time) and by isolating man's cosmic quarrel in an uncluttered resting place
(that is, in a contemporary total institution where, as Goffman notes, a "sense of dead and heavy-hanging time" lingers over a "kind of dead sea in which little islands of vivid,
encapturing activity appear"),[51] Storey builds a symbolic
paradigm on solid naturalistic grounds.

FINALLY we realize that *Home* is playing with us. As in *Marat/
Sade*'s therapeutic revolution and as in *The Physicists*' compromised scientific community, in *Home* madness is both
actual and virtual, in the sense in which Bernard Beckerman adopts Suzanne Langer's terms to the realm of theatrical activity:

"An image, something that exists only for perception, abstracted from the physical and causal order," Langer writes, "is the artist's creation." Through the artist's efforts, "a new appearance has superseded [the] natural aspect" of the raw materials, and the resulting image "is, indeed, a purely virtual 'object.' " An object, enlarged here to include activity, is virtual, not because it does not exist, but because the center of its existence is appearance. Miss Langer makes it quite clear that she is not restricting the term "image" to the class of visual phenomena. It is applicable to all forms of creative practice, regardless of the sense to which it appeals. Thus, the magician's act is virtual while the acrobat's act is actual. The first does one thing while trying to create the illusion that he is doing another; the second is actually doing what he appears to be doing.[52]

In these plays, madness is also relentlessly explored as a central myth of our neoromantic age. As Susan Sontag observes in her discussion of the romantic transfiguration of TB in the nineteenth century, "In the twentieth century, the repellent, harrowing disease that is made the index of a superior sensitivity, the vehicle of 'spiritual' feelings and 'critical' discontent, is insanity." Citing parallels between "the fancies associated with tuberculosis and insanity," Sontag writes:

> With both illnesses, there is confinement. Sufferers are sent to a "sanatorium" (the common word for a clinic for tuberculars and the most common euphemism for an insane asylum). Once put away, the patient enters a duplicate world with special rules. Like TB, insanity is a kind of exile. The metaphor of the psychic voyage is an extension of the romantic idea of travel that was associated with tuberculosis. To be cured, the patient has to be taken out of his or her daily routine.
>   . . . Not TB but insanity is the current vehicle of our secular myth of self-transcendence. The romantic view

1. *The Hothouse*. The warehouse-like set reflects Pinter's satiric view of a mental institution as a storage ground for defective human merchandise. (Photo by Constance Brown of the American premiere at the Trinity Square Repertory Theater, Providence, Rhode Island.)

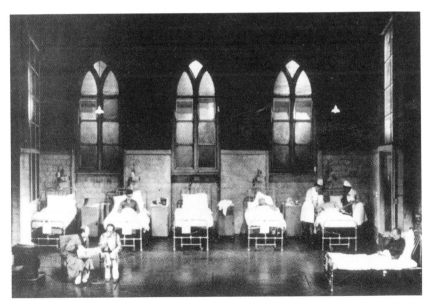

2. *The National Health*. Nichols's "snapshot"-precise hospital ward enforces the implied parallel between the total institution onstage and the outside world. (Photo by Reg Wilson of the 1969 National Theatre production at the Old Vic.)

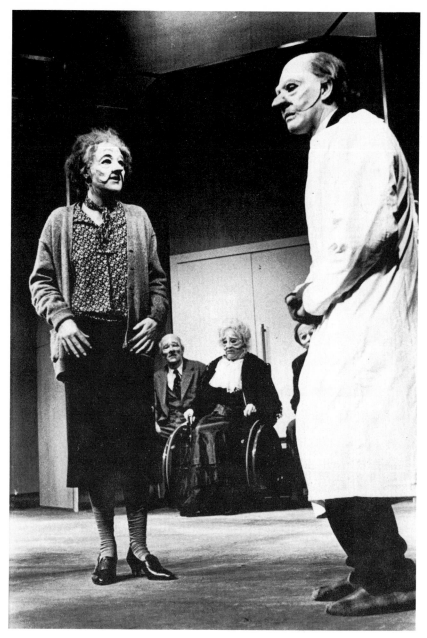

3. *The Happy Haven*. Arden calls for masks representing old age and a stylized hospital setting to create a "formalized presentation" of a social Structure. (Photo by Roger Mayne of the 1960 production at the Royal Court Theatre, with Rachel Roberts as Mrs. Letouzel [l., foreground].)

4. *Wings*. Kopit's hospital setting is not an objective image, but a projection of the patient's subjective response to the trauma of illness and to the encompassing Structure in which she is lost. (Photo by Bill Smith of Constance Cummings in the 1979 New York production.)

5. *Marat/Sade*. A few sparse, cold props recreate the bath house of Charenton, which also serves as Sade's makeshift stage. Thus, the 20th-century audience is equated with the 18th-century oppressors. (Photo by Morris Newcombe of the 1964 Royal Shakespeare Company production at the Aldwych Theater.)

6. *Marat/Sade*. Under Peter Brook's direction, Charlotte Corday (Glenda Jackson) whips Sade (Patrick Magee) with rhythmic tosses of her long hair, evoking in the audience a visceral sense of what Artaud means when he writes that the stage demands a "concrete physical language" to express *"metaphysics-in-action"* and that "everything that acts is a cruelty." (Photo by Morris Newcombe of the 1964 RSC production.)

7. *The Physicists*. Seeking a haven from the madness of the outside world, the physicists take refuge in an asylum, which is ultimately revealed to them as an intensification of the outside world at its worst, totalitarianism. (Photo by Reg Wilson of the 1963 Royal Shakespeare Company production at the Aldwych Theater.)

8. *Home*. Watching what at first appear to be two middle class gents chatting, the audience gradually assumes an asylum setting from clues dropped in a disintegrating conversation. The apparent normalcy of Jack (Ralph Richardson) and Harry (John Gielgud), along with the lack of a distinct physical asylum onstage, heightens the connection between the characters' hopelessness and our own. (Publicity photo of the 1970 English Stage Company production.)

9. *The Brig*. Our vision of the play is filtered through barbed wire, a constant reminder that this Structure of impasse is violently divided into three zones: the audience, the guards, and the prisoners. (Photo by Morris Newcombe of the 1964 Living Theater production at London's Mermaid Theater.)

10. *The Quare Fellow.* Behan's satire of the human condition is grounded in hard facts. The setting and costumes convey prison life with a harsh, worn specificity, while the characters' behavior—here, inmates jokingly inspect the condemned man's last meal—universalizes the way people react when walled-in. (Photo by J. V. Spinner of the 1956 Theater Workshop production.)

11. *The Hostage*. Like many satires set in social Structures, Behan's play finally abandons its comic pose to reveal the raucous brothel-world as a battleground where disguises are deadly weapons. In the foreground at the table, Mr. Mulleady, a secret policeman, talks with the captive English soldier. (Photo by John Cowan of the 1958 Theater Workshop production.)

12. *Deathwatch*. The claustrophobic, nightmarish cell of Genet's play is an image of entrapment, an inverted, clandestine Artaudian double of the world outside. Here, Maurice (Harold Scott) and LeFranc (Vic Morrow) will engage in a savage "dance" of games. (Photo by Ben Mancuso, Impact, of the 1958 New York off-Broadway production.)

13. *Chips With Everything*. Our response to the setting of a play of impasse changes in the course of the action. Early in this play, for example, the conscripts' hut, realistically depicted, is warmed by a game of "cowboys and Indians" played by boys with their newly issued rifles. Later on, however, when military games are played in earnest, the hut will take on a larger, darker meaning as a Structure for the ritual transformation of boys into men. (Photo by Sandra Lousada of the 1962 English Stage Company production at the Royal Court Theater.)

14. *Chips With Everything*. In contrast to the conscripts' routine, the midnight coke-yard raid is a welcome moment when choreography breaks the tension of impasse. (Photo by Sandra Lousada of the 1962 English Stage Company production at the Royal Court Theater.)

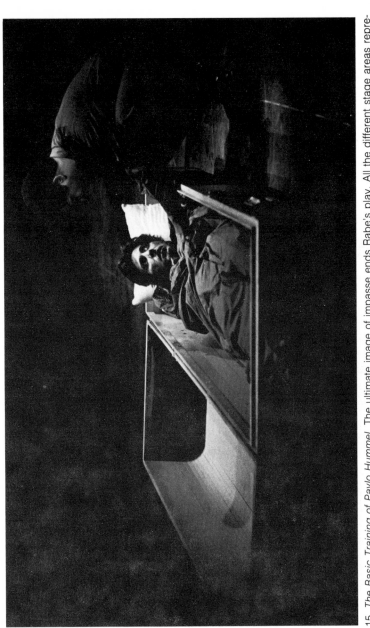

15. *The Basic Training of Pavlo Hummel.* The ultimate image of impasse ends Rabe's play. All the different stage areas representing Pavlo's tour of duty—the barracks, the parade grounds, the whorehouse, the pool hall, the hospital—finally radiate from a single point that is both actual and metaphorical, the pine box in which Pavlo will be shipped home. (Photo by Bert Andrews of the 1977 Theater Company of Boston's revival, with Al Pacino as Pavlo.)

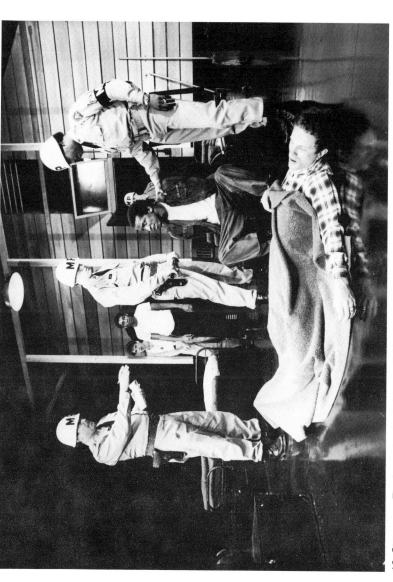

16. *Streamers*. The barracks, kept clean and tidy as a "house" by its inhabitants, can be transformed in a flash into Carlyle's vision of the army, a raging image of violence and destruction, an exploding world with no holds barred and no way out. (Photo by Martha Swope of the 1976 New York Shakespeare Festival production.)

17. *Endgame.* Nagg (Georges Adet), Hamm (Roger Blin), and Clov (Jean Martin) strain unsuccessfully to pray. This is a silhouette of the action of *Endgame* as a whole, and indeed, a distilled image of impasse in general. When prayer fails, they seek out other ways to face the monumental task of killing time. (Photo by Roger Pic of Roger Blin's original 1957 Paris production.)

is that illness exacerbates consciousness. Once that illness was TB; now it is insanity that is thought to bring consciousness to a state of paroxysmic enlightenment.[53]

Insanity is indeed romanticized in *Marat/Sade, The Physicists*, and *Home*, plays in which the metaphor of breakdown is evidenced time and again, plays in which the vehicle of revelation is madness.

But *Marat/Sade, The Physicists*, and *Home*, like many plays in the contemporary mode, also self-consciously comment on that process Sontag identifies as a neoromantic transfiguration of madness and the asylum. For all three plays ultimately locate our "secular myth of self-transcendence" in a sanatorium which mirrors life outside even as it locks its inmates in. In plays of impasse, neoromantic clichés about the transcendent side effects of pain are blasted. Holding no old saws sacred, plays in the contemporary mode are at bottom tough and unsentimental. Even the asylum's power to displace and dehumanize, to normalize, is overridden by the playwright's reordering of social institution as conceit. In this bleak, ironic world view, even the madhouse has room enough for everybody. An eighteenth-century snake pit, an atomic age political frameup, and a progressive island of rest—the settings of *Marat/Sade, The Physicists*, and *Home*—make the contagion of unreality, disbelief, and loss of faith concrete.

The institutions of madness, then, rendered clear and with poetic resonance, most profoundly smash neoromantic myths of individual escape and psychic voyages. Freed of these myths, audiences can go home following the dictum of Genet's Mme. Irma, the ringmaster of his dream *Balcony*, his grand whorehouse of Illusions, his whorehouse stuffed full of transcendence fantasies. Go home, Genet's Mme. Irma says to the audience, "Everything—you can be quite sure—will be falser than here."[54] This jaded contemporary view of masks of self and deception even when one is alone, even looking in the mirror, is most sharply felt in plays of impasse set in asylums. For like one of R. D. Laing's typical *Knots*—

> There is something the matter with me because I do not feel anything the matter with me[55]

—asylum-set plays of impasse, *Home* in particular, turn irrevocably inward, drawing the audience into a real place that also holds the promise of an elusive state of mind, the promise of a serenity we can no longer trust.

PASSING TIME BEHIND BARS

Kenneth H. Brown's *The Brig*,
Brendan Behan's *The Quare Fellow*
(and Behan's *The Hostage*),
and Jean Genet's *Deathwatch*

Shukhov went to sleep fully content. He'd had many strokes of luck that day: they hadn't put him in the cells; they hadn't sent his squad to the settlement; he'd swiped a bowl of kasha at dinner; the squad leader had fixed the rates well; he'd built a wall and enjoyed doing it; he'd smuggled that bit of hacksaw blade through; he'd earned a favor from Tsezar that evening; he'd bought that tobacco. And he hadn't fallen ill. He'd got over it.

A day without a dark cloud. Almost a happy day.

Alexander Solzhenitsyn,
One Day in the Life of Ivan Denisovich

THIS INVENTORY of small victories which add up to *One Day in the Life of Ivan Denisovich* indicates the negative capability required for survival in a prison camp. Solzhenitsyn's Shukhov ends his ordinary day content; his sentence stretches out before him with monotonous certainty, and so, within that space of "three thousand six hundred and fifty-three days . . . from the first clang of the rail to the last clang of the rail,"[1] he finds his freedom in his mind. Minor gains seem momentous; commonplace pleasures are savored; the avoidance of punishment is its own reward.

147

The ordeal of the prisoner, the understated subject of Solzhenitsyn's fictionalized account, is a constant of penal systems. On the stage and in films, too, life behind bars has been traditionally a popular subject usually broached for either social reform or romantic escape. Kenneth H. Brown's *The Brig* (produced by the Living Theatre in 1963), Brendan Behan's *The Quare Fellow* (first presented under the direction of Joan Littlewood in 1956), and Jean Genet's *Deathwatch* (first performed in 1949), however, are prison plays which transcend romanticism, melodrama, and reformist realism. All three of these plays reconstruct a prison, a total state, onstage; all three transform a recognizable setting into a societal model and a protorevolutionary document; and all three show how imprisonment breaks down the barriers of the self. These are sharply etched plays of impasse, set in contrastingly styled versions of the same total institution: Brown's *The Brig* evokes the terror of the total institution in a documentary drama of arbitrary rules; Behan's *The Quare Fellow* combines music hall material with gallows humor; and Genet's *Deathwatch* ritualizes eroticism and obsessive cruelty.

Brown, Behan, and Genet all had first-hand experience of the ordeal of the prisoner, and all three bring the impact of that experience to bear on their approaches to drama.[2] In their attention to spatial design, to blocks of time, and to the sounds and gestures signalling freedom's end, these three playwrights display the range of contemporary theatrical assaults on prison walls, within which they locate particularly stark and brutalizing plays of impasse.

The Brig

Kenneth H. Brown's *The Brig* is a seminal work of contemporary documentary drama. First produced by the Living Theatre under the direction of Judith Malina in May 1963, *The Brig* reconstructs in copious detail an ordinary day in a Marine base prison in the Far East. Like Peter Weiss's *Marat/Sade*, Brown's play has become closely identified with

the extraordinary nature of its filmed, definitive production.[3] For like *Marat/Sade*, *The Brig* is foremost a blueprint
for production. Brown's script is as sparse as is his barren
setting. Six scenes, divided into two acts, cover the activities
of a typical day in *The Brig* from dawn to bedtime. The
prisoners are eleven numbered men who, according to
Brown's stage directions, *"make up a cross-section of American
society."*[4] Behind the barbed wire which separates them from
us, these prisoners are repeatedly put through their humiliating paces. Discipline is carried to a dehumanizing
extreme here: the warden and three guards are also stereotyped figures empowered to play a terrible cat-and-mouse
game with their charges. An infraction of a random rule
can cause a catastrophe. One false move can precipitate a
blow. Dignity is denied. The prisoner must always be on
his guard.

Set in a Marine base prison, the play calls our attention
to one total institution within another total institution. Both
an American Marine and a military prisoner, an inmate of
The Brig has a double identity imposed on him by his environment; his individuality is obscured by his official military status, and once he is sentenced to *The Brig*, even his
individualizing rank is denied. Assigned only a digit to dif-
ferentiate himself from his fellow prisoners, an inmate of
a brig must endure the most extreme form of institutional
control. For two of the most formidable American institutions are the prison and the Marines. Both strip their
subjects of their names, personal possessions, connections
outside the institution, and self-determination. There are,
of course, significant ideological differences governing subjects: though attempts may be made to reform him, a prisoner is primarily being punished; a Marine, on the other
hand, theoretically seeks to alter his sense of self to suit a
military image. But when these two settings merge, this
ideological distinction is blurred. A military prison can thus
be the most terrifying of all total institutions devised for
punishment and/or reform. A prisoner who is also a Marine
must reckon with the paradox of his punishment, for unlike

an ordinary prisoner, the inmate of a brig supports—in theory at least—the goals of those abusing him. Unlike his civilian counterpart, then, he must "take" his punishment in earnest. Within a brig, Brown envisioned *The Brig*. His naturalistic model of selfhood being denied matches the austerity and power of its equivalent in reality.

Though it is filled with incidents and activity, *The Brig* is essentially plotless. As in *Marat/Sade*, the affective strength of *The Brig* derives from a director's organization of the behind-the-scenes routines of inmates who populate an open space. In the audience of *Marat/Sade*, after all, we find the inmates on the periphery of the play-within-the-play as fascinating to watch as are those participating in Sade's supposedly therapeutic pastime. Likewise, in the audience of *The Brig*, we are engrossed by our suddenly graphic exposure to a previously secret society and by a documentary form of drama that is original and demanding. *The Brig* even dares to obstruct the audience's direct view of the stage. Going even further in this regard than did the film version of *Marat/Sade* (which put bars between the camera lens and the action to evoke the feeling of danger— something accomplished exceedingly well onstage by the presence of live actors), the action of *The Brig* is obstructed from our view by an actual boundary: barbed wire encloses the compound. And here, as in *Marat/Sade*, a naturalistically reconstructed area becomes a magic circle of symbolic acts when the rhythms of the performance exalt a daily routine. As Judith Malina suggests in her notes on "Directing *The Brig*" appended to the play:

> The marching is a ritual of great beauty only grown hideous because it stands for the marches towards the fields of death in battle and because it has come to signify the loss of character that ensues when all of life becomes routed into this exactitude. And because you cannot stop. Meanwhile the rhythm of mutuality entices the kinetic senses. The sense of moving in a mutual rhythm with one's fellow man. (p. 97)

Under Malina's direction, the drills, the marches, the end-less exercises, and the energetic scrubbing and swabbing of the compound are invested with communal rhythms which transmute routines into rituals. With a kinetic poetry of the theater, *The Brig* can absorb us in the rhythmic beauty of order.

The object of the Living Theatre's production of *The Brig* was to demonstrate how the beauty of order is blas-phemed by the brutality of the Structure. As Malina puts it in her director's notes, "Violence is the darkest place of all. Let us throw light on it. In that light we will confront the dimensions of the Structure, find its keystone, learn on what foundations it stands, and locate its doors. Then we will penetrate its locks and open the doors of all the jails" (pp. 106–107). The play is a thesis drama; it deplores the debasement of pure form by obscene power, and it ap-pealed to Malina because of its revolutionary potential.

To Julian Beck, *The Brig* also had the potential of a rev-olutionary manifesto. In his introductory essay on the Liv-ing Theatre in the published version of the play, he writes:

> *The Brig* is the Theatre of Cruelty. In that it is the distillation of the direction of The Living Theatre's history. You cannot shut off from it, as from a dream. It is there, real, in the pit of your stomach. Defy the audience. Tell them you don't want to involve them. Don't run into the aisle to embrace them. Put up a barricade of barbed wire. Separate until the pain of separation is felt, until they want to tear it down, to be united. Storm the barricades. (p. 34)

Through a sharp-edged fence we see the system in action, and we feel emotions like pity and fear. Simultaneously, *The Brig* instructs us in the ways of the prison world, and it incites us to break down the walls of that world. It calls for revolution, for the barbed wire of *The Brig* objectifies the paradox of action and meaning in this play where er-ratic rules cut into human dignity. As Beck concludes, "Ar-taud's mistake was that he imagined you could create a horror out of the fantastic. Brown's gleaming discovery is that horror is not in what we imagine but is in what is real" (p. 35). Indeed, *The Brig* is at once a factual model and a brutal image. This photojournalistic use of the stage is also an Artaudian assault on the senses.

The double aesthetic which governs *The Brig* permeates every aspect of the play. The presence of the barbed wire, for example, immediately strikes us as a provocative naturalistic device *and* as an annoying innovation. In place of the imaginary fourth wall with which we are comfortable, we find an obtrusive barrier to conventional audience response. Caging becomes a constant reminder of the truth of the representation *and* of the representational nature of the truth; barbed wire becomes at once a naturalistic device *and* a theatrical one. Enclosing a clean, well-lighted place which is usually off limits to the audience, the wire obscures our vision of secret rites enmeshed in a ruthless siege of stage space. In *The Brig*, Artaud's aesthetic, that "in our present state of degeneration it is through the skin that metaphysics must be made to re-enter our minds,"[5] is concretized in a visual metaphor of accurate physical dimensions.

The lighting of *The Brig* also clarifies the Structure on more than one level. The play begins in complete darkness. A dim light focuses on two guards—Tepperman, a black man from New York, and Grace, a short and stocky Midwesterner. They are whispering and smiling together. Alone, in the dim light of early morning, the guards are at ease. The routine of their day has not yet begun, and we catch a glimpse of them before they assume their roles for the day. Our first impression of the play is, in this moment, neutralized: we felt threatened by the unorthodox barrier constructed between us and the stage; but as the play proper begins, we feel reassured. Brown's guards are not dehumanized figures in a strident morality play; rather, they are people getting ready to perform their duties. They are men in uniform, but they whisper and smile at dawn. Eventually, however, the naturalistic dimness takes on a sinister glow. After some preliminary moves, Tepperman unlocks the door to the inner compound, enters the sleeping area, and awakens a sleeping prisoner by tapping him on the head with a billy club. According to the stage directions, "*only this is visible, since the dim light has followed* TEPPERMAN" (p. 49). Spotlighted in the darkness, Tepperman assaults and humiliates a new arrival (prisoner Number Two). When it is time to wake the others up, Grace "*flicks a switch on the wall near his desk, and suddenly the stage is bathed in light— bright, white, electric. At the moment the light goes on,* TEPPERMAN *crashes the can cover down the middle of the inside compound, making a resounding noise*" (p. 50). The audience, like the newcomer, is startled by the sudden bright light and piercing noise. In the brief time of this opening sequence, Brown barrages us with naturalistic details which also evoke the malevolent nature of a Structure.

In his depiction of guard/inmate interaction, especially, Brown overshadows symbolic pronouncements with naturalism. The action of *The Brig* moves from guards to inmates, and from inmates to guards, to record the events of a day objectively. This see-saw technique gives the play a surface validity as a social document. Brown's fair treatment of his guards also has a more subtle cumulative effect, for *The Brig* teaches us a game peculiar to prisons and elevated here by military codes of behavior. The prison game poses unique strategic problems for its players, for as Goffman points out in his *Strategic Interaction*, in the "prisoner's dilemma" game, where "mutual trust is not situationally generated," one team of players—the guards— has nothing to lose, and the other team of players—the inmates—cannot win. This is the catch. Why, then, do they play at all? The prisoner plays along with the prevailing game to avoid punishment. He is caught in a literal "enforcement system," a situation which, according to Goffman's study, combines the factors "constraint to play, structuring of choices, commitment to moves made, intrinsic payoff." In a prison, an inmate can only gain time (i.e., parole for good behavior) and might even lose status among his fellow prisoners for playing along with the guards; in *The Brig*, however, where such an agreement is particularly binding and one-sided, the prisoner can also gain stature as a regular Marine by playing the rugged game with a constant mustering of "emotional self-control."[6]

Gradually, then, we discover that a brig guard is more than a keeper of captive bodies; rather, he is a Marine with a specific mission. According to Pierre Biner, a chronicler of the Living Theatre, "The Marines use depersonalization as the method of 'rehabilitating' those who have committed infractions."[7] The impersonal nature of Brown's *Brig*—its anonymous cruelty—is naturalistically grounded. In a context he cannot challenge, the prisoner in *The Brig* is the double of his guard; both are following the orders imposed on them of their own initial volition. Brown plays upon this paradox to heighten our sense of the Structure as a microcosm of anonymous actions.

The villain of this piece is ultimately the comprehensive Structure. Brown's guards, like his prisoners, make up a cross-section of American society; and when we catch them off-guard we see the human double of the institutional shadow. When, for example, in Act One, Scene Three, two more shotgun-toting guards arrive to complete some paperwork, they all engage in some brigade banter. The backstage talk of the guards among their peers forces the audience to recognize that they, too, are subservient to an encompassing social institution:

> GRACE *goes to his desk, takes two sheets of paper from it, and hands one to each man. They greet him with a smile and*: "How are you?" "How did it go last night?" *and* "We had a ball in town last night."
>
> GRACE. Everything's O.K. so far. (*And then to the last remark.*) Wait till tomorrow night when you guys are sweating it out in this joint.
>
> (pp. 57–58)

154

This telling moment is what Artaud would call a signal through the flames: Brown's guards are suddenly Marines "sweating it out in this joint," too; like the prisoners, the guards are also biding time in the brig. Their assigned duty is to bully and berate their prisoners into a thick-skinned brotherhood. In this sense *The Brig* has a psychodramatic dimension: within a representative space, forces of conformity dominate forces of self-expression.

With its emphasis on social and psychological power plays, *The Brig* stirs us as a dynamic conflict between social norms and human instincts. This kind of dynamic tension inspired Julian Beck to wonder at those halting, humanizing remarks of the guards cited above:

> Brown, panting, never stops, accuracy after accuracy with no blank space in between, and there, documented, were all the crimes of abstract feelingless authoritarianism. A play in which the two dim moments of real speech, "Did you get to Tokyo last night?" and "We had a ball in Tokyo last night," are thrilling even in their feebleness. They speak to us from the abode where the immortals are. It is speech, no matter how stuck in the throat, it is the blessed speech that communicates friendliness, and if there were more of it, so softly spoken and rising from the warmer regions of the body, enough of it to displace the rest of the language of the play, all the sentences that begin with "Sir," why then we could get off this arid plateau, to the next, where the problems of life will be less deranging and still more beautiful.   (p. 5)

Beck's characteristic rhapsody about the potential of the liberated human spirit applies specifically to the inner predicament to be abstracted from the arid political plateau of *The Brig*. Indeed, the play, significantly sandwiched in its published version between a diatribe by Beck and director's notes by Malina, is a concept which exemplifies both the political strategy and performance style of the Living Theatre.

155

The Living Theatre repeatedly creates theater pieces which fit social parts into a psychodramatic framework. Its kinetic quest is to transcend the boundaries of society, the stage, and the self. To foster revolution, one must override the barricades of civilization and overcome the inhibitions of the self. This unremitting thesis of the Living Theatre is made tangible in *The Brig*, where the tension between inner turmoil and its double in external action becomes manifest.

This interpenetration of psychodrama and sociodrama, a hallmark of the Living Theatre, is apparent most profoundly in *The Brig*; it is most obvious, however, in the group's production of *Frankenstein*, which has ideological and formal affinities with *The Brig*. An intentionally primitive piece, *Frankenstein* begins with a manhunt by executioners who round up their victims from the auditorium, "book" them according to American police procedures, and lock them into solitary cells on a tiered stage. In addition to becoming a microcosmic machine of enslavement, performance, and death through which the Creature moves, the compartmentalized tiers onstage are revealed in silhouette to form the profile of a man's head. The figure of the Creature itself is created by means of a pyramid of actors within the framework. *Frankenstein* is, as Pierre Biner suggests, like the prison,

> the essence of *The Brig*: both stand for the world man has built for himself. . . . The three levels and everything that takes place on them are . . . solitary compartments of the Creature's mind, modern man's mind. . . . The superman (the Creature) becomes the subman. Frankenstein protests being imprisoned in a punitive structure that he did not intend to create; nevertheless, the structure is the very result of his best intentions—his work has produced the antithesis of what he had hoped to create, and he himself is a victim of his own creation. . . . Everything has turned against him. The prison, a large soulless machine, functions only because its gears—the prisoners—are well oiled.[8]

Frankenstein, a revolutionary drama of ideas, may be seen, then, as a striking visual equivalent of *The Brig*. *The Brig*'s dimensions—as microcosm, psychodrama, and image of impasse—are all present in that silhouette of *Frankenstein*.

Still, the Living Theatre's most disciplined formal organization of psychological states into a polemic is its clockwork production of *The Brig*. The guard/inmate game enacted before the audience witnessing this unrelenting play moves from mimesis to parable to self-conscious clarity all behind the white line, "the Line beyond which we cannot co-operate." That white line, "drawn alike by prisoner and guard" according to Malina (p. 103), is a powerful emblem of impasse in the contemporary theater.

Our sense of our own place in the audience of *The Brig* is constantly shifting. One of the particulars marking the way of Malina's production was, in fact,

> how the author, in the opening scene, enters the character of Prisoner Number Two whose "night it is," and how at first we see the Brig through his staunch, frightened eyes, but later in the day he is immersed in the fraternity of not suffering alone; not knowing his fellow's name, he learns to live in silent empathy with him, till the author's ego and the actor's individuality and the audience's sense of personal uniqueness are swallowed up in the narrow strictures of the Brig's confining rules. (p. 104)

In the opening sequence, then, using the conventional means of audience identification with an uninitiated newcomer, Brown conditions his audience to the enforced etiquette governing guard/inmate relations. During the half-lit segment of the one-sided welcome which is our naturalistic introduction to *The Brig*, the two guards who whispered and smiled together in the predawn darkness now gang up on the new prisoner, testing his mettle, making his acquiescence to authority as painful and humiliating as possible. The new prisoner is insulted, ordered to parrot the insult, beaten without provocation, and threatened with more violence. Multiple forms of inmate mortification, instances of what sociologists identify as "forced deference patterns" and "verbal or gestural profanations"—typical violations of the "territories of the self" in penal institutions[9]— are consolidated into this rite of initiation. In the audience, we are stunned by the first blow of *The Brig*. Prisoner Number Two, half-awake, is verbally and physically attacked; his human response—he doubles over in pain—is, as Malina intends, "repeated *inside* the body of the spectator" (p. 98). Our sympathies are at once with the victim; we respond to his helplessness with an "imitative reflex action" (p. 98).

Unconventional methods of audience initiation characterize many plays that seek to place the audience in a social reality. In these plays of extreme naturalism, fictive situations edge towards documentary drama. To jolt a jaded audience into a new awareness of the theater as a real place with the potential power to change our perceptions, indeed, to change our lives, innovative playwrights and directors may reshape the environment of the theater to suit the play rather than to comfort us in a familiar upholstered-on-the-aisle darkness. Innovative techniques of greeting and seating the audience, common to many plays of impasse, are also used by the Living Theatre in attempts to engross the audience in a new concept of performance. Its production of *Paradise Now* (in which the audience members were accosted by actors upon entering the auditorium) is a notorious example. Environmental theater companies such as Richard Schechner's Performance Group have adapted this practice to such a large extent that it sometimes loses the immediacy of its initial impact. An unusual environmental effect was achieved, too, in Megan Terry's *The People vs. Ranchman*, when seemingly armed guards escorted a startled audience to their seats in a courtroom/theater. Similar "shock" treatments of arriving spectators now abound in theaters both on and off Broadway. What was once guaranteed to strike an audience as a jolt of reality, came in time, after frivolous overuse (in plays like *Hair*, for example), to lose its political and psychological power as it gained commercial exposure. When such a method was fresh, however, and even now, whenever its use is integral to a mode of performance, it can still jolt us into a new appreciation of the real time and real space that theaters can occupy in our lives. When we first enter the theater housing Malina's production of *The Brig*, for example, we are handed copies of the "Brig Regulations" which Brown lists in the preface to his play (pp. 45–47). Malina calls these rules of military discipline "the basic stage directions of *The Brig*" (p. 92), and so they are. Not only are these rules printed in our programs, they are also demonstrated before us. In the course of the play, we are taught the jargon and the rites of this passage from military protocol. We witness frisks and shakedowns, a field day and a sound off, an exercise drill and a head call. We come to recognize the pure terror of the white lines which must not be crossed without permission.

The ritualized request for permission to cross the white line signals another level on which we acknowledge *The Brig*. The redundancy of the dialogue and action are rooted in fact, but they also suggest an archetypal pattern of hierarchical power. A children's game of giant steps is amplified by the sounds of stamping feet stopping short of a deadly mark on a concrete floor of a brig. A place in time ("Time: March 1957 / Place: Japan" [p.43]) becomes a metaphysical fragment of common experience. Grown men play a perpetual game in earnest here, and gradually, the monotonous pecking-order activities which mirror reality also reflect the gestures of ritual. Prisoners are initiated, berated, pummeled, released, intimidated, etc.; nothing—not even the mental breakdown of one of them—can halt the functioning of this reformatory mechanism within a military world. *The Brig* continues like clockwork. As Malina observes:

159

The sparseness of human activity is demonstrated by the prisoner's day. It is the minimal man, confined to needs. He rises, washes, cleans his quarters, urinates, eats, smokes, is searched, works, eats, is frisked, works or cleans his quarters thoroughly, eats, writes a letter, showers, shaves, and sleeps. He also leaves the Brig, enters the Brig, flips out, marches, and has the living daylights beaten out of him. It isn't much. But where there is very little each action carries a greater burden of a man's suffering, as well as greater inklings of his smothered glory. (p. 90)

These are the minimal actions of a minimized man: the reductive Beckettian universe, the eclipsed world of *Endgame*, for example, has an affinity with the Brig as a way of life.

The only relief from the tedium of this mode of being is an occasional outburst or attack by a guard. These moments of gratuitous violence clarify the naturalistic and symbolic nature of *The Brig*. Like the prisoners onstage, we in the audience learn to dread those unpredictable moments of violence or venom which animate *The Brig* and which break the compelling rhythm of monotonous labor. As Malina notes, "The theory of deterrence is the discipline of The Brig" (p. 104). Our primary response to the cruelty of the play is on this level of sympathetic physical fear. Like the new prisoner who is hastily initiated in Act Two, Scene Three, we in the audience soon develop a resistance to the belligerent rebukes which punctuate enforced silences.

Recovering from the initial pain we witness, we wonder at the pain: why is it inflicted? and by whom? We see instances of inmates conspiring in their own pain. At the end of Act One, for example, the guards initiate a make-believe bombing. A garbage can is turned over on Prisoner Number One "to protect him from shrapnel" (p. 62), and Prisoner Number Two is directed to "pick up the G.I. can cover and run in a circle around One, who is armored government property . . . and each third time around . . . hit the can with the cover" (p. 62). As Prisoner Number Two runs around in circles, "*screaming his general order and clanging the cover on the can,*" and the other prisoners are vigorously exercising to the commands of another guard, the guards begin laughing out loud. The absurdity of misrule is objectified; illogic commands the compound, for the distubing games organized by the guards are played with determination by inmates who are being accorded the cruelest nonperson treatment. They perform in a Marine Corps scenario improvised endlessly by the guards on duty, though internally, perhaps, they are playing private mind games of their own. After all, their complicity in humiliating games may be hard to bear in the theater, but in real life—and real life is what *The Brig* commits its audience to witness— such behavior is a survival tactic. To maintain one's sanity in the incessant enforced performance of a meaningless task, it becomes necessary to play mind games, to impose a meaning—however contrived—from within oneself. Shukhov does this in the wall-building episode of *One Day in the Life of Ivan Denisovich*. There are other accounts of the effects of meaningless tasks on concentration camp inmates.[10] So in *The Brig*, too, in a play that is true to life rather than to stage conventions of heroics, the bodies obey. At the climax of the play, the prisoners accord "civil inattention" to a troubled fellow inmate, and when they close their eyes to the anguish of James Turner, Prisoner Number Six, they are forced by circumstances to survive in silence.

Because of its rarity, a guard's informal address to a prisoner breaks the impersonal rhythm of a uniform community. Only once do the guards speak with audible warmth to each other, and only once do they lower the barriers between the self and the other to speak with compassion to a prisoner. In Act Two, Scene Two, one of the prisoners is released from the brig. The docile boy exits through the "freedom door" to the outside world which is a Marine base. The irony of his release into a larger social institution is intensified by the guard's farewell. Tepperman slams the

door shut and gloats at the remaining residents of his "house":
"Back to your manuals, and someday, if you are good mag-
gots who clean under their short hairs every day, you may
be free" (p. 72). All the prisoners—except for Prisoner
Number Six, a rough-looking man of thirty-four—heed the
command. While the others are systematically paging
through *The Guidebook for Marines* (the only reading material allowed in the brig, and required reading whenever
they are not otherwise occupied), Prisoner Number Six
suffers a mental breakdown. He screams, falls to his knees,
and weeps. The other prisoners first jump with fright, but
immediately return to their reading. They have learned
how to recover from the blow; if this moment of impact
does hurt them, they do not show it. Like the audience,
they remain bystanders as madness breaks down the barriers between the mind and body. Tepperman, billy club
in his grip, rushes toward Number Six. The other prisoners
avert their eyes to their guidebooks, a silent chorus of in-
carcerated Marines.

This is the climax of a communal tragedy. The foundation of the Structure is momentarily threatened by a
rebellion of the spirit. This moment of defiance is the test
of *The Brig*. Seeing the freedom door slam shut behind a
"rehabilitated" offender, Six loses the self-control required
for survival and release by this cold manifestation of the
Marine creed. He breaks the fundamental rule of the game:
he looks up at the guard, but he talks to the man: "I am
thirty-four years old. For God's sake, let me out of this
madhouse. I'm not one of these damned kids. I can't stand
it any more" (p. 72). His appeal, made on the man-to-man
level, is denied on an impersonal level. "I told you to get
on your feet, Six," Tepperman answers. Suddenly, Six lunges
at the figure of the guard. He fights savagely with the three
guards who violently subdue him and take him off to a
solitary cell out of our sight. But we can still hear him. He
continues to scream, "My name is not Six. It's James Turner.
Let me out of here" from within the cell (p. 73). Promptly,
he is straightjacketed and removed from the brig. As he is

carried out, babbling incoherently, one of the guards consoles him with a single exchange of human kind. "Just relax, James Turner," the guard reassures Six. "You are getting out of here" (p. 73).

Of course, the kindness of the guard's remark is deceptive, for James Turner is not really "getting out" at all; he is merely being transferred to another realm of the same military regime. Still, the guard's comforting remark is gratuitous: he has called a prisoner by a name instead of a number, and he has shown sympathy for his double under duress. For a breathtaking moment the game is interrupted. According to Malina:

> He screams because he has broken out of the system. Because he has isolated himself forever. Because he cannot go back. He is afraid. And he is not afraid because he has gone crazy, but because he has gone sane. . . . This is the only instance in which a prisoner is referred to by his name. For an instant the prisoner is deluded that the minion of law and order has restored him to the status of a man. He relaxes, and this is the fatal moment when they bind him and carry him out on a stretcher, as he says "Thank God."
>
> But *where* are they taking him? He has a rendezvous out there with an unknown, impenetrable, giant Brig called the Looney-Bin where tomorrow's hospital-prisons are already a-building on the ruins of the ancient dungeons. (pp. 104–105).

This moment realizes Judith Malina's vision of *The Brig* as an allegory in which the individual is swallowed by the villainous Structure. And with the play's kindest gesture being accompanied by straightjacketing, at the moment of James Turner's release, the brig is also clearly an Artaudian Structure, where "everything that acts," every human gesture, is a cruelty.[11]

But this moment passes and the guards resume their roles. The captive team has lost a player, but the predetermined game goes on. The rebellion is doomed on the social level, and so, as long as the impervious institution stands, the rebel can only turn inward and destroy himself. For the odds are heavily against Six; his name is disregarded here, and his shrieks are muffled by the brick walls which batter his spirit. He breaks down himself instead of the walls of his prison; and even though he is released, we know that he will not be freed. According to Malina, "The body of the prisoner is totally captive. The soul of the prisoner is potentially totally free. The trip between these two points is the crucial experience of the play" (p. 101). This spiritual trip is demonstrated in naturalistic steps, and its philosophical destination—the only way to end the impasse, to break the deadlock—is revolution.

BALANCED at the edge of documentary, *The Brig* focuses on the beauty and terror of the encompassing Structure. In this annex of military life bracketed onstage, defeated, anonymous figures finally merge in a mechanical rhythm. This emphasis on the endurance of the Structure rather than on the individual pitted against it becomes the strength and terror of *The Brig*. Behan's *The Quare Fellow* and Genet's *Deathwatch*—two other contemporary plays using imprisonment as the metaphor *and* the reality of a spirit battered by a social institution—share with *The Brig* its premise of pain and loss as well as its prison setting. Yet both these plays contrast with *The Brig* in their focus: unlike the depersonalizing *Brig*, both *The Quare Fellow* and *Deathwatch* are institutional endgames lost by a singular convict. In each of these plays, the experience of *The Brig*, a play that strikes us as a continuous image of men marching in place, is incarnated in *one* inmate running in circles towards his own death. Still, the timetable of everyday, the pastimes passing for action in jail, and the paring down of those old conventional "unities" to an indicative present, a static essence, an impasse, is the same. The doubleness of guards and inmates—keepers and criminals, oppressors and victims—each of them a reflection of the hated, admired other in a dialectic of the imagination, is the same. And the philosophical destination beyond play—the vision of power in such plays of extreme situations, both psychological and social—is the same.

The Quare Fellow (and The Hostage)

Brendan Behan's *The Quare Fellow* parallels both *The Brig* and *Marat/Sade* in its formal fidelity to a social institution. All three plays are spectacles of ideas: *Marat/Sade* is a debate between freedom and restraint, madness and sanity; *The Brig* is a didactic docu-drama, inciting us to reform by calling our attention to a Marine camp prison as an *objet trouvé*; and *The Quare Fellow* is a moral tonic, a satire, a jocular musical with a somber theme which is, as John Russell Taylor phrases it, "the inalienable dignity of man—inalienable, that is, in that nobody can take it away from him except himself."[12] This theme, a singularly recurrent one in the plays considered here, is coupled with Behan's dramatic absurdism—his willingness, in Martin Esslin's terms, to "face reality in all its senselessness; to accept it freely, without fear, without illusions—and to laugh at it."[13] The product of Behan's union of his social concern with his absurdist sense is an original concept of prison and performance. Like *Marat/Sade* and *The Brig*, *The Quare Fellow* is aimed at the audience's mind; and in its own surprising way, it, too, assaults us "through the skin" with Artaudian weapons of theatrical efficacy.

The Quare Fellow shares with *Marat/Sade* and *The Brig* another important element: a collaboratory relationship between playwright and director. Like Weiss and Brown, Behan avoids conventionally following a story line by attenuating action onstage. When the playwright diffuses his focus to include an expansive setting, the director has the task of synthesizing bits of stage business into a cohesive form. The director must congeal the flow of action into art. Peter Brook dazzled us with his work on *Marat/Sade*; Judith Malina turned the skeletal script of *The Brig* into a highly coordinated military operation. Joan Littlewood's

165

productions of *The Quare Fellow* and *The Hostage* were even more collaboratory in nature. Somewhat less credit is due to Littlewood for *The Quare Fellow* than for Behan's later *The Hostage*, which Littlewood claims to have wrenched from his pen; as one commentator tartly put it, after the success of *The Quare Fellow*, Behan became "a strictly C.O.D. man."[14] Still, Littlewood's contribution to the final, published version of *The Quare Fellow* is also substantial.

There are, of course, alternative versions concerning the extent of Littlewood's midwifery in the execution of this play. John Russell Taylor contends that *The Quare Fellow* was originally an amorphous argument against capital punishment encumbered by uneven comedy. In his opinion, the undisciplined Behan's theatrical sensibility was formed "by the taste and theatrical flair of Joan Littlewood," under whose influence the play underwent theatrical metamorphosis:

> His first play, *The Quare Fellow*, was written in 1955 and sent finally to Joan Littlewood, who read the first five pages, sent off a telegram at once accepting it, and spent the next few months licking it into shape, tightening, sharpening, eliminating the sentimental passages—all with the help of the author from the safe distance of the pub over the way.[15]

Even earlier changes in the original script of *The Quare Fellow* are recalled by Alan Simpson who, with Carolyn Swift, gave the play its first production at the small Pike Theatre in Dublin. According to Simpson:

> Brendan's happy-go-lucky, slapdash approach to his writing should, in the ordinary way, have prevented his work from ever being produced. *The Quare Fellow* breaks pretty well all the rules for good play-writing. It is rambling, without plot, and the principal serious character (Warder Regan) doesn't appear consistently throughout the play, which perhaps tempted Miss Littlewood to form the amalgamation with Donnelly. . . .

The two principal comedy characters, Dunlavin and Neighbour, don't appear at all in Act Three, although they are heard briefly as "voices off." Actually, in my Pike production, I slightly ameliorated this latter deficiency by having their cell windows visible to the audience. This was a wildly implausible departure from realism, but once the audience had accepted the twelve by twelve Pike stage as the exercise yard of Mountjoy Prison, they were ready for anything, and the fact that these characters appeared like Jack-in-the-boxes seven feet above stage level didn't seem to trouble them at all.

Simpson expresses his regret that in the Pike production, and to a greater extent in Littlewood's Theatre Workshop production, characters became more schematized than they had been in Behan's original concept of the play:

> There were twenty-nine characters in the original play, which we reduced by doubling, to twenty-one. The number was reduced further in Theatre Workshop, which, I think, was a pity as it destroyed some of the continuity of characterization. This was particularly evident in the amalgamation made by Joan Littlewood of Donnelly and Warder One. Donnelly, in the original version, was the warder who opened the play. In the Stratford production, Warder Regan was given his lines at this point. They are, in fact, very different characters; Donnelly being a gruff, no-nonsense type of man, but essentially decent and kindly. Regan, on the other hand, is a highly sensitive, almost neurotic Catholic. . . . It is through Regan's mouth that Brendan gives us his own philosophy, and this does not match up at all with Donnelly's bluff, unthinking approach to life.[16]

When Ulick O'Connor traces the history of *The Quare Fellow* from its first production, he, too, catalogues shifts in focus from the original script. By his account, Carolyn Swift recalls that she "had to transfer passages from one part of the play to the other, as it was rather confused." According to O'Connor, Joan Littlewood later altered the play for the Stratford presentation, "to make it more acceptable to a cosmopolitan public." The effect, in O'Connor's opinion, was not only to "internationalize the local atmosphere of *The Quare Fellow*," but also to eliminate from the play sections which "helped to project [Warder] Regan as the major character in the play." O'Connor misses the more fully realized version of Warder Regan; he believes "Regan is the most striking of the characters which Brendan created for the stage. He is a Christian humanist with an Irish sense of irony which enables him to walk a tightrope between duty and compassion." Yet O'Connor sees the director's rationale for the changes in the script. "Of course it can be argued," he writes grudgingly, "that the play is a series of tableaux in which the ritual of hanging is unfolded and that the inclusion of a fully drawn character would overbalance it."[17] Under Littlewood's direction, this is indeed *The Quare Fellow* that emerged: a series of densely humanized tableaux against which the ritual of hanging is measured.

By all these accounts of Behan's habits and his easygoing playwrighting, then, *The Quare Fellow* was a mercurial script. Though undisciplined, Behan was a cooperative playwright with a flexible, vivid script, a dream of a play for any contemporary director. Like many of those involved with plays considered here (Peter Brook, Judith Malina, John Dexter, for example), the director, Joan Littlewood, became involved in the creation as well as the realization of *The Quare Fellow*. The result was the performance-oriented rather than text-oriented final version of the play. Typical of contemporary plays of impasse, this final version of *The Quare Fellow* emphasizes the Structure teeming with everyday, routine life at the edge of doom, and it pays little mind to heroes. Only David Rabe's *The Basic Training of Pavlo Hummel* was so spliced and reshaped in rehearsal; only Peter Weiss's *Marat/Sade* had so dense a script as to make the notable production by Peter Brook, like the production of

The Quare Fellow by Joan Littlewood, inimitable, textured by the director as powerfully as by the playwright. No other play included in this study equals *The Quare Fellow* in its subjugation of script to staging.

Joan Littlewood organized the comic lyricism of Behan's *memento mori* within the comprehensive framework of a prison. Like Judith Malina, who molded Brown's chronicle of incessant orders and drills into an experiential pattern of military imprisonment, Littlewood brought stability and formalism to the mobile, loosely arranged elements of *The Quare Fellow*. Indeed, her rehearsal technique for the play bears a striking resemblance to that which would later be used by Malina to discipline her troop of actors according to an institutional model. As one of the actors from Little-wood's Theatre Workshop remembers the experience:

> For the first week of rehearsals of *The Quare Fellow* we had no scripts. None of us had even read the play. We knew it was about prison life in Dublin, and that was enough for Joan. None of us had ever been in prison, and although we could all half-imagine what it was like, Joan set out to tell us more—the narrow world of steel and stone, high windows and clanging doors, the love-hate between warder and prisoner, the gossip, the jealousy, and the tragedy—all the things that make up the fascination of dreariness. She took us up on to the roof of the Theatre Royal. All the grimy slate and stone made it easy to believe we were in a prison yard. We formed up in a circle, and imagined we were prisoners out on exercise. Round and round we trudged for what seemed like hours—breaking now and then for a quick smoke and furtive conversation. Although it was just a kind of game, the boredom and meanness of it all was brought home. Next, the "game" was extended— the whole dreary routine of washing out your cell, standing to attention, sucking up to the screws, trading tobacco, was improvised and developed. It began to seem less and less like a game, and more like real. By

degrees the plot and the script were introduced, although some of us never knew which parts we were playing until half-way through the rehearsals. The interesting thing was that when she gave us the scripts we found that many of the situations we had improvised actually occurred in the play. All we had to do was learn the author's words.[18]

The Brig and *The Quare Fellow* depict distinct penal systems, the one American military, the other Irish; and the styles of Brown and Behan are very different, the one objective and terse, the other subjective and satirical. Nevertheless, both these plays are rooted in the experience of systematic condemnation, both are closely associated with their directors who fixed them in an image of authenticity, and in both, even in rehearsal, the games of the Structure hold sway.

The Quare Fellow, like *The Brig*, derives much of its power onstage from its fidelity to the institution it reconstructs. As Alan Simpson observed, "the authentic atmosphere of *The Quare Fellow* is all important."[19] Luckily for Behan, with his free-wheeling style, the history of penology reveals that the jails of Ireland are considered part of the vanguard of progressive approaches to imprisonment. Flexibility is their hallmark. According to one observer:

> The Irish Free State has one other distinction besides having Europe's smallest relative prison population; it shares with Belgium and Sweden a system of short furloughs home for inmates of its three prisons who have "earned" them, or who have good records and are near discharge. Despite the Irish reputation for violence, there are so few prisoners that after the Free State was founded twenty-one jails were closed because they were empty.[20]

Unlike the real model for *The Brig*, an oppressive total institution that prohibits comic relief, the heterodox institution in which *The Quare Fellow* is housed accommodates

Behan's own flexibility as a playwright. Characterized in reality by a less inhibitive atmosphere than is common in prisons of many other countries, Behan's jail gives its inmates enough rope to ease the tension of imprisonment. The model for his prison setting suits Behan's heterogeneous style.

Within a framework of naturalism, Behan's prisoners crack jokes, sing songs, and commit pardonable offenses. His play engages us with the deceptive frivolity of humorous types and their prison-yard pastimes. But this music-hall revue of prison life is finally an unsentimental review of life measured out in prison. In Behan's play, songs, sound effects, and ingenious prison games are at once dramatic equivalents of a real prison routine, self-conscious theatrical routines, and echoes of an off-key dirge for a funny world gone wrong.

Singing is Behan's primary technique for merging ironic commentary with authentic prison behavior. As the curtain rises to reveal a wing of a city prison, an offstage prisoner who, according to the opening stage directions, is *"in one of the punishment cells"* sings a refrain of prison routine:

> To begin the morning
> The warder bawling
> Get out of bed and clean up your cell,
> And that old triangle
> Went jingle jangle
> Along the banks of the Royal Canal.[21]

This song of the offstage balladeer immediately establishes the place and the mood of the ensuing action: as in *The Brig* (and as in *One Day in the Life of Ivan Denisovich*), in this play time is measured out in the days of a sentence; each day to be served is virtually indistinguishable from the rest; and after a while, a prisoner's absurd sense of a clockwork reality transfigures an institutional routine into a ritualistic pattern.

As the opening song in the Littlewood production of *The Quare Fellow* established the mood of life on schedule, it

171

also signaled Behan's double emphasis on naturalism and ironic symbolism. Ulick O'Connor recalls:

> The mixture of grimness and gaiety in *The Quare Fellow* enthralled the audience. When the curtain went up on the first night at Stratford, a superb set by John Bury showed the stage open to the back wall, so that the bricks and central heating pipes of the theatre gave the impression of the bleak interior of a prison. Then Brendan's ringing voice, with poetry hidden somewhere in its stridency, intoned the opening song, "The Old Triangle."[22]

By exposing the backstage area to the audience, Littlewood's production called attention to the mechanics of staging. The voice of the playwright in the role of the unseen singer also added a heightened awareness of the play as performance. At the same time, however, both the unpretentious setting and the authentic sound effect contributed to the audience's first impression of naturalistic "grimness" as well as to its immediate sense of the self-conscious boundaries of a playing space.

Much as the barbed wire encases *The Brig*, the recurrent singing from the offstage punishment cell frames the action of *The Quare Fellow*. It, too, persistently sets the pace of stage business according to the tone of the institution being reconstructed onstage. In fact, the song proves immediately prophetic, for it is drowned out by the sound of the "jingle jangle" of the triangle being beaten "*loudly and raucously*" by an approaching warder (p. 40). On his third verse, the singer continues: "The screw was peeping / And the lag was weeping . . ." (p. 40). Ironically, at this very moment the guard is in fact peeping through the cell door spyholes. We in the audience see that the song of the man in solitary is a melodic transformation of routine into art; the song is a comic signal of the beauty in rhythm and order—even in the rhythm and order of an Irish jail. The song extols the ritualistic certainties of an organized program; and in the course of the play, the recurring song itself becomes an organizing principle, shaping the discordant variations on the theme of imprisonment into a dirge for the condemned man of the title. The singer in solitary, like the quare fellow, never appears onstage. Both shadowy figures lurk in the background of Behan's comedy. Like Green Eyes and Snowball in Genet's *Deathwatch*, the two formidable presences of Behan's play dominate his prison setting. There is, however, an important difference: Genet's dreamlike drama radiates from one cell, the claustrophobic one of the condemned man; Behan's authentically set burlesque demonstrates the triumph of immutable order over the lives of many men on an expansive cul-de-sac stage.

The first spoken words of the play are the early morning threats of the warder. With a menacing shout, he puts an abrupt halt to the offstage singing which opens the play. The warder calls out his own tune of prison routine: "The screw is listening as well as peeping, and you'll be bloody well weeping if you don't give over your moaning" (p. 40). This characteristic bellow of a guard is doubly striking. For the guard not only ends the opening song by shouting it down in the performance of his duties, he also spontaneously incorporates the familiar lyrics of the prisoner's morning song into his own sarcastic litany. For the audience, the truth of the song is verified both by the guard's simultaneous enactment of the lyrics and by his irritated reaction to them. Before the play proper has even begun, we are alerted to the omniscience of the offstage singer. At regular intervals throughout the play, choral commentary will be provided for us by a clear, melancholy, disembodied voice.

Songs, the adhesive element of this prison variety show, emerge as just one musical aspect of a very musical piece. In addition to the unseen chorus below, for example, the Hangman and Jenkinson, his melancholy assistant, perform a duet to the accompaniment of a concertina in Act Three, Scene One as they make the necessary preparations for the morning. The Hangman introduces the song as a hymn which is "very moving about hanging and mercy and so forth" (p. 117). The ironic relevance of the hymn is given added weight by the Hangman's simultaneous reckoning of the drop required to balance the weight of the quare fellow. His calculations counterpoint the song of mercy:

> JENKINSON. Though thou hast grieved me sore,
> My arms of mercy still are open wide,
> I still hold open Heaven's shining door
> Come then, take refuge in my wounded side.
>
> HANGMAN. Now he's only twelve stone so he should have eight foot eight, but he's got a thick neck on him so I'd better give him another couple of inches. Yes, eight foot ten.
>
> JENKINSON. Come now, the time is short.
> Longing to pardon and bless I wait.
> Look up to me, my sheep so dearly bought
> And say, forgive me, ere it is too late.
>
> HANGMAN. Divide 412 by the weight of the body in stones, multiply by two gives the length of the drop in inches.
>
> (p. 118)

This song is followed by a plaintive Irish song sung by the young lad homesick for Kerry. His song is the bridge between the night patrol and the appointed morning. At the first sound of his lone voice, the two warders recognize its funereal intonation:

> PRISONER C (*sings from his cell window*). Is e fath mo bhuartha na bhfhaghaim cead chuarta.
>
> WARDER REGAN. Regular choir practice going on round here tonight.
>
> CRIMMIN. He's singing for . . . for . . .
>
> WARDER REGAN. For the quare fellow.
>
> (p. 119)

As his song dies out, morning fades in onstage. The hanging is carried out offstage and the play closes on another everyday vignette underscored by a wistful song.

The last routine of *The Quare Fellow*, ironically followed
by the last strains of the offstage singing, is a quarrel among
gravedigging prisoners, battling over possibly salable letters
scrawled by the condemned man on the eve of his execution. The prisoners distance themselves from their gravedigging roles by making what sociologists call "secondary
adjustments" to a prison situation. As Goffman characterizes this system common to guarded communities, such
secondary adjustments are

> practices that do not directly challenge staff but allow
> inmates to obtain forbidden satisfactions or to obtain
> permitted ones by forbidden means. These practices
> are variously referred to as "the angles," "knowing the
> ropes," "conniving," "gimmicks," "deals," or "ins." Such
> adaptations apparently reach their finest flower in pris-
> ons, but of course other total institutions are overrun
> with them, too. Secondary adjustments provide the in-
> mate with important evidence that he is still his own
> man, with some control of his environment; sometimes
> a secondary adjustment becomes almost a kind of lodg-
> ment for the self, a *churinga* in which the soul is felt
> to reside.[23]

The Irish jail in which Behan sets *The Quare Fellow* differs
significantly from its American counterpart (after which
The Brig is modeled) in the nature of the secondary adjustments made by prisoners. Behan's comedy is benefited
by the instances of face-saving, role-distancing, and secondary adjustments drawn factually from his model; the
institution is much looser than its sober American military
counterpart (imprisonment is a less dangerous game), and
so, the secondary adjustments of Irish prisoners are a naturalistic resource, supplying Behan with comic material
for the stage.

Focusing on the secondary adjustments made by different vaudevillian types of prisoners and guards, *The Quare
Fellow* finally unites these two uniformed factions in a contrapuntal struggle within the social system. In *The Brig*, the

focus is also on secondary adjustments; but within the naturalistically imposed framework of Brown's play, options for survival within the system are severely limited. In *The Brig*, only by madness, death, or total submission of individual will to institutional whim could an inmate hope to work his way out of the prison and get through that symbolic yet concrete "freedom door." And death and madness, the prisoner's first two options, are certainly *not* secondary adjustments. In *The Quare Fellow*, however, Behan presents us with a civilian institution which is riddled with loopholes through which an enterprising inmate may find momentary release from the boredom of the cellblock. The options here are plentiful, so in Behan's play, as opposed to Brown's uncompromising barrage on our senses, a grim idea of the theater is expressed by grimacing buffoons. His play translates into the theatrical idiom the farcical details of a system of secondary adjustments to a total institution. The loopholes available to *The Quare Fellow*'s enterprising inmates make their awareness of the impasse at bottom of their situation all the more painful. In *The Brig* there is no illusion of freedom, not even any small choices. All fight is futile. But in *The Quare Fellow*, where song and comedy fight institutionalization, as in other parodic treatments of social institutions—*The Happy Haven* and *The Physicists*, for example—the temporary release found in play, the flexible, shifting Structure, and the feeling of retained individuality combine to encourage an illusion of autonomy that keeps inmates looking, hoping for a way out. The looking and the hoping underscore the actual impasse of their imprisonment—the white line beyond which they finally cannot go, no matter how clever their ruses.

Behan's play is a lively rendition of clever ruses. In particular, the complementary team of Dunlavin and Neighbour, two old "lags" (men doing at least three years of "penal servitude" [p.60]), are past masters at prison games. They drink the alcohol with which the warder rubs their rheumatic limbs; they keep an eye out for dog-ends of cigarettes strewn about the exercise yard; they take bets on the quare fellow's chance for a reprieve; they connive to get letters of recommendation from Healey, the complaint collector sent around by the Department of Justice. In their spare time, they gossip with other prisoners, watch for "the mots from the laundry over on the female side hanging out the washing in the exercise yard" (p. 54), and teach the criminal trade to apprentices who arrive eager for knowledge. Young Prisoner 2, for example, remarks half-jestingly to an older convict: "When you're over here, there's always a chance of getting a bit of education about screwing jobs, and suchlike, from experienced men. Do you think Triplex or celluloid is the best for Yale locks, sir?" (p. 48). Much of the dialogue is, in fact, delivered in such a half-jesting tone. For the jest is coupled with the dramatic irony of extenuating circumstances. The members of Behan's penitentiary underworld project an existential optimism by means of their secondary adjustments to prison life.

A note in the program of Littlewood's production said, "This is not a play about prisons, but a play about people."[24] How appropriate, for *The Quare Fellow*, like other plays of impasse, focuses on human behavior in a pinch—reactions to extreme situations—rather than on a program for reform of a specific social institution. With songs and institutional lingo, with double takes and buddy relationships, and with contrapuntal bits of stage business that are based on real secondary adjustments to imprisonment, *The Quare Fellow* affects us as a series of comic turns celebrating the small victories of men over the system. With the broad gestures of slapstick and with the variety of a music hall bill, Behan's prison play reconstructs a prison on the eve of a hanging, and by extension, an absurd universe on the eve of destruction.

Although singing is Behan's primary affective technique, other sound effects are also used ironically. Details drawn from reality are underscored here so that Behan's play, like Brown's, contains moments that call forth expressions of anguish, moments that cry out from the depths of human despair. While Neighbour and Mickser exchange prisoners' insults in Act Two, for example, they catch the attention of some of their fellow inmates in the exercise yard. Suddenly, however, according to the stage directions, "*A WARDER passes, sounds of the town heard, factory sirens, distant ships. Some of the prisoners pace up and down like caged animals*" (p. 82). At this moment of *The Quare Fellow* stage action is energized by sound, and by means of sound a social institution of restraint takes on larger suggestive qualities. The sounds of this play evoke a mood of specifically located imprisonment, and beyond that, they create a more generalized atmosphere of impasse, of whistling in the dark, of foreboding, anticipation, and dread.

Later that night, as the time for hanging draws near, "*a faint tapping is heard intermittently*" (p. 105); and the two warders on watch remark on the "yapping" among the prisoners which builds traditionally to a piercing crescendo whenever an inmate is executed:

WARDER 1. Have you ever been in one of these before?
WARDER 2. No.
WARDER 1. They'll be at it from six o'clock tomorrow morning, and when it comes a quarter to eight it'll be like a running commentary in the Grand National.
(*Tapping.*)
WARDER 1 (*quietly*). Shut your bloody row! And then the screeches and roars of them when his time comes. They say it's the last thing the fellow hears.
(*Tapping dies down.*)
WARDER 2. Talk about something else.
(*Tapping.*)
WARDER 1. They're quietening down a bit. You'd think they'd be in the humour for a read or a sleep, wouldn't you?
WARDER 2. It's a hell of a job.
WARDER 1. We're in it for the three P's, boy, pay, promotion and pension, that's all that should bother civil servants like us.

(p. 106)

This reassurance of one warder to another is an ordinary bit of role-distancing by guards faced with a distasteful task. For a moment here, we see the warders backstage at their job. Like the guards of *The Brig* who talk among themselves about a night off in Tokyo and about taking turns "sweating it out" in the brig, the warders in *The Quare Fellow* talk matter-of-factly about their tasks, and as they do, they seem to be realized characters, not just types. With their catalogue of the "three P's, boy, pay, promotion and pension," they remind us that the routine of imprisonment can have a demoralizing or numbing effect on guards as well as on inmates. So just as the guards of *The Brig* go about their dehumanizing business, the "screws" of *The Quare Fellow* perform assigned tasks in an institutional rhythm aligned to the movements of a rigidified dance. Although *The Quare Fellow*, especially in its sympathetic characterization of Warder Regan, is more even-handed in its treatment of both inmates *and* guards than either *The Brig* or *Deathwatch*, still, here, too, the Structure steals the show. Throughout that interchange between warders quoted above, for a crucial example, the sound of the prisoners' tapping continues, an eerie counterpoint taking center stage.

When the time for hanging arrives, Behan's musicality and comedy again intensify the irony and pathos of his prisoners' situation. In a comic moment of men facing death, Warder One's forewarning description of the ritualized mourning for a murderer rings true. An eyewitness account rendered into sportscasting jargon by the prisoner, Mickser, is accompanied by the sound of the clock chiming the hour; according to the stage directions, "*each quarter sounds louder*" (p. 121). As Mickser travesties the rite with role-distancing mockery, the other prisoners listen for the hour to strike. So the race towards death begins with Mickser's announcement of a spectator sport about to start:

> We're off, in this order: the Governor, the Chief, two screws Regan and Crimmin, the quare fellow between them, two more screws and three runners from across the Channel, getting well in front, now the Canon. He's

making a big effort for the last two furlongs. He's got the white pudding bag on his head, just a short distance to go. He's in. (*A clock begins to chime the hour. Each quarter sounds louder.*) His feet to the chalk line. He'll be pinioned, his feet together. The bag will be pulled down over his face. The screws come off the trap and steady him. Himself goes to the lever and. . . .
(pp. 120–121)

Offstage, the quare fellow reaches the finish line, the clock strikes, the warders cross themselves, and the prisoners howl.

The execution itself, although narrated in Mickser's parodic sportscast, is sidestepped in Behan's slapstick tragedy. The emphasis here is on people kept in the system rather than on a single human dilemma, so we never even see the quare fellow, the fulcrum of Behan's play. In contrast to Green Eyes, the condemned man who dominates Genet's compressed endgame, the "quare fellow" of Behan's title awaits his hanging in a cell of this liberally run prison out of our sight, and out of the sight of the other prisoners. True to its life model, Behan's stage prison segregates condemned men from the other inmates. The inmates themselves seem to prefer to keep their distance from one whose crime and punishment are ugly, terrible, awesome. Once he is sentenced to death, even the prisoner's name is traded in for an impersonal euphemism. Like the balladeer who is his ironic counterpart (his lone voice drifting from beyond Behan's vaudevillian stage, from a solitary punishment cell below), the quare fellow gains symbolic stature by his physical absence from the stage. He becomes a representative figure ironically akin to an institutional everyman, the title character of a comic rendition of prison life-in-death.

Behan himself alluded to the universality implied by the slang term he appropriated for his title. Dominic Behan quotes his brother on the genesis of the play and of its title:

"I saw Pierrepoint twice," he said, "once in Walton Jail in Liverpool, and again when he came to top Barney Kirwan in Mountjoy. Remember that fella, Christie?" "I do, Brendan, cut his brother up like a pig and fed him to the pigs." "Of course," said Brendan, "he didn't deserve to be hanged. A nut he was. Complete nut. But then accordin' to their own law a man should not hang if he's not responsible for what he does by reason of insanity. They had him examined by a trickcyclist. Trickcyclist how are yeh! Should have come to me. I'd have told them. He used to ask the screw to get me to sing for him so that he'd hear a nice young voice when he was goin' for the long drop. So bloody gentle. And yet he carved his brother up. One screw told me that on the mornin' of his execution Kirwan took up a glass of water and balanced it on the back of his hand saying, 'There's nerves for yeh. From a man that's on his way to his Maker.' And they said he wasn't potty! I've written a play about it. And I hope someone has the sense to do it, called, it was, what we used to call him. Nobody ever likes to refer to a condemned man by name; sticks in the throat; used to call him the quare fella." "In the camp you were calling it *The Twisting of Another Rope*," said Christie. "Yes," said Brendan, "in jail the deed of hanging, the act is the enemy. Outside, yeh can think of the victim."[25]

Just as the unseen singer gives the play its cohesion and consistency, so the universalized victim—the quare fellow—gives the play an omnipresent representative of its central thesis. The singer turns an everyday routine into a musical round, but the execution of the condemned man is a still point that punctures the routine organization of the play. When his death offstage is punctuated by the striking of the clock and by a *"ferocious howling"* from the prisoners (p. 121), an idea of the theater, an impulse to break through the impasse, to "storm the barricades," as Beck puts it, is enacted in sound. At the moment of his hanging, then, the

quare fellow interrupts the rhythm of the prison; a cacophony of inmates accompanies his death. But as in *The
Brig*, a cry of chaos is short-lived. The warders shout "Shut
up," and gradually the noise subsides.

But that momentary howl of Behan's prisoners echoes
in the mind of the audience. More strident than the even
sounds of the prisoner's song, this communal cry lingers
in the silence of the prison yard like the air of the Kerry
boy who, according to one of the prisoners, "sings an old
song betimes. It's very nice. It makes the night less lonely,
each man alone and sad maybe in the old cell" (p. 96). This
harsh cry suddenly pierces the orderly musical arrangement of the preceding action. The doubleness of Behan's
play—its social commentary and its symbolic resonance—
is most vivid in that prisoners' howl, a theatrically expressed
idea about capital punishment,[26] and a shriek of sympathetic feeling for all who must stay or die.

The dialectic of Behan's play, then, is not represented
by opposing forces of guards or inmates; rather, as in the
more rigid *Brig* and the more dreamlike *Deathwatch*, it is
finally to be found in the play's formal organization, in the
polarity of the self vs. the Structure. This dynamic tension
is reinforced throughout the play by means of ironic counterpoint. Immediately following the hanging, for example,
the warders who cross the yard carrying an inert body
explain that this is not—as we in the audience might assume—the body of the quare fellow. It is, rather, the body
of Crimmin, the novice guard who fainted at the ceremony.
A touch of comic relief undercuts a grim moment as it
underscores the humanity—and vulnerability—of guards
and inmates alike.

Only the Structure endures whole, and only the Structure is finally an active force onstage. Here, as in other
plays in this contemporary mode of human stasis, the grim
rite of passage out of an institution is followed by the confused reactions of powerless bystanders. Plays such as *The
Quare Fellow, The Brig,* and *Deathwatch* as well as *Chips With
Everything, The Basic Training of Pavlo Hummel, The National*

Health, and *Marat/Sade* share this plot element of the death of a representative figure to be communally, briefly mourned. Such plays recall the medieval morality play in their use of character types within a system suggesting the *theatrum mundi* metaphor, and they are, in essence, a series of episodes leading to the death or destruction of a representative figure. Significantly, however, such plays differ from medieval morality plays in their focus *not* on the everyman figure, but on the world he leaves behind, on reactions to his death. His death is rarely transcendent; more often, it is a sign of his defeat by that formidable world.

IN ITS RESEMBLANCE to a modern morality play, as well as in its use of songs and ironic counterpoint, *The Quare Fellow* prefigures Behan's *The Hostage.* In *The Hostage,* too, the sacrificial central character is a universal type drawn from ordinary life. Both of Behan's completed plays alternate the comic patterns of a closed system's population with a plot which breaks the patterns of all concerned. The plots of these two plays are also essentially similar: life goes on as usual for all but one character; he is scheduled to die, and this single instance of impending death takes on symbolic overtones for those who must continue their daily routines.

There is, however, a difference between the quare fellow and the hostage, the doomed title characters of Behan's two completed plays. And this difference pertains directly to the striking effect achieved by contemporary drama when it emphasizes a pure Structure, a cannibalistic setting, rather than a conventional, sympathetic hero in that setting. To varying degrees in contemporary drama, heroes are swallowed up by powerful settings; the more potent the Structure in which he eats, sleeps, works, and plays, the less likely is the hero's chance of dominating the play. After all, a hero's odds of winning, of beating the world onstage, are hurt by his reduction to a number by a Structure demanding multitudes, *and* demanding their anonymity. Plus, the variable of free will is at least compromised, or at most, eliminated by a formidable Structure that even may go so far (in plays like *The Brig, Marat/Sade,* or *The National Health,* to mention some extreme examples) as to take over the stage, to transform it into a documentary image of real pain and terror in the Structure which is at once a social reality, a psychodramatic construct, an analogy for the world as it is since the end of World War II, and an ironic idea of universal play. The nature of this mode that finds humanity locked in a shell is most devastating when it is stark, pure in its emphasis on a Structure that siphons out life and methodically eliminates or upstages potentially threatening, individual figures such as Prisoner Number Six in *The Brig,* Green Eyes in *Deathwatch,* or Behan's quare fellow. But the nature of this mode is also present, although to a lesser degree, even in a sentimental play like *The Hostage* which allows Leslie, its title figure, its sacrificed hero, to be a real boy and a central figure, as well as a shadow of a universal soldier.

Embodying the war which victimizes him, Leslie unites the dramatic poles of Behan's boarding house. Engagement in a cause and escape in a song merge in a single figure, for the hostage brings both pleasure and pain in exchange for his room. His songs and later seduction of Teresa are comic contributions to a bawdy house revue, but his imprisonment and inevitable execution are political. The logic of war, like the logic of theatrical performances, is absurd in its redundancy: the hero dies, but he rises to play again; the encompassing Structure remains the same.

As befits a resident of the fleabag hotel where he is forcibly lodged, Leslie displays good-humored tolerance. At the close of Act Two of *The Hostage,* however, Leslie realizes that he is doomed, and he grows understandably agitated. While everybody is dancing to rock-and-roll music and Miss Gilchrist is singing a pious tune, the Soldier reads about himself in the evening paper. Suddenly, he calls out, "Shut up, this is serious," and he reads the newspaper account aloud. In disbelief, he turns to the revelers:

SOLDIER. Does it really mean they're going to shoot
me?
MULLEADY. I'm afraid so.
SOLDIER. Why?
MONSEWER. You're the hostage.
SOLDIER. But I ain't done nothing.
OFFICER. This is war.
SOLDIER. Surely one of you would let me go?
(*They all move backwards away from him, leaving him
alone in the room. They disappear.*)
Well, you crowd of bleeding—Hey, Kate, give us
some music.
(*He sings "I am a Happy English Lad."*)

(p. 206)

With that broken line, "Well, you crowd of bleeding—Hey,
Kate, give us some music," the Soldier moves to a more
serious mode, and he shifts the balance of the Act Two
curtain. Leslie's immediate reaction to the news of his unfortunate state is incredulity. But when he appeals to reason, he is answered with rhetoric. Numbed by the blank
stares of those dancing and encircling him, the Soldier grows
angry and fearful. He is trapped. Realizing the awful truth
of patriotic entrapment, Leslie accepts his role. As the captured Soldier, he recovers quickly from the shock of certain
death, and he sings a song (as he did in Act One) to bring
the curtain down. The patriotic lyrics of "I am a Happy
English Lad" are tinged with a spirited irony. This ironic
retreat into type is Leslie's final defense of selfhood, for
the logic of war is absurd, and rather than discuss the issue,
the Soldier transcends it with music hall flair.

In Act Three of *The Hostage*, the conflict of ideas is ironically resolved. Though the Soldier expects to be shot to
balance the death of the I.R.A.'s boy in the Belfast jail, he
is shot instead by a stray bullet in the confusion of a raid
on the house in which he is a stranger. The raid on the
sometime brothel sends its inhabitants scurrying about in
comic directions. Leslie is caught in the middle of another

war which does not concern him, and he dies by mistake. Despite its comic pose, then, Behan's brothel-world is finally a battleground in which disguises are deadly weapons. For example, Mulleady, a buffoon behind in his rent, described by Meg as a "gouger and bowsey" (p. 138), emerges in the play's final moments as an undercover policeman; Princess Grace, the hotel's flamboyant homosexual resident, is likewise revealed. Even as disguises slip away, Behan reminds us theatrically that disguise remains an integral part of his dramatic technique:

MONSEWER. Who are you?
MULLEADY. I'm a secret policeman and I don't care who knows it. . . .
(*Two nuns scurry across the room and up the stairs, praying softly. . . . They are the two I.R.A. men in disguise.*)

(p. 235)

On the contemporary stage, a fact of contemporary life is brought home. Beneath the mask is what Pirandello called the naked mask; social masks can never be totally stripped away. When one mask falls, another slips into place. Theatrical truth is the only certainty. According to Behan's music hall ontology, only the stage is real.

The solitary reality of the stage world is asserted in the hostage's finale. It is a contrived curtain call, a musical release for the sudden tension of tragic action. The dramatic progression of the last act matches that of the two preceding ones. As in the first and second acts, a crowd gathers in a circle around the Soldier; and as before, their melodramatic dialogue is counterpointed by an irreverent refrain sung by the Soldier. By this point in the play, of course, the audience is accustomed to Behan's playful disregard for the conventions of staging. We may even anticipate a final song. We do not, however, expect the Soldier to sing it.

Behan sets us up for his theatrical coup. The lodgers gather mournfully around the Soldier's dead body; they listen with us to Teresa's O'Caseyan eulogy:

186

MULLEADY. Cover him up. . . .
TERESA. Leslie, my love. A thousand blessings go with
   you.
PAT. Don't cry. Teresa. It's no one's fault. Nobody
   meant to kill him.
TERESA. But he's dead.
PAT. So is the boy in Belfast Jail.
TERESA. It wasn't the Belfast Jail or the Six Counties
   that was troubling you, but your lost youth and
   your crippled leg. He died in a strange land and
   at home he had no one. I'll never forget you, Leslie, till the end of time.

(p. 236)

Having said her melodramatic piece, Teresa "*turns away*"
according to the stage directions. Through Pat, the playwright has indulged in the intentional fallacy of wartime
casualties, and through Teresa, he has manipulated the
audience towards a sentimental response. Her last sad and
bitter farewell has the deceptive rhythm and sound of a
closing speech. Some audience members may even mistak-
enly take her speech as their cue to applaud. But Behan
has the last laugh. One more time, the Soldier rises to the
occasion, and like an Elizabethan fool, he sings ironically
of the action we have just witnessed. His instantaneous
resurrection onstage intensifies the irony of his sacrilegious
ditty:

> The bells of hell,
> Go ting-a-ling-a-ling,
> For you but not for me.
> Oh death where is thy sting-a-ling-a-ling?
> Or grave thy victory?
> (p. 236)

The Soldier's final music hall number, a jovial taunt by a
death's mask, is Behan's show-stopper. A dance-of-death
brings the curtain down. This is, after all, Behan reminds
us, meant to be a theater of embodied ideas, not a drama
of easy emotions.

187

Shot down by "*shadowy shapes of the forces of law and order*" (p. 233), the Soldier's spirit (an intact idea of individual freedom incarnate) remains unbroken. The ominous armed figures cannot suppress his ironic will. In this way, the play's power derives from the theatrical resilience of its title character isolated in a world apart. *The Hostage* is a sort of morality play for an age in which survival itself demands an everyday suspension of disbelief: its uninitiated Everyman is betrayed and abandoned by representative figures who surround him in an absurd setting; yet by embracing his formal role in the setting as metaphor, he achieves a spiritual victory over individual death.

LESLIE, the innocent soldier who is sacrificed in *The Hostage*, is clearly the hero of that play; he is strongly individualized; and though he is killed, he remains undefeated by the system which controls his destiny. The quare fellow of Behan's first—and indeed purer—play in the contemporary mode, however, is far from the hero of that play; in fact, he does not even appear onstage; from hearsay we learn that he slaughtered his brother and dismembered the body; he remains a phantom, his condemned presence hovering over the action of the play. His doom is sealed from the start: not only does the brutal violence with which he committed his crime prohibit a merciful reprieve from the representatives of authority onstage, but we never see him, so no direct appeal is ever made for our pity. On the contrary, the grisly details of his alleged fratricide appall us. Yet we join the other inmates—and the guards, as well—in their communal deathwatch, for *The Quare Fellow*, though it shows the lighter side of human behavior at odds with a penitentiary code, is nevertheless primarily concerned with a total institution which subordinates individuals within its range. So like *The Brig*, for example, *The Quare Fellow* has a cyclic rather than a linear progression; it is disrupted but *not* concluded by a single incident; it, too, explores an essentially static situation, a situation of impasse.

The contrast, finally, between Behan's two plays in which

a deadly framework permits no action, only *reaction* to its regular movement, may also be seen in David Rabe's two plays of military stasis and communal inertia, *The Basic Training of Pavlo Hummel* and *Streamers*. Behan's first play, *The Quare Fellow*, is more extreme in its focus and more demanding of its audience than is his second play, *The Hostage*. The same contrast holds true for the first and third plays of Rabe's Vietnam trilogy: the first, purer, more expansive play focuses on a model of reality mechanically snuffing out life, even the life of the title character who is a zero; the later, more conventional, more compressed play favors one individual, an innocent who makes a laughing stock of our war-torn world by transcending it.

The final scene of *The Quare Fellow*, with its focus on prisoners distancing themselves from their gravedigging roles by making a secondary adjustment to a prison situation, contrasts especially sharply with the heavy-handed irony and pathos of the Soldier's own finale in *The Hostage*. In *The Quare Fellow*, Behan's stronger, less sentimental play, the Everyman figure—like Rabe's very ordinary Pavlo Hummel—is purely ironic; he resists the tendency to which Behan allows his *Hostage* to succumb: he resists representative martyrdom. At the close of *The Quare Fellow*, instead of mulling over the cold fact of lawful murder or the routine discarding of a dead man's missives, Behan's gravedigging prisoners bargain for the "bloody letters . . . worth money to one of the Sunday papers" (p. 124). Their business transaction at a prison grave site becomes a mime accompanied by the anonymous single voice whose song of the prison routine opened the play. His haunting refrain is an effective theatrical reminder of both the permanence of the prison as Structure and the artifice of the staging.

Deathwatch

The Quare Fellow and *Deathwatch* revolve around a similar dramatic situation: in both plays a man is condemned to die for a hideous crime of passion. But while *The Quare*

Fellow translates a slang prison term for the doomed one into a dark vaudevillian routine, *Deathwatch* transforms a prison routine into a danse macabre. In this minimal play, Jean Genet glorifies an image of Green Eyes, the killer set to die, a manipulator with nothing left to lose.

Deathwatch, Genet's first play, was probably written about 1944–45, but was not performed until 1949, three years after the first performance of *The Maids*.[27] Like *The Brig* and *The Quare Fellow*, two other first plays, it is modeled after the penal system most familiar to the playwright. In contrast to the novice Brown and the delinquent Behan, however, Genet's underworld experience was international and categorically criminal. By 1926, Genet had begun a decade and a half in which a jail cell was his only real home, and in between sentences he reveled in crime:

> "I used to live from theft," he observes with pride and self-abasement, "but I like prostitution better. Less effort." Albania, Yugoslavia, Italy, Austria, Czechoslovakia, through Hitler's Germany to Antwerp: arrested, jailed, deported, arrested, jailed, deported. In Germany he loses his taste for robbery and blackmail: He is among thieves and theft loses its meaning. Crime is good only if it exalts Evil in the face of society.[28]

The real prototype for Genet's metaphysical cell is probably the French prison system which, until recent reforms, was notoriously backward in its treatment of prisoners. One commentator has noted that "As recently as 1931 Belbenoit described the Central Prison of Beaulieu, where he awaited transportation, as having its inmates sleep barefoot, clad only in trousers and tunic, under a thin blanket on the bare stone floor; and he described also the dark, damp dungeons of its disciplinary department, where men lay in irons, fed on bread and water."[29] These traditional emblems of imprisonment—tattered uniforms, stony surroundings, bare feet, and iron chains—are all integrated into the minimal setting of *Deathwatch*.

The entire action of *Deathwatch* is confined to one prison

cell crowded by three convicts. The setting has a dual nature in this play: it includes both elements of the stark reality described in that 1931 account ("walls of hewn stone," "a barred transom, the spikes of which turn inward, " "the bed . . . of granite," "a barred door")[30] *and* elements of distortion. The distorted aspect of *Deathwatch*, its danse macabre quality, is a hallmark of Genet's style. The opening description of the setting for this self-proclaimed "dream" play calls for stylization in all aspects of staging:

> The entire play unfolds as in a dream. The set and costumes (striped homespun) should be in violent colors. Use whites and very hard blacks, clashing with each other. The movements of the actors should be either heavy or else extremely and incomprehensibly rapid, like flashes of lightning. If they can, the actors should deaden the timbre of their voices. Avoid clever lighting. As much light as possible.   (pp. 103–104)

In the colors of the costumes, the intensity of the lighting, and the gestures of the actors, Genet intends to transform a prison, based on a real model, into an imagistic dream.

Deathwatch is Genet's most elemental play; in form as well as in substance, it foreshadows many of his later plays. The prison cell of *Deathwatch* is shared by Green Eyes (a convicted killer), Lefranc (a burglar), and Maurice (a delinquent youth). Here, a love triangle among persons of ambiguous sexuality erupts in an act of violence which is an attempt to consolidate an illusion into essence. The violence is ineffectual, however, for the insistent image looms larger than its human double. In *Deathwatch*, Genet's players revere the role of spiritual outlaw; the glorified image is one of criminality.

The theme of this lengthy one-act play has been identified by Lucien Goldmann as "the individual's struggle for moral recognition where the only things of moral value are those which ordinary society condemns. This divides the world into two kinds of men: the weak—the petty thieves and crooks, and the strong—the natural murderers whose criminal character is part of the natural order." As Gold-mann remarks:

> Genet's theatre offers a very interesting object for sociological study. He is the product of the French underclass of petty thieves and homosexuals; he describes and transposes his underclass experiences in his early works. But what makes Genet truly interesting (as an example of the relation between modern industrial society and literary creation) is the encounter in his work between an implicit but radical rejection of society and the problems of a still active European intelligentsia which is hostile to today's corporate capitalism. The underclass has been expelled from respectable society. But Genet has interiorized this expulsion and raised it to the level of world vision.[31]

This characteristic of Genet's theater—his elevation of the depths of society and the self to a visionary theatrical plane—is most marked in *Deathwatch*. Genet's prison cell, like the waiting room of *No Exit* (Sartre's play set in a self-service hell, first performed in 1944), is a stylized reflection of both public and private—real and imagined—underworlds.

As in Beckett's *Waiting for Godot* (first performed in 1953), the action in Genet's economically organized space revolves around symbiotic characters passing—serving—time. As in *Waiting for Godot*, the three prisoners in *Deathwatch* depend on each other to lessen the weight of time. And as in *Waiting for Godot*, the primary means of making time less of a burden is to combine in games of entertainment and momentary release. The dreamlike aspect of the *Deathwatch* setting and characters, however, affects the nature of games played. In this prison cell that is at once singular *and* generic, Genet puts forth Artaud's idea of theater "whose only value is in its excruciating, magical relation to reality and danger."[32] In his preface to *The Theater and Its Double*, Artaud proselytizes: "If our life lacks brimstone, i.e., a constant magic, it is because we choose to observe our acts and lose ourselves in considerations of their imagined form instead of being impelled by their force. . . . But no matter how loudly we clamor for magic in our lives, we are really afraid of pursuing an existence entirely under its influence and sign."[33] Genet shares Artaud's conviction. A driving force in *Deathwatch* is Artaud's idea of a dark, metaphysical theater where ceremonies are performed in the sense that, as Genet's Chief of Police says in *The Balcony*, "the outside world says a mass is celebrated."[34]

The play progresses through a series of violent and fantastic games which make up its through-action of passing time with a passion. The three inmates show off for each other's sake; performances are reciprocated. The effect of watching these performances becomes double. While we, the audience, witness secret rites of initiation into a literal—criminal—underworld, the characters onstage, trapped in their own minimal world of death-watching, also witness and participate in secret rites of initiation into a symbolic—magical—underworld that is, finally, Artaud's idea of a theater. With a "poetry of the senses" and a "concrete physical language," the members of the audience are advised of "their dark power, their hidden force" by Genet and his characters in *Deathwatch*, who invite them "to take, in the face of destiny, a superior and heroic attitude they would never have assumed without it."[35]

In *Deathwatch*, Genet realizes Artaud's vision (which is Genet's dream as well) of a pure theater in which communion is possible. In "A Note on Theatre," Genet puts forth this dream of the theater itself as a taboo underworld: "A clandestine theatre, to which one would go in secret, at night, and masked, a theatre in the catacombs, may still be possible. It would be sufficient to discover—or create—the common Enemy, then the Homeland which is to be protected or regained."[36] *Deathwatch* puts just such a clandestine theater—the cellmates' secret games—before us onstage. We witness the prisoners' experience of what Artaud terms "renewed exorcisms."[37] At the same time, by juxtaposing a series of incidents to be apprehended sensually, Genet attempts to make the play itself an instance of clandestine theater. The effect is one of a savage "dance" of games (p. 132), which flows into and out of center stage, leaving the participants exhausted and frustrated. The cellmates' fusion within a dreamlike dance of games, their "renewed exorcisms," are sudden and short-lived; each is finally alone with his own pain.

Though the action of *Deathwatch* suggests the spiraling logic of a dream and a kinetic poetry of the theater, Genet balances this with the authentic sounds and gestures of street life. Throughout the play, characters speak in the vernacular of street violence; the playwright directs them to recite their lines "with the characteristic deformations that go with the accent of the slums" (p. 104). Even the most lyrical passages of *Deathwatch* maintain this naturalistic coloration in performance. The clandestine theater in the cell of *Deathwatch* is in this way like the "essential theater" to which Artaud aspires in his essay on "The Theater and the Plague"; in this cell, "the revelation, the bringing forth, the exteriorization of a depth of latent cruelty . . . are localized."[38]

By localizing larger-than-life desires in a single cell, Genet transforms a specific place into an image of one. *Deathwatch* derives much of its power from its setting in that simple cell. Like this first play, all of Genet's other plays have been described as takng place in "private hells (each a paradise to him) in which the Usual Order is interrupted." As one commentator explains:

> In these special places—prisons, barracks, the Mass— the real Game is played. . . . And yet these secret societies, these places of "difference," have an attraction: They are a terrain for art, microcosms of the wider outside world to which a Genet can apply special rules. They are places of secret languages; of shorthands by which like recognizes like; of accepted hierarchies. They are places from which the Alien is excluded; they are abstract, impersonal.[39]

In the special place—the prison cell—of *Deathwatch*, Genet's convicts play their "real Game" of release and escape. In this underworld of degrading, sordid rituals, Genet's idea of dignity subverted by social systems is made concrete. Here, in this economically constructed play, Genet's aesthetic of categorical Structures is underscored.

Deathwatch is one of the earliest plays to expose the prison setting from a formal rather than a melodramatic or social realist standpoint. It turns a prison cell into an inverted—clandestine—image of our world, its referent. The character Green Eyes, too, like the cell that contains him, has an analogous significance here. The dominant personality of the *Deathwatch* triangle, Green Eyes has been condemned to die for an especially terrible crime of rape and murder. He is a formidable stage presence; the chains on his feet fail to subdue his movements; instead, they intensify our constant awareness of his dangerous nature. His role as the prison personified informs his every gesture, physical and verbal. The character filling his setting becomes a living poem for Genet.

In their progressive complexity, the speeches of Green Eyes parallel the movement of the play. His transcendent soliloquies, especially, have a theatrical polyvalence. They are at once colloquial remarks, social pronouncements, psychological purges, and ritual incantations. After he recounts and reenacts his definitive crime for his cellmates, for example, Green Eyes' heightened belligerence becomes most overdetermined. As he warns his fellows, he reinforces himself:

> You've just learned something about me that the police were never able to learn. You've just seen what I'm really like inside. But look out! I may never forgive you. You've had nerve enough to take me apart, but don't think I'm going to remain there in pieces. Green Eyes'll pull himself together. Green Eyes is already getting reorganized. I'm building myself up again. I'm healing. I'm making myself over. I'm getting stronger,

more solid than a fortress. Stronger than the prison. You hear me, I *am* the prison! In my cells I guard big bruisers, brawlers, soldiers, plunderers! Be careful! I'm not sure that my guards and dogs can keep them back if I loose them on you! I've got ropes, knives, ladders! Be careful! There are sentinels on my rounds. There are spies everywhere. I'm the prison and I'm alone in the world. (pp. 136–137)

By alternately referring to himself in the third person and to the prison in the first person in this pivotal speech of *Deathwatch*, Green Eyes bridges the chasm between his inner and outer worlds by means of his own body. He identifies himself with the brute force that contains him, which gives him life, and which will kill him.

The ontology of Genet's world is an inversion of its real counterpart: here, criminals are kings, and the essence of existence is evil. Only Green Eyes thrives in this subculture. The prison is his exterior double, for he is the muscular personification of Genet's concept of an underworld. He is a *client du matin*, the French equivalent of a "quare fellow." In contrast to Brown's *The Brig*, *Deathwatch* individualizes its character types and elevates one of them to translate the thesis of the play into dramatic action. Here, as in the metaphysical brothel of Genet's later play, *The Balcony*, a unique figure dominates the stage. Green Eyes, like *The Balcony*'s Mme. Irma, is a master of ceremonies *and* an idea of the theater. As Genet writes in his "Letters to Roger Blin," his idea of the theater includes a vision of the actor as larger than life, a vision of the actor as a force of nature:

The actor must act quickly, even in his slowness, but his speed, lightninglike, will amaze. That and his acting will make him so beautiful that, when he is snatched up by the emptiness of the wings, the audience will experience a feeling of sadness, a kind of regret: they will have seen a meteor loom into view and pass by. This kind of acting will give life to the actor and to the play.

Therefore: appear, shine, and, as it were, die.[40]

196

The dialectic of *Deathwatch* also parallels that of *The Balcony*. The clashing images of illusion and reality which merge in the mirror of *The Balcony* are in Genet's first play, too. In *Deathwatch*, the playwright adheres most rigorously in the French tradition to the unities of time, place, and action; he also invents a formal coherence appropriate to his restrictive setting. Here, as in *The Balcony*, the paradox of a power struggle is dynamically represented. The unseen other of Mme. Irma, the madame of *The Balcony*, is the real Queen; the unseen other of *Deathwatch* is the offstage prisoner, Snowball. In both plays, also, an antithetical figure is finally merged with the central character as two personified sides of a single illusion of power. The antithesis of Mme. Irma, the ruler of *The Balcony*, is the revolutionary figurehead, Chantal; the antithesis of Genet's Green Eyes, the quintessential prisoner, is the Guard.

Snowball plays an important role in the idea of imprisonment at the quick of Genet's play. Though he never appears onstage, Snowball's presence is diffused in the atmosphere of conflicting desire which seeps beyond the cell walls into the audience. The play begins, in fact, with a battle about him. Maurice and Lefranc are characteristically bickering with each other, this time about the comparative merits of Snowball vs. Green Eyes. Lefranc glorifies the image of the absent black prisoner:

> Snowball? He's out of this world. All the guys in his cell feel it. And in the cells around too, and the whole prison and all the prisons in France. He shines. He beams. He's black but he lights up the whole two thousand cells. No one'll ever get him down. He's the real boss of the prison. . . . His chains carry him. Snowball's a king. . . . And his crimes! (p. 107)

Maurice, however, champions Green Eyes. In Maurice's rhapsody, Snowball is defined as a negative image of Green Eyes, a dark double of this cell's mastermind: "You might even call him a Green Eyes with a coat of shoepolish, Green Eyes with a smoke-screen, Green Eyes covered with mud, Green Eyes in the dark" (pp. 106–107). Abruptly, Green

Eyes quiets his cellmates, cautioning them to dispense with their petty squabbles and popularity contests. "In prison, no one's a king," he proclaims (p. 108). This royal edict signifies Green Eyes' acknowledgment of the ultimate sovereignty of the prison itself. Within this controlling framework, neither he nor Snowball—two charismatic candidates for dominance in any setting outside this institution—can ever reign supreme. Conscious of the final subjugation of the self to the prison, Green Eyes abdicates to his unseen other. In two months, he knows, he will be decapitated, and so he advises his jealous followers to switch their allegiance to Snowball:

> Don't you see my situation? Can't you see that here we make up stories that can live only within four walls? And that I'll never again see the light of day? You take me for a fool? Don't you know who I am? Don't you realize that the grave is open at my feet? . . . The axe, gentlemen! I'm no longer alive! I'm all alone now! All alone! Alone. Solo. I can die quiet. I've stopped beaming. I'm frozen. . . . Frozen! You can get down on your knees before Snowball. You're right. The Number One Big Shot is Snowball. The Big Shot! (p. 124)

Frozen into an image of criminality, Green Eyes awaits the executioner. In essence, he considers himself already dead; he merely waits for this essence to be enacted into fact. Already, however, Green Eyes concedes defeat to the "four walls" of the prison, and he resigns his underworld position in favor of his dark double, whose offstage presence hovers over the frenetic action of *Deathwatch*.

The ultimate impotence of the individual in the prison, the fixed situation of Genet's play, is demonstrated in *Deathwatch* by Snowball's absence from the stage. In characteristically negative terms, Genet expresses his central dramatic thesis: the action of *Deathwatch* seems to follow a traditional formula of jealousy and triangular betrayal, but the requirements of the prison prevail over the conventional demands of the stage. Genet encloses his magic circle within the walls of one cell. So despite extensive expository passages concerning his history and his personal stature, Snowball cannot be cued to appear onstage in *Deathwatch*. The three men sharing this limited space recount their stories and retrace their steps, creating a pattern out of half-remembered actions. Their sense of suffocation and restriction gradually infects the audience with similar emotions, and as in the audience of *The Brig*, we are affected by the situation onstage so that the minds and bodies of the spectators may respond in kind to the pent-up feelings of the prisoners. We, too, feel the frustration shared by the three outlaws trapped together in a cage-like world they cannot control. As an audience, we can also sense the dramatic possibilities of a character such as Snowball. By depriving us of the stage presence of Snowball, Genet reminds us, by means of what does not—what *cannot*—happen on the contemporary stage, of the impasse implicit now in a prison setting, an impasse felt even when that prison is located in a dream of last rites.

Throughout *Deathwatch*, there is a constant tension between opposites. This governing aspect of Genet's theater is most apparent in the tug-of-war between Maurice and Lefranc. As a game, they quarrel over the difference between Green Eyes and Snowball. In a more urgent game, however, they vie for the attention and approval of Green Eyes alone, their living model marked for death. The tattooed image of a girl, inked beneath the surface of Green Eyes's skin (p. 155), becomes an emblem of their struggle for a sign of preference. Lefranc, especially, longs to mirror his idol, and so he strives to become him: first, he corresponds for the illiterate Green Eyes with his girl; second, he draws the name "Avenger" on his own chest; and third, he commits a murder of his own in Green Eyes' domain. All three of these attempts to imitate and thereby possess Green Eyes are failures: Lefranc's Cyranoesque letters arouse the girl's suspicions (as Lefranc had jealously hoped) but they anger Green Eyes, who offers the unseen girl to his favorite prison guard; the legend of the "Avenger," emblazoned as a criminal title on Lefranc's chest, is exposed as a forgery drawn from reading rather than earned by experience; and the murder of Maurice, an act of will to win Green Eyes' favor, seals Lefranc's fate as a cheat and a parasite in the hierarchy of jail.

The action of the play moves in slow motion towards this murder: Lefranc strangles his rival hoping to gain criminal stature by performing a violent rite of initiation. But Green Eyes repudiates this premeditated love token. The murder which caused *him* to be condemned was a passionate act; his crime was an uncontrollable spasm which he relives in prison:

> . . . everything began to move. There was nothing more to be done. And that was why I had to kill someone. . . . And I was scared. I wanted to back up. Stop! No go! I tried hard. I ran in all directions. I shifted. I tried every form and shape so as not to be a murderer. Tried to be a dog, a cat, a horse, a tiger, a table, a stone! I even tried, me too, to be a rose! Don't laugh. I did what I could. I squirmed and twisted. People thought I had convulsions. I wanted to turn back the clock, to undo what I'd done, to live my life over until before the crime. It looks easy to go backwards—but my body couldn't do it. I tried again. . . . My dance! You should have seen my dance! I danced, boys, I danced!
> (p. 131)

Carried away by his own history, Green Eyes reconstructs his crime before us. According to the stage directions, *"He contorts himself silently. He tries a spiral dance, on his own axis. His face expresses great suffering"* (p. 132). When his dance is done, Green Eyes recalls the frenzied moment which fixed him in an image: "I had some lilacs between my teeth. The girl followed me. She was magnetized. . . . I'm telling you everything, but let it guide you. Then . . . then she wanted to scream because I was hurting her. I choked her. I thought that once she was dead I'd be able to bring her back to life" (p. 134). "I'm telling you everything, but let it guide you," Green Eyes cautions his captive audience. For his crime is an act of aggression which is love. It cannot be imitated; it can only be invoked in ritual. And so, Lefranc's homicidal gesture is comparatively insubstantial. Its willful nature merely offsets the horrible beauty of Green Eyes' inexplicable crime of passion.

Lefranc feels bitterness and inadequacy in this no-exit situation. In Green Eyes' presence, he is always odd man out. When, for example, the Guard and Green Eyes—two equal forces of subdued power in the prison hierarchy—exchange gifts, Lefranc expresses his resentment of the exclusive transaction being carried out above him. The Guard has brought Green Eyes a message and cigarettes from Snowball, and Green Eyes, in turn, does the Guard a favor. He gives the Guard the go-ahead to try and win over his girl. Lefranc seethes:

> Green Eyes gets his orders from the other world. They send him cigarettes—from where? From the other side of the water. Brought by a special guard, in full uniform, who offers him his friendship on a platter. A message from the heart. . . . All the prisoners are divided into two warring camps, and the two kings toss smiles at each other above our heads—or behind our backs—or even before our very eyes. And at the end they make a present of their girls. . . . (pp. 143–144)

But Green Eyes silences his presumptuous cellmate with a reminder of his superior status. "If I felt like it, I'd make you circle round and round like the horses in a merry-go-round," he tells Lefranc (p. 144). For like Snowball and like the Guard, Green Eyes knows himself and his place in a specialized scheme. "I've understood my crime. I've understood everything and I'm brave enough to be all alone. In broad daylight," he boasts (p. 145). In the same tone he tells Lefranc, "Maybe some day you'll know what a guard is. But you'll have to pay the price" (p. 145).

In the course of *Deathwatch*, Lefranc does, in fact, pay the price to which Green Eyes refers. After going around and around in circles, he commits a violent act which transfigures him. Lefranc kills Maurice in a conscious effort to prove his manhood. The stage directions to the actors at this moment are explicitly sexual: *"He blocks* MAURICE *in a corner and strangles him.* MAURICE *slides to the floor between* LEFRANC'S *spread legs.* LEFRANC *straightens up"* (p. 159). As he has consistently done throughout the play, at this moment of *Deathwatch*, Genet incorporates an authentic detail of imprisonment (the incidence of homosexuality) into his ritualized danse macabre. As Lefranc freezes himself into an image, *Deathwatch* telescopes behavioral norms of prison life, the alternative code of an inmate subculture, into a single, symbolic gesture of cruelty which could be love in an isolated cell onstage. Lefranc, a man in motion, is suddenly fixed in his own image. And that—his crime—is the personal prison from which there is no escape.

Deathwatch ends with a silent affirmation of the mutual understanding between Green Eyes and the Guard, two embodiments of apparently antithetical values. Especially after the conventions of the staging make clear to us that the presence of Snowball, the alternate larger-than-life image pitted against Green Eyes, cannot be made physical, we come to perceive the special relationship between Green Eyes and the Guard—between the glorious criminal and his keeper—that sets them apart from the others. These two figures of power are equals in the prison hierarchy. Yet the Guard, the only character with freedom to move from one cell to the next, is not finally just the *opposite* of the condemned killer; he is his double. When, for example, the Guard enters Green Eyes' cell and notices an unmade bed, he responds to Lefranc's insolence by explaining himself and defending his role in this predetermined conflict between the superior individual and the formidable institution:

> You see what happens when you want to be nice? Can't be done with guys like that. You end up by becoming inhuman. And then they claim that guards are brutes.

(*To* LEFRANC) If you weren't so thick, you'd have realized I was doing my job. No one can say I pick on
you. You may think you're smart, but I'm way ahead
of you. . . . You don't know what a prison-guard has
to see and put up with. You don't realize that he's got
to be the very opposite of the thugs. I mean just that:
the very opposite. And he's also got to be the opposite
of their friend. I'm not saying their enemy. Think about
it. (pp. 139–140)

The vernacular in which the Guard speaks lends authenticity to his self-defense. By generalizing about the type of
part a guard must play in a prison, he also suggests that in
performing a social function, he is obscuring an essential
part of himself. This hidden dimension of his personality
has its psychodramatic counterpart among the prisoners in
this dream vision of a cell. Like Green Eyes, the Guard
serves Genet as an individualized character, a sociological
type, a psychodramatic part of the self imprisoned, and an
embodiment of an idea. Leaving Lefranc to ponder the
meaning of a prison guard, the Guard turns to the prisoner
who stands on his level as an idea incarnate and as an image
of power within bounds. Opposite him stands Green Eyes,
who is not his foe, but his negative; not just his opposite,
but his double.

This doubleness of Green Eyes and the Guard is dynamically represented in the final moment of the play. After
Lefranc has killed Maurice, Green Eyes confronts him with
the fraudulence of his crime. Their discussion, in which
Green Eyes exalts a crime of passion and demeans a crime
of will, is at the quick of Genet's dialectical dream play.
And now, the alliance beneath the skin of Green Eyes and
the Guard is crystallized, for the last act of Green Eyes is
his betrayal of Lefranc. According to the stage directions,
Green Eyes "*raps at the door,*" calling for the Guard, and
finally, there is the "*Sound of a key. The door opens. The*
GUARD *appears, smiling. He leers at* GREEN EYES" (p. 163).
Genet himself was guilty of Green Eyes' last crime, the

ultimate crime according to an outlaw's code: betrayal of another criminal to the police. But as Genet explained to an interviewer, police are different from judges or juries or the abstract authority of the state. Genet admires police as he glorifies Green Eyes, for "They kill. They do the job with their own hands, not at a distance or by proxy."[41] In Genet's inverted ontology, that final tableau is a silent affirmation of the common ground of a transcendent killer and leering authority.

Both the killer and his guard are still subverted by the Structure, however. Even their combined strength is no match for the prison. Their loss of free movement, a common denominator of all social institutions—and that includes the theater itself—makes itself felt on the contemporary stage. Fundamental to plays of impasse are the spatial and temporal limits of action, the line not to be crossed, the individual cornered in a cul de sac. The prison setting is a popular choice for plays of impasse, because here the common properties of impasse can be expressed directly and naturally. After all, the first thing prisoners lose is the ability to move freely, and this restraint inevitably has an effect on the movement of dramatic action, leading the playwright to heighten an everyday cycle rather than invent a linear plot. For no matter how strong their motives, characters sublimated to a contemporary dead-end setting in a prison house of spatial, temporal, *and* metaphysical dimensions cannot enter or exit at will. This bleak given of contemporary plays of impasse—an immobilizing world—is clearly pronounced in *Deathwatch*. Focusing on one cell among hundreds, Genet magnifies and glorifies an image of immobility, and he elevates a concentrated struggle among prisoners and a guard to the level of prototype. As Genet writes in an essay, "The strange word *Urb* . . .":

> Where shall we go from here? Towards what form? The theatrical site, containing the stage and the auditorium?
>
> The site. I told an Italian who wanted to build a

theatre whose elements would be movable and whose architecture flexible, depending on what play was being performed—even before he had finished his sentence I said that the architecture of the theatre still remains to be discovered but that it must be stationary, immobilised, so that it can be held responsible: it shall be judged by its shape. It's too easy to put one's trust in the movable. Let anyone who wants to work towards the perishable, but only after the irreversible act by which we shall be judged or, if you prefer, the fixed act which judges itself has been accomplished.[42]

From the opening of *Deathwatch*, we sense the magnetic power that Green Eyes wields within his domain. Nevertheless, the "barred transom, the spikes of which turn inward" (p. 103) looms constantly over the figures strutting in the shadows of their cell. Like the preliminary vignettes which give Genet's *The Balcony* its theatrical power, the entire action of *Deathwatch* reveals to us the secret ceremonies and condition of impasse in one small room which, when multiplied in our minds, produces an image of endless corridors linking similar rooms strewn apart by the centrifugal force of the institution.

As THESE PLAYS by Brown, Behan, and Genet show, the prison is a logical setting for plays which end up counting down to the death of the individual in an extreme situation. All three of these plays go beyond the melodramatic pitfall of old prison dramas, for the prison—the total institution depicted in each—is *not* subject of these plays; rather, the prison becomes the vehicle for expressing impasse in a world of internecine conflict.

The prison setting, especially when its cruelties and codes are arbitrary, has a particularly powerful effect on a post-World War II audience freighted with the weight of recent history and influenced to the core by photographs and accounts of death camps and Gulags, total institutions that mobilized nations and harnessed advanced technology to a barbarous cause. In his essay, "Individual and Mass Behavior in Extreme Situations," Bruno Bettelheim coined the term "extreme situation" to describe the reactions of adults in early German concentration camps. "These reactions," he writes in another essay in the same collection, "Schizophrenia as a Reaction to Extreme Situations," "in many aspects different from person to person, were all responses to one and the same psychological situation: finding oneself totally overpowered. Characterizing this situation were its shattering impact on the individual, for which he was totally unprepared; its inescapability; the expectation that the situation would last for an undetermined period, potentially a lifetime; the fact that, throughout its entirety, one's very life would be in jeopardy at every moment; and the fact that one was powerless to protect oneself."[43] The contemporary audience, finding a prison awaiting them onstage, cannot help but feel at the core of their being a connection between such a setting and the totalitarian machines that seared an image—put a death mask—in postmodern consciousness.

The prison, then, the Sartrean situation of entrapment, is a natural home for plays of impasse, goading a usually distant audience to respond from the gut, to be implicated as witnesses, to enter the theater of cruelty. As Julian Beck puts it, such plays "Separate until the pain of separation is felt, until [the audience] want[s] to tear it down, to be united. Storm the barricades."[44] The separation, the barricades, the Structure dominate these plays: *The Brig* brings home with fact and brute force the waste of noble gestures behind barbed wire; *The Quare Fellow* reveals with grim humor some secrets of survival in a music-hall-framed prison; and *Deathwatch* gives a mythic dimension to the dark side of the human soul, projected like a shadow on a prison wall. There are no heroes here.

ACTING TOUGH IN THE BARRACKS

Arnold Wesker's *Chips With Everything,*
David Rabe's *The Basic Training of*
Pavlo Hummel,
and Rabe's *Streamers*

There was only one catch and that was Catch-
22, which specified that a concern for one's own
safety in the face of dangers that were real and
immediate was the process of a rational mind.
Orr was crazy and could be grounded. All he
had to do was ask; and as soon as he did, he
would no longer be crazy and would have to fly
more missions. Orr would be crazy to fly more
missions and sane if he didn't, but if he was sane
he had to fly them. If he flew them he was crazy
and didn't have to; but if he didn't want to he
was sane and had to. Yossarian was moved very
deeply by the absolute simplicity of this clause
of Catch-22 and let out a respectful whistle.
    "That's some catch, that Catch-22," he ob-
served.
    "It's the best there is," Doc Daneeka agreed.
                    Joseph Heller, *Catch-22*

SINCE THE PUBLICATION in 1955 of Joseph Heller's grisly
comedy of combat, the term Catch-22 has entered our vocabulary as a shorthand way of saying you can't beat the
system, the system will second-guess you every time, they're
always one step ahead of you, the system will win. Purring
along smoothly, the system makes up the rules. The military

system in particular achieves such a clear, solid victory of order and regulations that it is to be admired even by those young men who fuel it. Heller's Yossarian sees the army's spiraling Catch-22 "clearly in all its spinning reasonableness. There was an elliptical precision about its perfect pairs of parts that was graceful and shocking, like good modern art, and at times Yossarian wasn't quite sure that he saw it all, just the way he was never quite sure about good modern art."[1]

The "elliptical precision" that is at once "graceful and shocking" in good modern art is, as Yossarian discovers, at the heart of military life. As in modern art, in the military there is a special logic governing the syncopation of parts. So there is order all right, but it eludes the untrained eye. What basic training does, then, is to make that order clear to recruits. This military metamorphosis, with its implicit toughening of the muscles, skin, and spirit, is a rite of passage.

War has always served dramatists well: bloody battlefields and heroic soldiers are perennial sources of sure-fire entertainment. A military setting suggests adventure and, perhaps, romance to the public. Especially in the past generation, however, attitudes towards military plays have shifted dramatically. Playwrights no longer glorify service; their goal seems merely to describe it, to evoke it, to recreate on stage the "elliptical precision" that civilians cannot fathom. Recent plays set in military institutions exhibit the docudrama aspect of plays of impasse in the most pronounced way. For in the military, the "white line" is actual, the boss barking orders is deafeningly ever-present, and the rules of conduct are rigidly codified. *The Brig*, the play shot as a "newsreel" by the director who filmed it,[2] is the most extreme instance of this kind of military world, seen with precision and seen without hope. That play's weakness is in its almost total authenticity, its want of dramatic shape beyond the social system it exposes. It wants narrative; it wants a sense of the individuals caught in the cage, lost in the numbers, lost in what Judith Malina called "the beauty and terror" of *The Brig*,[3] lost to an "elliptical precision" that is at once "graceful and shocking." Arnold Wesker's *Chips With Everything* (first produced at the Royal Court Theater in London in 1962) and David Rabe's Vietnam trilogy, particularly his *The Basic Training of Pavlo Hummel* (first produced at the New York Public Theater in 1971) and his *Streamers* (first produced at Connecticut's Long Wharf Theater in 1976), are special in their infusion of narrative into a stubbornly no-exit setting. Plays by both these playwrights do not only transcend the pomp and circumstance tradition of conventional military drama, they also go beyond *The Brig*'s newsreel limitations and the limitations of military plays driven by politics—plays which proliferated especially during the Vietnam years. Plays by Wesker and Rabe, two playwrights who are by no means apolitical, transcend topical significance. Their military plays transform the stage into an encompassing social institution as they follow recruits through their paces.

It is exciting to consider how and why these three plays feel so different to an audience. After all, they all share the military setting and use it to evoke in the audience a sense of what it must be like to go through a military mill, and they all drain us with their grueling theater verité styles and military business. They all seem to induct us, and they all finally let go of us, leaving us weary from drills and training and relieved at being dismissed. But the similarity of setting aside, these three plays explore in very different ways the contemporary dramatic form of enclosure, impasse, and loss of self to the system. Wesker's *Chips With Everything* has a strong clockwork narrative plot about class distinctions; it is matter-of-fact, linear, and peopled by psychologized, highly appealing characters. Rabe's *Pavlo Hummel* is a dream play of guerrilla warfare; its title character is a loser, a naive recruit sleepwalking through basic training and shrapnelled across a treacherous mental landscape. Finally, Rabe's *Streamers* encloses its characters in a box of a play, treating the barracks like a coffin; this tight shot of a conforming world within a conforming world, a barracks in an American military camp, is spare, sharp, and bloody, a messy, military endgame.

Like Brown, Behan, and Genet, all of whom had first-hand experience of imprisonment, both Wesker and Rabe color their plays with their own memories of service.[4] So as we watch boys become soldiers in these plays of precise detail and telescoped action, we see different sensibilities at work in transforming military routines into formal meanings. Most important, we see different ways in which the rigidly ordered world onstage can emerge as a vital metaphor for the human condition, a blistering image of the way things are.

Chips With Everything

Arnold Wesker's *Chips With Everything* is a chronicle of the drills and broken wills in an R.A.F. training hut. With the new conscripts onstage, the audience encounters the rigors of basic training. Through a series of vignettes showing enforced submission to the circumstances and ceremonies of national service, Wesker's play strives for a complex effect. At the end of *Chips*, says Wesker now, "Synthesis would be the spark of light, the illumination the audience goes away with, in that they have hopefully understood a little bit more of the complex machinery of human behavior and the nature of society."[5] For *Chips With Everything* is above all about the actual experience of basic training: each scene demonstrates with documentary accuracy another aspect of military life drawn from reality. Simultaneously, however, *Chips* is a symbolic parable: the play focuses upon the exploits, education, and conversion of Pip, a new conscript whose initial defiance gives way to his ultimate co-opting by the system.

Like his compatriots Peter Nichols and David Storey, Wesker hints at the double nature of his institutional setting by means of a punning title. Just as *The National Health* and *Home* both refer to Britain as well as to specific settings, so, too, *Chips With Everything* depicts the national service in particular and the national state in general. In the second scene of the play, Pip, an upper-class boy whose father is a banker and a general, joins in the banter of the barracks. He recalls a stroll through the East End, a common café, and a peeling menu stained with tea upon which was written "Chips with everything." Pip translates this side-dish into a dismal sign of national life, and he berates the lower-class recruits for the sameness of their everyday existence: "Chips with every damn thing. You breed babies and you eat chips with everything."[6] At this point, Pip's self-right-eous diatribe is interrupted by the booming voice of Corporal Hill, who orders all the conscripts to sleep. The next day, however, Pip reasserts his elitist position. As the boys march away from the lecture hall where they have just been barraged with demands for conformity of mind and body, Pip intones, "You have babies, you eat chips and you take orders" (p. 314). With this phrase remembered from a tea-stained menu, Pip connects the demanding tedium of life itself to the belligerent commands of the military world.

In his first play, *The Kitchen*, Wesker took painstaking care to create a microcosm of drudgery and desire behind the scene of a restaurant. In his Introduction to that play, he acknowledged his use of the stage setting as an analogy for modern society:

> This is a play about a large kitchen in a restaurant called the Tivoli. All kitchens, especially during service, go insane. There is the rush, there are the petty quarrels, grumbles, false prides, and snobbery. Kitchen staff instinctively hate dining-room staff, and all of them hate the customer. He is the personal enemy. The world might have been a stage for Shakespeare but to me it is a kitchen, where people come and go and cannot stay long enough to understand each other, and friendships, loves and enmities are forgotten as quickly as they are made.[7]

In *The Kitchen*, Wesker also utilized what would become the title of his R.A.F.-world play. Here, when Michael dreams aloud, "One day I'll work in a place where I can create masterpieces, master bloody pieces. . . . Beef Stroganoff, Chicken Kiev, and that king of the Greek dishes—Mousaka," Gaston replies by belittling bland British tastes. "Never," he tells Michael. "You'll never create a Mousaka. Chips you can make—chips with everything."[8] To Wesker, those chips that come with everything in a British restaurant are indicative of the stale monotony of the modern world.

In his introduction to a more recent play, *The Journalists* (1975), set for the most part in the main offices of "The Sunday Paper," Wesker puts forth a parallel intention to use a setting as a metaphor:

> *The Kitchen* is not about cooking, it's about man and his relationship to work. *The Journalists* is not about journalism, it's about the poisonous human need to cut better men down to our size, from which need we all suffer in varying degrees. To identify and isolate this need is important because it corrupts such necessary or serious human activities as government, love, revolution or journalism.[9]

Wesker's introductory remarks to both these work-plays apply as well to his *Chips With Everything*, a play set in an environment even more inclusive than a work place. As Wesker notes, "The three of them [*The Kitchen*, *Chips With Everything*, and *The Journalists*] are set inside institutions, but *Chips* is outside that, because it's not a work institution. . . . It's conscription, and you are commanded by law and government to serve that period. I think that makes an important difference from the other two plays."[10] Indeed, a conscript in the R.A.F. is in a total institution; he must live in a controlling environment morning, noon, and night. To his greatest degree, then, in *Chips With Everything* Wesker turns a real place of work into a microcosm.

IN *Chips*, as in *The Kitchen* and *The Journalists*, the use of the setting as a microcosm is clear at the outset of the play.

212

It begins with the entrance onstage of nine new conscripts. According to the stage directions, they enter the R.A.F. hut *"subdued, uncertain, mumbling"* (p. 303). So our first glimpse of the conscripts is a backstage peek: we catch them off-guard and anxious. They are awaiting the arrival of Corporal Hill, the man who will teach them their new roles. At first, they are unaware of his presence at the door of the hut. We see him before they do, but as soon as they notice him, their nervous chatter ceases. The boys rise to attention, and after *"a long pause"* the N.C.O. (non-commissioned officer) addresses his novices. In the time between his appearance and his first booming speech, Corporal Hill becomes a physical stage presence of menacing authority. The play proper begins with his vulgar rebuke. Immediately, he teaches the boys a lesson in military protocol which is also an exercise in self-discipline:

> CORPORAL HILL. In future, whenever an N.C.O. comes into the hut, no matter who he is, the first person to see him will call out "N.C.O.! N.C.O.!" like that. And whatever you're doing, even if you're stark rollock naked, you'll all spring to attention as fast as the wind from a duck's behind, and by Christ that's fast. Is that understood? (*No reply.*) Well, is it? (*A few murmurs.*) When I ask a question I expect an answer. (*Emphatically*) Is that understood!
> ALL (*shouting*). Yes, Corporal!
>
> (p. 303)

To this first imperative question, the individual soldiers respond in sudden unison. They learn fast that even if individuality is undermined by rank, it is also protected in a faceless crowd.

Corporal Hill immediately introduces the recruits (and an attentive audience) to the hierarchy and the code of the R.A.F. In his opening address, he verbally assaults and assigns duties to the conscripts. Their orientation is on three levels. First, they are conditioned to the R.A.F. as fact. "Right, you're in the R.A.F. now, you're not at home. This hut, this place here, this is going to be your home for the next eight scorching weeks," he informs them (pp. 303–304). Secondly, they are warned of the R.A.F. as model. "You're going to go through hell while you're here, through scorching hell. Some of you will take it and some of you will break down," he tells them (p. 304). The warning analogy is issued; the hut is not only a real place of rigidly defined roles (the chorus of recruits having already learned their limited lines, "Yes, Corporal!"), it is also a hellish system from which one cannot retreat. And thirdly, the conscripts are teased into joining the R.A.F. as game. "But I'll play fair. You do me proud and I'll play fair," the Corporal promises them (p. 304).

The play element of the R.A.F. extends immediately beyond the official games into the private games of the recruits. The moment the Corporal leaves the boys alone at the end of Scene One, they begin to mimic and deride their superiors. Scene Two flows smoothly from this backstage insubordination. With an ironic barracks song lamenting lost innocence and several speeches quickly individualizing the various conscripts, Scene Two underscores the feelings of authenticity and of a microcosmic world onstage that we got from Scene One. Pip, Smiler, Charles, and Wilfe all start to emerge as distinct personalities and socioeconomic types. Then, once each boy stands out for us as an individual, Wesker submerges them all in a marching crowd. Scene Three reduces their humanity to a blur, as Corporal Hill marches his new squad across the parade ground at morning.

These first three scenes of *Chips* are faithful to reality. The barking of Corporal Hill, the barracks talk, and the early morning drill sound remarkably authentic, especially in performance. For like other playwrights working in this mode, Wesker is foremost a selective artist; the R.A.F. serves him theatrically as an *objet trouvé*. This is evident even in the first drill sequence, for example, upon which Wesker has commented:

In fact a great deal of the drill was written in by myself and one whole section was discovered by Frank Finlay [one of the actors] out of the R.A.F. Drill Manual which he learned off by heart and Sergeant-Major Brittain [a specialist in the official Manual of Drill] simply took the boys on a number of parades in which he instructed them how to move.[11]

As the play progresses, however, we gradually discover that those sections of redundant action which seem the most fiercely rooted in fact are precisely the moments which are theatrically vivid and symbolically charged. In a much-quoted interview, Wesker remarked: "I have discovered that realistic art is a contradiction in terms. Art is the re-creation of experience, not the copying of it. Some writers use naturalistic means to re-create experience, others non-naturalistic. I happen to use naturalistic means; but all the statements I make are made theatrically."[12] Wesker repeatedly comes back to this idea in his thoughts about drama. In his notebook he writes, "In art truth is like reality—an impossibility to re-create exactly. Art is *about* truth and reality. Unless this is understood we encourage a dishonesty and pretentiousness of approach, and it's this which I cannot pretend to believe in."[13] In conversation he also returns to this idea of a theatrical paradox. "You can't have realistic art," he begins, "but art is about reality. And the reason for making that distinction is that once you recognize that art is *about* reality, then you begin to reorganize your categories."[14] Understandably, Wesker resists arbitrary labeling, for as naturalistic as his play may be, it is nonetheless still a play with a meaning beyond accuracy, not a documentary.

The lecture hall sequence—Act One, Scene Four—of *Chips With Everything* is a good example of just how Wesker's drama goes beyond accuracy towards art, which he has so usefully defined as "the re-creation of experience, not the copying of it." In this sequence, the Wing Commander, the Squadron Leader, the Pilot Officer, and the P. T. Instructor give a series of coercive speeches. Each man's speech stresses the priority of the military machine, the limits of individual choice, and the goal of making recruits into military men. Those three aspects of military life made clear in the three introductory scenes—the R.A.F. as fact, model, and game— are emphasized again in the lecture hall. But here, the R.A.F. looms even larger. Its connection to the world outside grows symbolic in this scene as familiar rhetoric gives way to surreal speeches.

In their speeches, the officers all refer to the recruits as a single body of men. Just as the boys learned to march in time in the previous scene, so, too, they now learn to answer in time in the special vocabulary signaling submission to authority. The first speaker, the Wing Commander, for example, generalizes, "The human being is in a constant state of war and we must be prepared, each against the other. History has taught us this and we must learn. The reasons why and wherefore are not our concern. We are simply the men who must be prepared" (p. 311). The Wing Commander reduces mankind to a figure in eternal combat. To him the task is one of vigil, unrelieved preparedness to defend what is, what is right. This dogmatic watchfulness carries over into his welcoming address. He repeats his last admonition for emphasis, and he searches the faces of the recruits with mistrust. Rhetorically, he calls for questions:

WING COMMANDER. Any questions?
WILFE. Sir, if the aggressors are better off than us, what are they waiting for?
WING COMMANDER. What's your name?
WILFE. 247 Seaford, sir.
WING COMMANDER. Any other questions?

(p. 312)

There are, of course, no further questions. For the Wing Commander has clarified his position by answering a question of military strategy with a strategically worded question. His "What's your name?" effectively stifles possible inquiries. The Wing Commander has told the men to be

216

prepared, but by his hostile response to a direct question he has taught them a more important, lesson of service: they are to obey, and they are not to question why.

The next speaker in the lecture hall is the Squadron Leader. His text reinforces the Wing Commander's menacing object lesson in submission. In a brusque, authoritative address, the Squadron Leader puts the recruits neatly in place. "You are here to learn discipline," he informs them. "Discipline is necessary if we are to train you to the maximum state of efficiency, discipline and obedience. . . . That is what you are here to learn: obedience and discipline. Any questions? Thank you" (pp. 312–313). Obedience is recognized as an end in itself, and as the lecture hall speeches drone on more and more specifically, their effect on the recruits becomes visible. Questions are no longer posed; speeches are punctuated by boys rising hastily to attention.

One requirement leads to another. The Pilot Officer requires "cleanliness. . . . I want clean men. It so happens, however, that you cannot have clean men without rigid men, and cleanliness requires smartness and ceremony" (p. 313). But this exhortation to order, issued by the Pilot Officer, romanticizes the corps and it then extends oddly beyond normal expectations. "I want him so clean that he looks unreal," he continues. "In fact I don't want real men . . . I want unreal, superreal men" (p. 313).

The "superreal" expectations expressed by the Pilot Officer and by the next speaker alter the effect of this scene on the audience. The P. T. Instructor is blunt:

I want you like Greek gods. You heard of the Greeks? You ignorant troupe of anaemics, you were brought up on tinned beans and television sets, weren't you? You haven't had any exercise since you played knock-a-down-ginger, have you? Greek gods, you hear me? . . . I don't want your stupid questions! (p. 313)

This final speech is the most scornful and belligerent, yet it is also the most wistful reminder of the ideal of soldiering.

217

Such speeches are probably commonplace. Put-down pep talks are standard procedure in basic training. But in sequence here, they lift reality towards theater, towards a metaphor of service, towards an image of the gods.

After these first four sequences of group initiation, *Chips With Everything* focuses on individual conscripts, especially on Pip. The education of Pip is at the heart of Wesker's play. In his barracks storytelling to recruits, in his Christmas party machinations, and in his coke yard triumph in Act One, Pip emerges as the stubborn pivot about which Wesker's plot is built. The audience identifies with Pip as our clever, ironic surrogate onstage. He is a self-conscious character aware of the traditions of service and aware of the real predicament, and he seeks personally to transcend both in a game of will. But even clever Pip cannot beat the system. He is ineffectual in his defiance of the machine which will systematically place him above others in its hierarchy. Although Pip fancies himself to be a rebel, opposed to the military order, his ability to initiate and organize disruptive group efforts belies him.

One of the most memorable scenes of this play is the coke yard raid. This scene calls attention to Pip's imagination and leadership as he tries to "outwit" the R.A.F. (p. 334). The midnight escapade in the coke yard, a pantomime of intricate timing and coordination, is a welcome relief—for the audience as well as for the conscripts—from the tedium of following orders. This scene, like the whipping in *Marat/Sade*, like the chair-lifting in *Home*, like the dance in *Deathwatch*, is a breakthrough of choreography in a play of impasse. In it, everyday action soars. This scene stays true to its institutional setting, yet it works, too, as an isolating image, a silhouette of the action of the play as a whole.

The coke yard raid stands out in another regard as well. This funny, fast, and silent capsule of the play (like the gesture of the whipping with a toss of Corday's hair in *Marat/Sade*, for example) is a powerful instance of the collaboration of playwright and director in shaping plays of impasse, in exploring the theatrical idiom needed to express life in a parenthesis. Wesker's vision, implemented time and again by the direction of John Dexter, theatrically heightens the form and movement of the R.A.F. experience.

Throughout *Chips With Everything*, dramatic tension is felt in the contrapuntal arrangement of scenes, alternating between large military movements and those showing individuals either adjusting to or breaking down under stress. Scenes like the coke yard raid and the Christmas party in Act One are scenes of adjustment, scenes of relief from the military sameness. But in production even these two scenes are colored by the institution. Their rhythms, their teamwork, and the outcome of both scenes are bound to the total institution which tolerates them.

Like the reproduced drills and dreary routines which link *Chips With Everything* to their counterparts in reality, the Christmas celebration and show are also believably drawn aspects of life in the R.A.F.[15] Again, however, Wesker theatrically heightens such activities: just as the marches and the raid are choreographed, so, too, the musical entertainment enlivening the Christmas party is played up in this scene to call attention to the class-conscious hierarchy of the R.A.F. And like the coke yard raid, which Pip engineers and for which he is not punished, the Christmas party also demonstrates the inconsequential nature of Pip's rebelliousness. Here, when the Wing Commander condescendingly calls for a talent show, Pip directs the other conscripts in an old peasant revolt song. The song has a revolutionary subtext, but in the spirit of the Christmas celebration it is tolerated. The scene even ends with the Wing Commander offering a "truce" to Pip, the lad "from the same side" (p. 328).

Pip is clearly, inescapably officer material. As Wesker points out, this is not necessarily evil or a betrayal. Wesker says:

> It's not as easy as "There are bad men who want us to be automatons." There's a conflict between . . . those who have power and those who have none, and the

way in which this division exists is not simple, and on both sides there is neither simple virtue nor simple evil. So those working class recruits may be good boys and deprived and oppressed by the institution, but they are guilty of accepting an image of themselves such as in the Naafi scene when the Officer says, "Come on, let's have some performances." And Pip says, "You're more than what they think you are," and they [the conscripts] say they're not, and so they get up and they do something corny. But when pressed, they can see that they are capable of rather more. But their main fault is that for most of the time most of them accept this third rate image . . . of themselves. And on the other side, on the side of the oppressing or the ruling or the powerful class . . . there is the act of tolerance and forgiveness, which are virtues that we applaud. But paradoxically they lead to further acquiescence.[16]

In the course of Act Two, Wesker clarifies Pip's thematic function by balancing his superficial rebellion against the more substantial resistance of Smiler. The fate of these two conscripts dramatically states the central idea of *Chips With Everything*.

The turning point in Pip's military career is marked by the bayonet practice episode of Act Two, Scene Five. One by one, the boys must rush forward at a dummy hanging in the yard and, following Hill's example, they each scream and lunge with the "nasty weapon" (p. 346). Pip alone rebels. Instead of cutting the air with his bayonet, he *"stands still."* Hill first responds to this gesture of defiance by swearing to court-martial that "scorching, trouble-making, long-haired, posh-tongued, lump of aristocracy." When Pip still refuses to follow orders, Hill calls for the other recruits to form up a line behind Pip. In the presence of these witnesses, Hill issues a warning, legally worded. Once again he commands Pip to attack. "Failing to carry out this order," Pip is officially "charged under Section ten paragraph sixteen of . . . Her Majesty's rules and regulations" (pp. 346–347).

As at the Christmas celebration, at bayonet practice Pip singles himself out to make a moral statement about the military institution. Both the rigid language with which Hill chastises Pip and the rhythmic shrieks with which the other conscripts accompany their formal thrusts of bayonets are grounded in reality. The harsh words and rhythmic movements also lend a ritualistic quality to the bayonet practice sequence. An objective recreation of a military practice session, this scene simultaneously enforces a moral point: we watch the boys "run, scream, lunge" at a hanging dummy, and this rhythmic imitation of violent, unreasoning action performed with unyielding precision strikes us at once with what Judith Malina terms "the beauty and terror" of the total institution.[17] Pip's rebellion breaks the ritualistic rhythm. He refuses to play along with what even the N.C.O. recognizes as a game. ("This is only practice and no one can be hurt," the N.C.O. reassures the immobile Pip [p. 347].) As a result of his moral stance and sudden halting of rehearsal violence, Pip is court-martialed. But Pip's place in the R.A.F. has been predetermined by his class, and so, his court-martial turns out to be a bluff.

Now the military system defeats Pip; he is first rejected by his fellow conscripts:

ANDREW. No one's asking you to make gestures on our behalf.

PIP. Go off now.

ANDREW. Don't go making heroic gestures and then expect gratitude.

PIP. Don't lean on me, Andy—I've got problems.

ANDREW. I don't think I can bear your martyrdom—that's what it is; I don't think I can bear your look of suffering.

PIP. I'm not suffering.

ANDREW. I don't know why but your always-acting-right drives me round the bend.

PIP. I'm not a martyr.

(p. 348)

Indeed, the R.A.F. makes certain that he is not martyred.
He must merely be reassigned. In Act Two, Scene Seven,
the Pilot Officer speaks to Pip in off-the-record terms:

> It goes right through us, Thompson. Nothing you can
> do will change that. We listen but we do not hear, we
> befriend but do not touch you, we applaud but do not
> act—to tolerate is to ignore. What did you expect, praise
> from the boys? Devotion from your mates? Your mates
> are morons, Thompson, morons. At the slightest hint
> from us they will disown you. Or perhaps you wanted
> a court martial? Too expensive, boy. Jankers? That's
> for the yobs. You, we shall make an officer, as we
> promised. I have studied politics as well, you know,
> and let me just remind you of a tactic the best of rev-
> olutionaries have employed. That is to penetrate the
> enemy and spread rebellion there. You can't fight us
> from the outside. Relent boy, at least we understand
> long sentences.   (pp. 348–349)

Still, Pip insists, "I WILL NOT BE AN OFFICER," and
then the Pilot Officer teaches him about himself:

> Power. Power, isn't it? Among your own people there
> were too many who were powerful, the competition
> was too great, but here, among lesser men—here among
> the yobs, among the good-natured yobs, you could be
> king. KING. Supreme and all powerful, eh? Well? Not
> true? . . . You're destroyed, Thompson. No man sur-
> vives whose motive is discovered, no man. Messiah to
> the masses!   (p. 349)

After this chastisement and cruel education, Pip is given
another chance. As Wesker describes it:

> Pip *is* broken, he is corrupted, [according to] my very
> idiosyncratic definition of the word "corruption," which
> is that you present people with motives that they could

have but they don't actually have, and because they are sensitive, they believe they have. The officer says to him [Pip], "You want to be a messiah to the masses; now we've found you out." And that wasn't Pip's motivation, but he suddenly thinks, because he is a sensitive, intelligent human being, "My God, is that all I wanted to be. Well, if that's all I wanted to be, I won't have anything to do with that." So he says, "Right, I'll return to the officer class." So he's corrupted. One can't be simple about it.[18]

Broken by the system he sought to undo, Pip accepts the challenge. In Act Two, Scene Eight, the instructions are repeated. According to the stage directions, "PIP *pauses for a long while, then with a terrifying scream he rushes at the dummy, sticking it three times, with three screams*" (p. 350). Now Pip's conversion is confirmed; he conforms with a determination equal to his earlier resistance. Even in the formalized routine of bayonet practice, Pip's performance separates him from the other less shrill and less self-assured recruits.

Immediately following, in Act Two, Scene Nine, we return to the hut. Pip has been crying. Charles approaches him tentatively, wanting to learn "economics," really wanting to "find someone" to trust. But Pip, having just fulfilled that symbolic requirement of bayonet practice, has now committed himself to his validated role. According to sociological theory, "The acquisition of roles by a person involves two basic processes: *role-validation* and *role-commitment*. Role-validation takes place when a community 'gives' a person certain expectations to live up to, providing him with distinct notions as to the conduct it considers appropriate or valid for him in his position. Role-commitment is the complementary process whereby a person adopts certain styles of behavior as his own, committing himself to role themes that best represent the kind of person he assumes himself to be, and best reflect the social position he considers himself to occupy."[19] In this decisive moment in the hut, Pip shows both by his disconnected speech and by his alienating action that he has committed himself to his officially validated role in the R.A.F. He feels himself alone among the other conscripts. Pip's voice is distant. First, he quotes the Pilot Officer who told him, "We will listen to you but we will not hear you, we will befriend you but not touch you, we will tolerate and ignore you," and then he cruelly belittles the loyalty Charles offers him. Pip's new military bearing is based on class distinctions. "You're a fool, Charles, the kind of fool my parents fed on, you're a fool, a fool—" he says, and then this scene shifts, as do so many others in this play, to "*the sound of marching feet*" (p. 352). The emphasis on military stratification signifying stratification in society at large is sharp here. As Wesker sees it, this scene is central:

> My point is . . . if you analyze a work you will find there are many things you can say it deals with, but there is only one thing you can say it deals with mostly. The best productions and the best interpretations find what that one thing is. In *Chips* the one thing is the conflict between that in society which will limit expression and that which seeks to find what will encourage more expression. There is the main conflict between the military machine and the individual recruit, and then there is the story of Chas and Pip, which has his asking for education, for words. At an individual level he is saying, "I want to be able to do more, to say more, to understand more," and as a theme that runs through nearly all my work.[20]

Smiler's individual conflict with what Wesker calls here the "military machine" complements the education and conversion of Pip. Its meaning is also integral to the central theme of *Chips*, "the one thing it deals with mostly," as Wesker describes it. In contrast to Pip, Smiler is doomed to failure in the national service: the unfortunate alignment of his facial muscles insures his being singled out for insubordination. And Smiler's fate, like Pip's, is decided by class. He, too, is guilty of disrupting a ritualistic exercise.

In Act Two, Scene Two, Smiler fails to master the movements taught during a rifle drill. Though Pip's later breaking out of step is willful and Smiler's is merely due to sluggishness, Pip is excused; Smiler, on the other hand, is not given another chance. Having bungled on the parade ground, he is immediately court-martialed. In production, this plot development is scenically conveyed: *"The squad march off, all except* SMILER. *The wall of the guardroom drops into place"* (p. 341). The guardroom sequence which follows shows us unpreferential treatment of a conscript (in contrast with the later cajoling of Pip). The guardroom sequence is also similar—both in its torrential language and stylized movement—to Kenneth H. Brown's *The Brig.* Here, as in Brown's play of impasse, the abusive power of the intimidating Structure is wielded without a halt. In an enclosed space, the punishment is intensive, and the incessant attacks are personal.

During the guardroom sequence, two corporals join in a verbal assault on the callow Smiler. Their barrage of vulgar remarks about the boy's mother and his own worth is meant to teach him his place. Like the interrogation scene of Pinter's *The Birthday Party* (1958), this portion of *Chips With Everything* ends with a threat of individual extinction. "Stand still, boy. Don't move. Silent, boy. Still and silent, boy," commands the First Corporal in the eerie rhythm of dreamed echoes. Then Hill delivers a menacing farewell: "That'll do for a taster, Smiler. That'll do for the first lesson. Tomorrow we'll have some more. We'll break you, Smiler, we'll break you, because that's our job. Remember that, just remember now. . . . Remember, Smiler, remember" (p. 342). Hill proves true to his hypnotic speech, for Smiler is indeed broken by the deterministic machine. The next time we see him, Smiler is trying to break away. His mental breakdown, evidenced by his random ravings in flight, shifts the play's emphasis from a sociodramatic to a psychodramatic level of action.

After the New Year's Eve scene in the barracks where Pip, already defeated by this system which will absorb him in its class-conscious hierarchy, rebuffs Charles's friendship, Wesker shifts our attention to the inner process of conversion in the case of Smiler. To show us Smiler's conversion, Wesker takes a new tack. Pip's conversion was matter-of-factly traced, rooted in ordinary military actions. Smiler's experience, on the other hand, is shown in all its intensity. Taking his play beyond surface reality, beyond camera work, even beyond the highly suggestive sound effects of routine marching, Wesker now uses heightened language and accelerated action. The expressionistic sound effects of eerie voices and internal monologues give added force to Smiler's fall and to his ironically messianic function in the final movement of *Chips With Everything.*

As Act Two, Scene Nine ends with Pip's bitter self-knowledge and with his rejection of Charles, the scene shifts to an interior focus, to the expression of Smiler's confused inner state. According to the stage directions, *"Fade in the sound of marching feet and the* CORPORALS *repeating the insults they heaped upon* SMILER *and change to ... A roadway"* (p. 352). The nagging voices are used by Wesker as an expressionistic transition to interior action. The voices echoing in Smiler's head rise to a crescendo, and suddenly Smiler screams, "LEAVE ME ALONE! Damn your mouths and hell on your stripes—leave me alone. Mad they are, they're mad they are, they're raving lunatics they are" (pp. 352–353).

Act Two, Scene Ten unfolds in Smiler's mind. Riveted to a single spot onstage, he swears to get away. Still, he seems to be running in place. Unsuccessfully, he tries to thumb a ride home. "Home, you bastard, take me ho'ooooome," he calls to the sound of an engine which roars, then dies away (p. 353). He curses his tormentors, those men who "think that anyone who's dressed in blue is theirs to muck about, degrade," but somehow he ends up back where he began, trying to explain away his fixed smile ("It's not a smile, Corp, it's natural, honest, Corp. I'm born that way") to the aggressor who is not there.[21] This scene also falls directly into the next; it ends as Smiler

226

stumbles back into the hut. A very broken Smiler, exhausted from running around in circles and defending the natural twists of his face, returns to the camp which dominates the stage.

Some of the strongest scenes of *Chips With Everything* are set in the hut, the site of interpersonal, off-guard interaction among recruits. Though scenes between Pip and his working-class fellows sometimes seem set-ups for social debates, such a "fraternalization process" among "socially distant persons" who "find themselves developing mutual support and common counter-mores in opposition to a system that has forced them into intimacy and into a single, equalitarian community of fate" is a common phenomenon of total institutions.[22]

Back at the hut, then, a space already established as a place of relief and camaraderie for weary and lonely recruits, Smiler sways for a moment in Pip's arms, and then he collapses to the ground. The two sides of an individual's thwarted spirit—the officer and the ordinary soldier—fuse in an embrace with a symmetrical poetry of the theater. The momentary image of the Pietà, the offstage strains of "Auld Land [*sic*] Syne," and the ritualistic washing of Smiler's bleeding feet combine in a moment of sentimental irony. This moment is extraordinarily simple *and* complex. It fuses ordinary and symbolic action. Military camaraderie and an ironic image merge onstage. Wesker says, "The intention is that the square-bashing process attempts to give uniformity to people's behavior, and here is one person [Smiler] who is reacting against this by running away. In the process he hurts his feet. And the action of washing his feet is an action of solidarity, of sympathy, of love. It's not that he is the sacrificial lamb or being Christ-like; it's simply an action of comradeship."[23] And yet, this simple communal gesture, grounded in military reality, resonates.

The other men file into the hut. Returning from a New Year's celebration, their movements are *"wild and drunk"* until they notice Smiler, "lying there like a bloody corpse." Their entrance into the hut is heightened by Wesker's sudden contrapuntal arrangement of poetically overdetermined sounds. According to the stage directions, there is in succession, "*a long unconscious moan from* SMILER; *clock strikes midnight; sound of boys singing 'Auld Land [sic] Syne'* " (p. 354). Each of these sounds is linked to the others in a chain of associations connecting levels of action already established in Wesker's play of impasse. The individual's interior cry of pain and loss, the objective sound mechanically heralding a new year, and the communal farewell to old times combine in an aural pattern paralleling the levels of self, society, and performing expounded throughout *Chips With Everything.*

These suggestive offstage sounds are followed by the sound of a single voice shouting words into the night. Offstage, Corporal Hill reminds the conscripts of their imminent debut, and his voice, *"loud"* and clear, is a military reminder in syllabic measures:

> You pass out with the band tomorrow—rifles, buttons, belts, shining, and I want you as one man, you hear me? You'll have the band and it'll be marvellous; only you Smiler, you won't be in it, you'll stay behind a little longer, my lad—HAPPY NEW YEAR.   (p. 354)

There is, of course, an obvious dramatic irony in this goodnight address, for Corporal Hill is unaware of Smiler's escape and his subsequent return to the hut. Beyond this, there is a visual irony implicit in the staging of Hill's New Year's order: his offstage voice representing a perpetual system is underscored by the physical action of a group "as one man" right now. Together, the conscripts undress, groom, and bathe Smiler. This action is performed *"lovingly and with a sort of ritual"* according to the stage directions (p. 355).

Pip is also stripped in this scene, which objectifies metamorphosis. When Smiler is discovered by the officers and punishment is about to be meted out, Pip completes his own transformation (complementary to Smiler's) onstage. According to the stage directions, Pip changes his uniform

228

"from an airman's to an officer's" (p. 356). The accompanying dialogue, a verbal confrontation between Pip and the Pilot Officer, reverberates on several levels:

> PILOT OFFICER. Take the lot of them, I'll see them all in the guardroom.
>
> PIP. You won't touch any of them, Corporal Hill, you won't touch a single one of them.
>
> PILOT OFFICER. Do you hear me, Corporal, this whole hut is under arrest.
>
> PIP. I suggest, sir, that you don't touch one of them. (PIP *and the* PILOT OFFICER *smile at each other, knowingly, and* PIP *now begins to change his uniform, from an airman's to an officer's.*)
>
> (p. 356)

The new uniform he dons is a good fit: it is an outward expression of Pip's altered inner state. He has successfully challenged the encoded order, but in the process, he has acknowledged its validity. Pip's debate with the Pilot Officer over Smiler's prone body ends the battle he has fought throughout the play. Now stubborn opposites unite over the fate of a fallen man. The attenuated conflict between free will and a deterministic world ends in a visual draw, for once he dons the uniform of an officer, Pip becomes the Pilot Officer's double. Changed, Pip immediately takes on the kindly, superior tones of a sympathetic officer. He commends the airmen for their virtuous loyalty to Smiler; he paternally forgives them; and he reads out the permanent assignments list.

Wesker sees both sides of the issue. Referring now to Pip's transformation when he dons the officer's uniform, Wesker says:

> I don't think it should be described as a betrayal. Pip is very much a pragmatic Englishman. He sees that there is trouble, and he knows that he is in a position to save them. He takes on the mantle of the officer class, which fits him much better—he is more in har-

mony with that than with the recruiting class—but he doesn't become evil. What I think I'm saying is that one mustn't look at the other side in terms of evil. Pip says, "We're good honorable men; we applaud the virtues of courage and loyalty. We're capable of seeing them. Don't think badly of us," he says. And that is part of the nature of controlling bodies. So all I'm really engaged in is description, not in solutions. . . . The paradox is that in applauding them [the recruits], you diffuse them.[24]

So a new year begins; but with Pip as an officer, reading out the assignments list to the conscripts, the old order is reaffirmed. Basic training is over.

The last scene of *Chips With Everything* is a finale in full dress. The men march out before us "together—unity, unity," they salute the audience, hoist the R.A.F. colors, and perform the national anthem (pp. 357–358). Corporal Hill accompanies their synchronized approach with rhapsodic barks, "Lovely, that's lovely, that's poetry." Indeed, he is right. There is an unmistakable beauty in the even rhythms stamped out in the march in our time. Wesker says, "We have seen the spark of rebellion in them. But in fact they all go through that passout parade. And they are told by the commanding officers, 'We're very proud of you. You've served the Queen well.' Again, the paradox is I can remember when I did it. I loved it. I loved that passout parade. I was very proud that we were one of the best groups there."[25]

Quite naturally, then, *Chips With Everything* has such a patriotic ending. The presentation of the flag and the anthem—an old vaudeville trick to insure a standing ovation—is used here, as it is also used in Osborne's *The Entertainer* and in Nichols's *The National Health*, to achieve a double effect. Wesker is right: this moment is always thrilling, but in the context of his play, it is also ironic. This is called a passout parade, but by the time the conscripts get out, they have incorporated into their own individual outlooks the values of the system. The Structure has insinuated itself into their way of thinking about their lives, and in this way, the state of impasse, the place from which there is no escape, the trap (as Sartre puts it), has broken through to the self in ordinary society. Wesker's play ends with an exit through a freedom door of sorts; but the finale of pomp and order signifies a deeper notion of impasse, a profound sense of how the line beyond which one cannot pass can extend beyond the institution towards the place in which the self resides. When military movement literally becomes poetry in motion, then servicemen marching together stand out only as variations on a single patriotic theme. In Wesker's play of impasse, that theme is in one sense a national anthem. But there is another, more distanced sense in which to respond to the passout parade, too: the soldiers in step, the anthem, and the flag may stir us as usual, but we in the audience know we are watching a performance, *not* an actual parade. So we can finally watch the marching from two points of view: as members of a cheering throng *and* as members of a contemporary audience, all too aware of the exacting nature of service and of what Judith Malina called the dangerous "beauty and terror" inhabiting places, objects, and groups turned symbolic.

Chips With Everything has much in common in its thesis and in its form with such plays as John Arden's overwhelming *Serjeant Musgrave's Dance* (1959), an epic play about war and guilt that Arden based in part on his own television play *Soldier, Soldier*, and with Peter Nichols's *Privates on Parade* (1977), a burlesque show about the British Song and Dance Unit stationed in post-World War II Malaysia. A far cry from these plays, however, are many minor contemporary American military-based plays. Where *Chips With Everything* tends to be metaphorical, many recent American plays, particularly during and in the wake of the Vietnam war, have tended to be literal.

A surge of minor political plays, now dated, came forth

in response to the Vietnam war. Hastily composed and mounted, many have not held up well, although they made a very timely and important political impact in the 1960s through the early 1970s. Plays like Megan Terry's *Viet Rock* (1966), Denis Cannan's *U S* (first produced by the Royal Shakespeare Company in London under the direction of Peter Brook in 1966, released in a film version by Continental Films in 1968, and published under the title *Tell Me Lies*, edited by Michael Kustow, Geoffrey Reeves, and Albert Hunt), Barbara Garson's *MacBird!* (1967), and Peter Weiss's *Vietnam Discourse* (first produced in Frankfurt in 1968) abounded. Among the most effective as well as edifying of these dramatizations of military action were George Tabori's *Pinkville* (1971), the Open Theatre's production of Jean Claude van Itallie's *America, Hurrah* (1966), a play whose "Interview" segment featured a parodic treatment of television's bland digestion of war and violence, and, curiously enough, *The Lieutenant*, a 1975 rock opera by Gene Curty, Nitra Scharfman, and Chuck Strand based on the My Lai case. *The Trial of the Catonsville Nine* (1971) by Daniel Berrigan, one of the defendants, even made use of real courtroom transcripts.

There was, then, a bombardment of Vietnam plays, primarily during the war. On the whole, they were: (1) dramas against the war (such as those listed above); (2) plays which used the war as a backdrop for images of loss and anger (plays such as Michael Weller's *Moonchildren*, Mark Medoff's *When You Comin' Back Red Ryder?*, Ron Cowen's *Summertree*, Lyle Kessler's *The Watering Place*, and Tom Cole's *Medal of Honor Rag*, for example); and (3) guerrilla theater or street theater plays which sought to induce immediate social action.[26] But outside of such categories was Gerome Ragni and James Rado's *Hair*, an innovative rock musical which, in its first production at Joseph Papp's Public Theater, used the war not only as a plot, but also as an energizing force, a kind of fulcrum for a communal explosion of life. And also outside of such categories were the plays of David Rabe. *Hair* and Rabe's plays share an energizing sense of

232

community, and significantly, they shared the vision and commitment of Joseph Papp as producer. As one commentator noted in 1971:

> Papp is angered by bad war drama; of an example he saw at a college performance recently, he says, "When a guy starts talking about the Mylai massacre like that, I mean, man, you just pick up the newspaper, you don't have to listen to *this* guy. He sounds like the biggest fake in the world. If what you put on the stage is less than what you see in the newspapers, man, don't put it on the stage! . . . It is hard to keep the activist and the artist apart. Yet it is always much better, for example, to produce a good play on the war, than to protest personally." The first such play he has found worth producing opened recently: David Rabe's *The Basic Training of Pavlo Hummel*, which is about a Vietnam veteran searching out his identity.[27]

Even now, new plays about Vietnam occasionally surface. No longer politically motivated, they tend to use the war as an idea, a controlling metaphor of loss and anger. For example, Elizabeth Swados mounted a "rock war musical" based on Michael Herr's *Dispatches*. Performed in April 1979 in the Theater Cabaret in Martinson Hall at the New York Shakespeare Festival Public Theater, *Dispatches* was more of a concert than a play; but its songs, screamed with joyless abandon by a noncohesive ensemble, did incorporate bits and pieces of the powerful text of Herr's war journal. When the songs echoed Herr's vision of the soldiers whose terror and freedom he reported, the production demythified the Vietnam soldiers and had a tough, hard edge. A different stage adaptation of *Dispatches* was performed at the National Theatre's Cottesloe in 1979, directed by Bill Bryden.

A play that uses just two actors, some sliding screens, and a mythical country called Amboland to communicate the Vietnam experience with irony and an expansive imagination is *How I Got That Story*. It was written by Amlin Gray, playwright-in-residence at the Milwaukee Repertory Theater, and presented in December 1980 by the Second Stage, an off off-Broadway company in New York City. It was again presented in Spring 1981, with some changes, at the Folger Theater in Washington, D.C., and then again in New York City, this time off-Broadway, in February 1982. *How I Got That Story* follows the adventures of a Reporter from Dubuque who covers Amboland for the Trans Pan Global wire service. The play, a vaudeville, satirizes the Pavlo Hummel-like naive straight man out to get his scoop. At the same time, it satirically recreates almost two dozen embodiments of the Historical Event (all played by one chameleon-like actor) that he encounters in a string of staccato scenes along the Via Dolorosa. This play transcends the local effects of a war to show the vaster, universal implications of a play of impasse by satirically raising large questions about responsibility and identity in the face of horror. It focuses on how the Reporter gets "imprinted" by the war, that is, how, in one interview after another— with a swearing G.I., a Saigon whore, a combat photographer who keeps getting hit, Madame Ing (Queen of the Imperial Palace), and so on—he attempts to cover a country; but instead, he loses his objectivity and his sense of self, and finally, "the country covers him."

Also among the most interesting Vietnam-based plays to emerge in recent years is David Berry's *G. R. Point*, which, following its engagement at the Center Stage in Baltimore, had a brief run on Broadway in April 1979. This play, using the members of a graves registration unit as types, tends towards melodrama. It is distinguished by its treatment of the unit as a microcosm and by its central character, Micah, an upper-class Amherst graduate, who, like Pip in *Chips With Everything*, is initiated into a cohesive group. The play's most powerful moment, deftly played by Michael Moriarty in William Devane's Broadway production, comes when Micah gradually unwinds after his first combat. Talking in fragments about the battle's effect on him, Micah slowly lets go, loses control, and confides the excitement he felt on the killing ground. His flailing arms, blinking innocence, and memory of terrible control become unbearable. The set designed by Peter Larkin was another powerful aspect of this production: a lunar landscape, where gravity does not seem to hold, leads down to the barracks and to the morgue. This play is seriously flawed by a creaky plot and by some awkward dialogue of camaraderie. But its spatial design, its central character, and its imagery of life at the edge bear the hallmark of the contemporary dramatic mode, much as David Rabe's more substantial plays do. Stuck working in a morgue at the edge of battle, literally living a life-in-death, the characters in Berry's play react to limited choices, pass the time with wisecracks and reminiscences, and wait to get out, to get, as they repeatedly phrase it, "home on the range," "back in the world." Still, they realize they will never be able to shake this experience; there really is no getting "back in the world" after being caught in this trap, this impasse of Vietnam.

Like Wesker's *Chips With Everything*, Rabe's two powerful Vietnam plays, *The Basic Training of Pavlo Hummel* and *Streamers*, depict military training with documentary accuracy, explore the defeat of the individual by an overpowering military world, and shape an image of loss out of a thesis about soldiering. Like *Chips*, *Pavlo Hummel* and *Streamers* condense action by means of heightened language and balanced figures at the edge of understanding their situation. And like *Chips*, the two plays convert a military setting into a metaphor for the world as it is, and they convert a sympathetic character into a man in uniform. But Wesker's play upon a national theme turns the R.A.F. into a microcosm of social order and psychological control and it *stops* there. Rabe, a Vietnam veteran drafted in 1965, is, however, particularly concerned with the human condition affected by the American involvement in Vietnam. This concern intensifies his dramas. Further, as a playwright, Rabe is more immediate, more jazzy than is Wesker. Of the two, Rabe is also by far the more pessimistic. Wesker still believes "in the possibility of change" even if he does "not believe it is easy."[28] Wesker's soldiers can count on each other's friendship and concern; they can rely on the spirit of the corps. Meanwhile, Rabe's young men are on their own. In contrast to Wesker's more hopeful play, in Rabe's entropic *Pavlo Hummel* the pulsating pop music, the shrill screams, the harsh lighting, the salutes, the drills, and the street language are all brought to bear on a lonely soldier fighting for a lost cause. Rabe's stage is stripped of all but the essential props of war, barracks, and the colors of camouflage. His rhythms are quick; the action of both his Vietnam plays is tight, fast, energized, like a clenched fist. His characters and his situations go beyond Smiler, who is saved by his friends in *Chips With Everything*. In Rabe's plays, breakdowns are violent, explosive, final.

Importantly, Rabe's Vietnam plays grab us not only with their force, but also with their transcendent, haunting quality. The aesthetics, the morality, and the dynamics of these plays—*The Basic Training of Pavlo Hummel* and *Streamers*, in particular—suggest a nexus of response to Vietnam. Going beyond that, as vital, enduring plays of impasse they suggest American life penetrated, shaken loose, and sharpened to a knife-edge by that war.

The Basic Training of Pavlo Hummel

David Rabe's Vietnam vision has shaped and colored virtually all of his plays. Of his five major plays that have been produced thus far, four of them deal with some aspect of his wartime experience. As one reviewer observed, "Rabe showed in *The Basic Training of Pavlo Hummel* that the Army was the military institutionalization of stresses in the society itself. And in the controversial *Sticks and Bones* he showed the American middle-class family as the basic combat team behind the bloody moral slapstick of Vietnam. . . . In *The Orphan* he continues to explore the moral morass of the Vietnam war, but he has chosen to draw parallels between that travesty of honor in action and the *Oresteia* of Aeschylus."[29] Rabe has himself commented on his return to Vietnam time and again in his plays as an aesthetic choice, not a political choice. "The specificity of my work certainly comes out of my experience," he told an interviewer. "You're obsessed with certain things and you write about them. But I don't think my real obsession is the Vietnam War." Rather, he claims that the sleazy, exploitive world of the go-go dancer in one of his few non-Vietnam-rooted plays, *In the Boom Boom Room*, "illuminates the real nature of the other plays."[30] The translation of the Vietnam war into myth and social metaphor also characterizes Rabe's most recent major play, *Streamers*, which zeroes in on a no-exit barracks situation.

The Basic Training of Pavlo Hummel, Rabe's most ambitiously constructed play, was first produced by Joseph Papp's New York Shakespeare Festival at the Public Theater in 1971. It mixes the metaphor of basic training with the grotesque image of battle. The result is a graphic blend of naturalistic action and representational characters who convey the harsh reality of the Vietnam experience to an audience already detached from newscasted atrocities. *Pavlo Hummel* is nevertheless not an antiwar play in the sense that its playwright entertained no hopes of its having an immediate political effect. In his introduction to *Pavlo Hummel*, Rabe writes that he sees war as a phenomenon which is "permanently a part of the eternal human pageant."[31] And so, his play stands apart from the many other plays written as specific responses to the Vietnam war alone, plays whose topicality now dates them. Rabe's *Pavlo Hummel*, on the other hand, leads its audience towards what Brecht's Mother Courage urged on a soldier: a long rage, not a short one.[32] This is achieved primarily by means of Rabe's counterbalance of the lethal permanence of war as a state of mind with the boyish aspirations of the central figure. (Rabe was, in fact, drawn towards William Atherton, the actor who first played Pavlo, because "he had a Huck Finn mix of innocence, toughness, and mischievousness" [Introduction, p. xviii].) The title character of the play is killed in the first scene of Act One. The rest of the play may be seen as his vision of life-in-death, lost in a state of mind called Vietnam.

The theatrical focus of Rabe's topical attack on an American system, then, is not on linear action as in *Chips With Everything*, but on an encompassing Structure which consumes naive boys. Pavlo Hummel, the pathetic-comic recruit, is the pivot about which a disconnected series of scenes from military life revolve. Unlike Pip in *Chips With Everything*, Pavlo is not officer material. Pip is conscious and critical both of himself and of his companions in the hut. Wesker sets him apart from the others: he is ostracized by the lower-class recruits and he is wooed by his superiors. Pavlo, however, is more closely related to the role played by Smiler in Wesker's military procession. As John Lahr observed in his review of the Public Theater production of the play, the character of Hummel has the "stumbling gullibility" of a "contemporary Schweik."[33] For Pavlo is a loser among the recruits in Rabe's play. His stage predecessors are vaudevillian types: the sad faced fall guy, the gullible simpleton who is the butt of countless cruel jokes.

In his note to the play, at the end of the published text, Rabe comments upon the nature of his title figure. He stresses the innocence, ineptitude, and irredeemable loss personified by Pavlo:

> If the character of Pavlo Hummel does not have a certain eagerness and wide-eyed spontaneity, along with a true, real, and complete inability to grasp the implications of what he does, the play will not work as it can. Pavlo is in fact lost. He has, for a long time, no idea that he is lost. His own perceptions define the world. . . . He has romanticized the street-kid tough guy and hopes to find himself in that image. It is Pavlo's body that changes. His physical efficiency, even his mental efficiency increases, but real insight never comes. Toughness and cynicism replace open eagerness, but he will learn only that he is lost, not how, why, or even where. His talent is for leaping into the fire. (p. 110)

In this play, insight is reserved for the spectators, not for the participant. Pavlo is fundamentally a simpleton trapped in the illogic of a morality play in a military world. He is a misplaced Everyman figure, and like all the other Everyman figures, this Willy Lomanesque boy is doomed from the start. Pavlo enlisted. His expectations of army life are all drawn from cinematic romances, adventure stories, and propaganda. In this respect, he is typical. During bayonet practice in basic training, Sergeant Tower taunts the men with the army's betrayal of their fantasy. He bellows at them:

> LONG THRUST, PARRY LEFT . . . WHOOOOOO!
> (*And the men growl and move, one of them stumbling, falling down, clumsy, embarrassed.*)
> Where you think you are? You think you in the movies? This here real life, Gen'lmen. You actin' like there ain't never been a war in this world. Don't you know what I'm sayin'? You got to want to put this steel into a man. (p. 46)

But Pavlo can never quite reconcile his grand illusions with the twisted reality he experiences in Vietnam. "I enlisted because I wanted to be a soldier, Sir, and I'm not a soldier here," he laments when he is assigned to hospital duty instead of to squad duty (p. 91). Pavlo's symbolic dream of military manhood clashes repeatedly with his assignment in Rabe's pageant.

THE ACTION of *Pavlo Hummel* begins in one corner of the open space of the stage. The preliminary stage directions, orienting us to the stage design, also clarify the military nature of the setting which will encompass all the locations of dramatic action:

> *The set is a space, a platform slanting upward from the downstage area. The floor is nothing more than slats that run in various directions with a military precision. It has a brownish color. The backdrop is dark with touches of green. Along*

the back of the set runs a ramp elevated about two feet off the floor. Stage left and a little down from the ramp stands the drill sergeant's tower. This element is stark and as realistic as possible. Farther downstage and stage left the floor opens into a pit two feet deep. There is an old furnace partly visible. Downstage and stage right are three army cots with footlockers at their base. Upstage and stage right there is a bar area: an army ammunition crate and an army oil drum set as a table and chair before a fragment of sheet-metal wall partly covered with beer-can labels. All elements of the set should have some military tone to them, some echo of basic training. (p. 7)

As the action of the play moves from one area of the sparse stage to another—from the bar area to the drill instructor's tower to the furnace room to the barracks area to the training ramp to a pool table and then back again to the barracks area, etc.—the total set remains intact. Each scene, harshly lit, has the same military coloration. The primary linking device used by Wesker in *Chips With Everything* is the sound of parade-ground drilling. *Pavlo Hummel* is schematically set, so no such linking between conventional scene changes is needed. Instead, across a fragmented stage, one interrupted sequence breaks abruptly into the next. The disorienting effect is strong and harsh, like the experience of basic training itself. Rabe's war zone spreads itself across a schematic stage. The bar and the battlefield, the barracks and the hospital ward, the training ground and the furnace room are all separate authentically suggested exteriors radiating from a central thematic point.

Throughout *Pavlo Hummel*, the chronological order of events is subordinated to a thematic organization of military activity. The authentic sounds of incessant drills are frequently counterpointed with the ritualized actions of military men. We are initiated into this constantly shifting pattern almost immediately. The opening scene of the play, for example, a barroom sequence in a whorehouse during which Pavlo is blown to bits by a grenade, ends abruptly.

According to the stage directions, "PAVLO *drops to his knees, seizing the grenade, and has it in his hands in his lap when the explosion comes, loud, shattering, and the lights go black, go red or blue. The girl screams. The bodies are strewn about. The radio plays*" (p. 9). The sudden blare of the radio, which starts out as a shrill continuation of the girl's scream, gradually blends into the next scene, a meeting between Hummel and another soldier, Ardell. The sound of the radio is now converted into an authentic detail: Ardell begins his straight-talk with Hummel by *"moving to turn the radio off"* (p. 9). After a brief, colloquial conversation during which Hummel realizes the extent of his wounds, the two men merge with a group of trainees being badgered by Sergeant Tower. The flow of the action, like the slang-filled dialogue, suggests a realistic progression distorted by the logic of a dream. The first encounter between Hummel and Ardell, for example, consists of a sardonically matter-of-fact assessment of a surreal situation:

ARDELL. What you get hit with?
PAVLO. Hand grenade. Fragmentation-type.
ARDELL. Where about it get you?
PAVLO (*touching gently his stomach and crotch*). Here. And here. Mostly in the abdominal and groin areas.
ARDELL. Who you talkin' to? Don't you talk that shit to me, man. Abdominal and groin areas, that shit. It hit you in the stomach, man, like a ten-ton truck and it hit you in the balls, blew 'em away. Am I lyin'?
PAVLO (*able to grin: glad to grin*). No, man.
ARDELL. Hurt you bad.
PAVLO. Killed me.
ARDELL. That right. Made you dead. You dead man; how you feel about that?
PAVLO. Well . . .
ARDELL. *Don't you know? I think you know!* I think it piss

you off. I think you lyin' you say it don't. Make
you wanna scream.
PAVLO. Yes.

(p. 11)

Suddenly, a whistle blows loudly, and again the scenic focus
shifts from one area of the stage to another. The whistle,
another authentically military sound effect, is used as a
surreal bridge, linking one exteriorized scene to its asso-
ciative destination in a dying man's mind.

Sergeant Tower's indoctrination of the trainees takes place
on the parade ground beneath the high tower on which he
stands. The drill sergeant's introductory speech typifies both
his familiar speech pattern and his swelled attitude:

SGT. TOWER. GEN'LMEN! (*As the men standing in ranks
below the tower snap to parade rest and* PAVLO, *startled,
runs to find his place among them*) You all lookin' up
here and can you see me? Can you see me well?
Can you hear and comprehend my words? Can
you see what is written here? . . . Tower. My name.
And I am bigger than my name. And can you see
what is sewn here upon the muscle of my arm?
Can you see it? ANSWER!
THE MEN (*yell*). NO.
SGT. TOWER. No what? WHAT?
THE MEN. NO, SERGEANT.
SGT. TOWER. It is also my name. It is my first name.
Sergeant. That who I am. I you Field First. And
you gonna see a lot a me. You gonna see so much
a me, let me tell you, you gonna think I you mother,
father, sisters, brothers, aunts, uncles, nephews,
nieces, and children—if-you-got-'em—all rolled into
one big black man. Yeh, Gen'lmen. And you gonna
become me.

(pp. 12–13)

In the course of the play, Hummel is repeatedly drawn
back to the tower beneath which he is drilled and reviewed.

Basic training becomes a state of mind, and Hummel often backtracks in his dreamlike progress across Rabe's graphic landscape of military life and lost illusions. He returns to the tower, and he looks up to the belligerent sergeant who threatens—and promises—to make him over in his own military image.

At the basis of Rabe's societal model, then, stand three individualized representatives of military types: Hummel, Ardell, and Sergeant Tower. Together, they are the vertices of Rabe's triangle of military images. Pavlo Hummel and Ardell, apparently antithetical embodiments of an idea of a soldier, eventually complement each other when they are confronted with the impenetrable Structure personified by Sergeant Tower. At first, however, Ardell and Hummel seem to be dialectically opposed figures. When we first see Ardell, he seems to rise out of the debris of the first fatal scene. According to the stage directions, immediately after the explosion of the grenade:

> A *black soldier*, ARDELL, *now appears, his uniform strangely unreal with black ribbons and medals; he wears sunglasses, bloused boots.* (ARDELL *will drift throughout the play, present only when specifically a part of the action, appearing, disappearing, without prominent entrances and exits.*)   (p. 9)

The superficially established opposition between the "cool" Ardell and the goofy Hummel in their adjustments to army life is resolved at the end of Act One. After a humiliating encounter in the barracks while awaiting his permanent assignment, Hummel inarticulately expresses his discontent and perpetual isolation. Ardell, his transcendent sidekick, expresses his feelings for him:

> ARDELL. I know. I know. All you life like a river and there's no water all around—this emptiness—you gotta fill it. Gotta get water. You dive, man, you dive off a stone wall.
> (PAVLO *has a canteen and paper bag in his hands.*)
> Into the Hudson River waitin' down dark under

you. For a second, it's all air . . . so free. . . . Do
you know the distance you got to fall? You think
you goin' up. Don't nobody fall up, man. Nobody.
PAVLO. What is it? I want to know what it is. The thing
that sergeant saw to make him know to shoot that
kid and old man. I want to have it, know it, be it.
ARDELL. I know.
PAVLO. When?
ARDELL. Soon.
PAVLO. If I could be bone, Ardell; if I could be bone.
In my deepest part or center, if I could be bone.

(pp. 55–56)

In his desperation to "have it, know it, be it," Pavlo Hummel
takes an overdose of aspirins and crawls under the covers
of his bunk to die. The rest of Act One is performed as if
in a dream. Hummel's attempted suicide is followed in
quick succession by an ironically apt monologue about the
importance of the North Star for those who are lost, delivered from his platform by Sergeant Tower, and by a
barracks-room card game set up on the bunk right next to
the prone figure of Hummel.

Finally, Pavlo Hummel's transformation is acted out before us, and the transformation is on the four simultaneous
levels common to plays of impasse: (1) on the authentic
level, the level of "new naturalism,"[34] Ardell is shaking Pavlo
out of his suicidal stupor; (2) on the sociodramatic level, a
half-dead soldier is snapped back to attention by a communal effort, for all the other men in the barracks now
move in to help dress him in his uniform; (3) on the level
of ritual this scene is a self-conscious triumph of mass-man,
for, as the stage directions suggest, the syncopated movements suggest "*a ritual now:* PAVLO *must exert no effort what-
soever as he is transformed*" (p. 61); and (4) the ritual of resurrection is symbolically heightened by the military
choreography:

ARDELL. Where you boots? An' you got some shades?
Lemme get you some shades. (*Walking backward*)

And tuck that tie square. Give her little loop she
come off you throat high and pretty.
(*As* ARDELL *exits,* PAVLO *sits on the footlocker.* PIERCE *and
the other soldier kneel to put the boots onto him.*)
HUT ... HOO ... HEE ... HAW ... (*Singing*) IF I
HAD A LOWER I.Q.
ALL THE MEN. IF I HAD A LOWER I.Q.
ARDELL. I COULD BE A SERGEANT TOO.
THE MEN. I COULD BE A SERGEANT TOO!
(*Across the back of the stage, two men march.*)
ARDELL. LORD HAVE MERCY, I'M SO BLUE.
(*The two men do an intricate drill-team step.*)
THE MEN. IT FOUR MORE WEEKS TILL I BE
THROUGH.
(*The two men spin their rifles and strike the ground smartly
with the butts, as* ARDELL *returns, carrying a pair of
sunglasses.*)
ARDELL. You gonna be over, man, I finish with you.
(PAVLO *stands up fully dressed.*)

(pp. 61–62)

As the stage directions make clear, this scene has the quality
of a sleepwalk: "*Everything* PAVLO *does is performed in the
manner of a person alone: as if* ARDELL *is a voice in his head.
The light perhaps suggests this.* KRESS, *all others, are frozen*" (p.
60). When Ardell leads Hummel to the tower, the four
levels of the scene are linked. The naturalistic, sociodramatic, ritualistic, and symbolic aspects of the action converge. Now, Ardell—the streetwise trainee, the stage presence of a surviving soldier—leads Hummel out of his delirium
by forcing him to see himself in his own projected image
atop the tower.

This moment of identity transference goes to the core
of *Pavlo Hummel.* As John Lahr observed in his review of
the Public Theater production of the play in 1971:

Hummel is gung-ho; but he is not the standard mad-
dog Marine. He's younger and more pathetic; the type
of smooth-faced soldier you see in his uniform on a

date; a soldier who wants to say "yes," not "no"; a
buffoon so impotent that he yearns for the power of
life and death over people; so lonely and lost that a
set of shades and his green dress uniform can give him
a new identity. "You so pretty you gonna make 'em
cry. What's your name?" Hummel answers: "Pavlo—
Mother-fucking—Hummel." In his fantasy world,
Hummel is looking tough; in his costume, he has—
what life denies—a heroic, even sexual destiny.[35]

Hummel's military transformation is at the exact center of
the play. Sporting the sunglasses and dress uniform in which
Ardell has outfitted him, Hummel stands atop that tower,
and he snaps to attention just as a blackout of the stage
signals intermission to the audience.

Pavlo Hummel revolves around the submission of the soldier to his destined anonymity, an idea which manifests
itself in the striking mirror image occurring at the precise
center of the play. Like Smiler, who is beaten by military
rule at the turning point of *Chips With Everything*, Hummel
is a misfit who plays in earnest and consequently loses himself in the game. He, too, is the victim of a system and a
prop which quickens when prepared by his fellows for a
ritual inspection. Wesker's play, however, also depicts the
education and conversion of Pip, a potential officer, in this
way balancing its Everyman with a superior figure in a play
which progresses in a linear as well as in a cyclic way.

Act Two of *Pavlo Hummel* consists mainly of an associa-
tively ordered barrage of military formations, flashbacks of
Hummel's civilian experiences, and graphic sequences of
Hummel in combat duty, in hospital duty, and off duty. In
a pattern similar to that of Act One, scenes of frustration,
confrontation, and bewilderment flow into and out of one
another with dreamlike rapidity. Each fragmented and interrupted sequence flows into the next.

In his introduction to *Pavlo Hummel*, Rabe candidly discusses the gradual genesis of his final version of the play,
especially of Act Two. Rabe makes clear that *Pavlo Hummel*

is indebted to its director, Jeff Bleckner (and to its producer, the ubiquitous, visionary Joseph Papp), for its kaleidoscopic stage design. According to the playwright:

> Five weeks into rehearsal of *The Basic Training of Pavlo Hummel*, the director, Jeff Bleckner, and I knew there were problems, and knew also the areas in which they lurked. The play spun out of kilter when it hit them, plopped down, and rolled about. Most of the problems were in the second act, but the key to all of them was in a kind of stylistic chasm between the two acts. The basic-training metaphor, meaning "essential" training (and intended to include more in this case than the training given by the army) had not been carried through in the writing or staging. The first act seemed rooted to an inextricable degree in documentary realism, while the second was fragmentary and impressionistic in a way that seemed to make any comprehensive and convincing sense of realism impossible.
>
> So we got Joe Papp in to see a run-through of the show. . . . He . . . deciphered many of *Pavlo*'s secrets, and the forces that were its substructure. . . . He urged a breakdown of the linear nature of the play. . . . His question was simple: what scenes in the second act could be moved into the first? . . .
>
> So we changed the position of two second-act scenes, rewriting them only slightly. Another pair of scenes in the second act were fragmented and restaged in a manner that allowed their implications to flow more freely back and forth: the man with one arm and everything amputated below the waist was on stage while Pavlo visited the whorehouse. To draw the metaphor of basic training as ritual throughout the entire fabric of the play, we decided to repeat a first-act drill scene in the middle of the second act and to put a formation at the very start of the second act.   (pp. xiii–xv)

In this disarming account of the collaborative creative process, Rabe calls our attention to the way in which he and his director organized symbolic action to heighten the effect of regimentation, fragmentation, and loss. The already-established triangle of military figures—Hummel, Ardell, and Sergeant Tower—is repeated, for example, throughout Act Two as a model both of a social hierarchy and of the divided self. Further, as Rabe's commentary suggests, *Pavlo Hummel* derives its considerable impact from the directorial vision which enlarged its scope to focus not only on the pathetic fool, but also on the stage world which engulfs and defines him.

So the play ends where it began: still posturing, Hummel is placed into his coffin and left alone *"in real light"* onstage (p. 109). In this way the play comes full circle: as one hallucination gives way to another, Hummel stands still at attention, the constantly reemerging essence of a specter of a soldier. Like the inundating static and rhythm of the pop American music occasionally accompanying the action, each profane gesture and aggressive movement of Rabe's play serves as a repeated motif in a ritualized tour of duty. Ultimately, the documentary reality, evoked in part by sounds of colloquial Americanisms, machine gun fire, and exploding grenades, is heightened and made dreamlike by means of flashbacks and flashforwards. The strategic placement of typical scenes in a contrapuntal pattern of attack and withdrawal lends a surreal quality to Rabe's vision of the Vietnam war as an episodic obscenity.

THE REALITY of pain—the wrenching of life by a bayonet, the ooze of blood from a wound, the bodies crumbling into "pink mud" (p. 95)—is what sets Rabe's plays apart from other theatrical responses to Vietnam. The random violence of *Streamers* would time after time cause audiences to shudder or run out. But even in the early *Pavlo Hummel*, Rabe touches a raw nerve and he deromanticizes violence. Death can happen here:

CAPTAIN. You want to get killed, don't you, Hummel?
PAVLO. No, Sir. No.

CAPTAIN. And they will kill you, Hummel, if they get the chance. Do you believe that? That you will die if shot, or hit with shrapnel, that your arm can disappear into shreds, or your leg vanish—do you believe that, Hummel? That you can and will, if hit hard enough, gag and vomit and die . . . be buried and rot—do you believe yourself capable of that? . . .

PAVLO. Yes . . . Sir. I . . . do . . .

(p. 92)

But Pavlo, inspired by war movies, never really does believe that. What Pavlo wants is to be in touch with the power that will make him a man among men. He wants to kill but not to die, to be a hero, to have within him the instinct, "the thing that sergeant saw to make him know to shoot that kid and old man. I want to have it, know it, be it. . . . If I could be bone . . . If I could be bone. In my deepest part or center, if I could be bone" (p. 56).

But, of course, Pavlo cannot be bone through and through. He is just flesh and blood, and the horrible, simple epiphany that death brings him is "we tear. We rip apart . . . we tear" (p. 97). The play insists on demythifying death: we discover when the opening scene is more fully played out at the play's end that Pavlo is exploded by a hand grenade tossed at him by an American sergeant in a whorehouse fight. The play insists, then, on having Pavlo's unheroic death graphically followed through in a speech directed straight out into the audience by the phantom figure of Ardell:

He don't die right off. Take him four days, thirty-eight minutes. And he don't say nothin' to nobody in all that time. No words; he just kinda lay up and look, and when he die, he bitin' on his lower lip, I don't know why. So they take him, they put him in a blue rubber bag, zip it up tight, and haul him off to the morgue in the back of a quarter-ton, where he get stuck naked into the refrigerator 'long with the other boys killed

249

that day and the beer and cheese and tuna and stuff the guys who work at the morgue keep in the refrigerator except when it inspection time. The bag get washed, hung out to dry on a line out back a the morgue. . . . (pp. 106–107)

Pavlo's epiphany, then, his last answer to the mocking question, "You tell it to me: what you think of the cause? What you think a gettin' your ass blown clean off a freedom's frontier? What you think a bein' R.A. Regular Army lifer?" is hollow. "It all shit! . . . It shit. . . . SHIT!" he chants (pp. 107–108), laughing at the miserable dream, the haunting rhythm he followed to Vietnam.

Streamers

The violence and the mortality at the heart of *Pavlo Hummel*, a play about an exploded myth of war, take center stage in Rabe's *Streamers*, probably his best play so far. In *Streamers* Rabe heightens his graphic focus on the U.S. army and its knot of Vietnam. Instead of the disjunctive force of the institution that swallowed Pavlo Hummel whole, in *Streamers* the organizing, cohesive force of that institution is driven home onstage. Here, in a stateside cadre room holding three bunks, three recruits, joined only by their basic training and their fear of the Vietnam riddle, make a safe place for themselves. Living in a barracks in Virginia in 1965, before they are shipped to Asia, the recruits pride themselves on their area, their shared space, what they call repeatedly their "house." The thrust of *Streamers* is towards senseless violence, towards a random explosion, a desecration of that temporary "house."

The energy of *Streamers* is again rooted in the experience of Vietnam; but here, even more profoundly than in *Pavlo Hummel*, Rabe explores that experience as a no-exit conceit. He has himself alluded to the aspects of his Vietnam trilogy that extend stateside beyond Vietnam. "In *Pavlo*," he says, "[I] took on misconceptions of manhood. In *Sticks* it was

250

the family, propagation, religion and above all guilt feelings. When I got through there was nothing left to hang on to." Although this trilogy revolves about Vietnam, Rabe continues, "What I do is to examine human beings and I must have been carrying all this material around back in Dubuque before I went to Nam. The war was the triggering device that forced me to write. If I'd never gone to war, I might be playing pro football."[36]

This idea of the war as a "triggering device" that "forces" a mode of action or a mode of art is crucial in this context. Rabe, like other American chroniclers of the Vietnam experience, insists on particularizing that war while at the same time probing it for universals, for postwar metaphors about the way things are. Michael Herr's powerful *Dispatches*, for example, ends with the haunting, echoic, "And no moves left for me at all but to write down some few last words and make the dispersion, Vietnam Vietnam Vietnam, we've all been there."[37] *Streamers* also penetrates the war and its casualties on this universalizing level. In fact, Rabe tends to see much experience this way. "I took [my son] to the circus and he didn't like it. I didn't either," Rabe told an interviewer, explaining, "A lot of mismatched people confined in an environment, like the Army."[38]

The metaphorical level of *Streamers* is present most insistently in the title and in the two lifers, the sergeants who sing the title song, "Beautiful Streamers," a punning adaptation of "Beautiful Dreamer." First, the sergeants turn that melody into a parachutist's dirge for the moment beyond bravado in mid-air when he knows his chute will not open. Finally, that melody is turned into a universalizing song about all meaningless deaths, sung in what the sergeant considers Oriental-sounding nonsense syllables. The song is a motif, then, for *everyone* fallen in lost causes, in absurd wars. Discussing the composition of *Streamers* with an interviewer, Rabe recalled the play's autobiographical origins and he recalled the play's need for a metaphor to cement it, to transcend memory, to shape anecdote into action. So *Streamers* began, Rabe told the *New York Times'* Mel Gussow, with "things I was thinking about, snatches of conversations, things I've heard about, or was involved in, or that came out of the air." But as the play evolved, Rabe said, he brought in two sergeants, and with them came a form and a metaphor. The sergeants and the title metaphor, he said, make it a play instead of an incident. "All of a sudden when the sergeants came to visit, I knew what the play was about."[39]

And just what *is Streamers* about? Mike Nichols, who directed the play first at Connecticut's Long Wharf Theater and then at Lincoln Center's Mitzi Newhouse Theater, where it won the New York Drama Critics' Award as the Best American Play of 1976, says, "If the engine of the play is fear—if everyone is plunging toward earth, as maybe we all are—then what every character in the play runs into is the varied impulse to grab someone else in the short time left, and the equally varied rules about how that can or cannot be done. That's what ties it all together." Discussing what Mike Nichols termed "the engine of . . . fear" in *Streamers*, Rabe said, "The play is about people misunderstanding each other. The violence comes out of everybody lying to each other—the games, the lies, the masquerading, the maneuvering, are what make the violence happen."[40]

IF WE LOOK at how Rabe describes the process of *Streamers*— the everyday games and strategic interactions out of which violence erupts and in which it is quelled—the play's doubleness, its representational premise and its sudden lurch beyond logic, makes affective sense. The play begins in a barracks with its focus on the three recruits who are yoked together by circumstance into sudden friendships. Roger, a black recruit, has "been on the street" all his life, and with his roommates he has been "tryin' to come outa myself a little. Do like the fuckin' head shrinker been tellin' me to stop them fuckin' headaches I was havin', you know."[41] Billy, who has been fast friends with Roger ever since they met in P Company, when Billy was "the first white person" to "talk back friendly" to Roger (p. 58), is a small-town,

middle-class, college-educated recruit who is full of anecdotes about the eerie violence that penetrates life back home
in Wisconsin and who wonders about Vietnam. "Be a great
place to come back from, man, you know?" Billy says in
Act One. "I keep thinkin' about that. To have gone there,
to have been there, to have seen it and lived" (p. 30). And
Richie, whose ostentatious show of homosexuality worries
his two roommates into plans and pep talks to set him
straight, also lives in this "house." The tension of *Streamers*
is rooted in this idea of the house, of domain, of sanctuary.
The violence of Act Two, in fact, erupts when Billy asserts
his rights on this score. "It ain't gonna be done in my house,"
Billy tells Richie and the confused Carlyle who wants to
join in a game of taking turns with Richie, a game he only
imagines is going on here. "I don't have much in this god-
damn army," Billy says, "but this *here* is mine" (p. 83).

The violence in *Streamers* erupts with Carlyle, but it has
been brewing all along, both inside Carlyle *and* inside the
army. Billy's and Roger's anecdotes about life back home
are riddled with violence: Roger describes a man stabbed
in a phone booth trying to hide his wound under a coat
"like he's worried about how he looks" (p. 29); Billy describes a neighbor in Wisconsin gone berserk "who came
out of his house one morning with axes in both hands" and
started "attackin' the cars that were driving up and down
in front of his house. An' we all knew why he did it, sorta"
(pp. 56–57). The stories told by the sergeants about falling
without a chute and about sitting on the lid of a literally
human powder keg (after dropping a grenade into a Ko-
rean's spider hole) are also violent. At the end of the play
Sergeant Cokes retells this story with sleepy compassion:

> I'm never gonna forget him—how'm I ever gonna for-
> get him? I see him and dive, goddamn bullet hits me
> in the side, I'm mid-air, everything's turnin' around.
> I go over the edge of this ditch and I'm crawlin' real
> fast. I lost my rifle. Can't find it. Then I come up
> behind him. He's half out of the hole. I bang him on

top of his head, stuff him back into the hole with a grenade for company. Then I'm sittin' on the lid and it's made outa steel. I can feel him in there, though, bangin' and yellin' under me, and his yelling I can hear is begging for me to let him out. It was like a goddamn Charlie Chaplin movie, everybody fallin' down and clumsy, and him in there yellin' and bangin' away, and I'm just sittin' there lookin' around. And he was Charlie Chaplin. I don't know who I was. And then he blew up. (p. 108)

The action of the play proper also begins with an image of blood, of violence prefigured. The very first person we see onstage is Martin, a recruit who has attempted suicide. According to the opening stage directions, Martin is alone with Richie, and he is "*pacing, worried. A white towel stained red with blood is wrapped around his wrist*" (p. 4). Like the song of *Streamers*, this opening image foreshadows an even deeper wound—the later senseless, bloody murder of Billy and then of Sergeant Rooney by Carlyle in his rage at not belonging.

Carlyle is the grenade of *Streamers*, waiting to explode. When he first appears onstage he is looking for Roger: he has heard that a black man shares this house, and he is lonely for a voice from home. "It is so sweet out there," he tells Roger. "I had such a sweet, sweet time. They doin' dances, baby, make you wanna cry. I hate this damn army. . . . And this whole Vietnam THING—I do not dig it" (p. 21). Later in Act One, Carlyle returns drunk and hurting, crawling "like I was taught in basic." And he tries to communicate his pain to the three boys who tell stories and pointed anecdotes while Carlyle just says what he wants, expressing directly what the others will not admit:

Oh, sure, you guys don't care. I know it. You got it made. You got it made. I don't got it made. You got a little home here, got friends, people to talk to. I got nothin'. You got jobs they probably ain't ever gonna ship you out, you got so important jobs. I got no job.

They don't even wanna give me a job. I know it. They
are gonna kill me. They are gonna send me over there
to get me killed, goddammit. WHAT'S A MATTER
WITH ALL YOU PEOPLE? . . . I don't wanna be no
DEAD man. I don't wanna be the one they all thinkin'
is so stupid he's the only one'll go, they tell him; they
don't even have to give him a job. I got thoughts, man,
in my head; alla time, burnin', burnin' thoughts a un-
derstandin'. (p. 50)

Carlyle's thoughts, "burnin', burnin' " in his head, drive
him into a corner. He wants to be part of this group, but
he does not know how. He misunderstands the dynamics
of the situation. When he stabs Billy his reason is "I STUCK
HIM. I TURNED IT. This mother army break my heart.
I can't be out there where it pretty, don't wanna live!" (p.
91). In the world of *Streamers* that reason is as good, or as
senseless, as *any* for living, dying, or killing. As Dorian
Harewood, the actor who played Carlyle to critical acclaim,
points out:

Carlyle has a reason. We don't ask audiences to forgive
Carlyle, but I get a chance to show them *why* he does
what he does. At least you know there's something
going on inside him. I mean, he wasn't born to kill
people. He wants to belong. He just happened to grow
up in a violent environment. . . . I assume his home
was on the street, with a gang. . . . Now he's trying to
get along better in the Army, which he hates. He's
looking for a gimmick. He thinks Roger and Billy are
having affairs with the homosexual guy, Richie, and if
he did that, too, he'd be part of the group, he'd be
accepted. Only reason he ends up stabbing anybody is
he was feeling they were really gonna be one big family,
he's standing in the clubhouse door, and all of a sudden
they say, "You don't belong here."[42]

The audience's shock at *Streamers* has to do not with the
killing onstage or with the plenitude of stage blood, but

255

with the blast of pent-up violence, the immediacy of dying, the sapping of life as a joke and death as actual. The violence of this play—its *slow*, bloody, meaningless deaths—disturbed many people in its audience. Rabe has "put death senseless on the stage," argued some critics—Walter Kerr for one.[43] But, as in *Pavlo Hummel*, that is precisely the point. "The law of realistic drama says that cause and effect operate in a procedural way—and I don't think it does in life," says Rabe. "If you stop somebody in a subway, you might get a lecture—or you might get a knife in the ribs. . . . The fact that [the violence in *Streamers*] is upsetting means it is not gratuitous."[44] Rabe has also responded to audience dismay at the violent core of *Streamers* by saying, "It's like I must be doing something right, finally; to make violence unbearable, not salable. If people watching a human being knife another human being ask themselves, 'My God, why?' instead of shrugging it off, well, is that noncommercial violence or what? To me, it's theater's ability to reach people."[45]

The play even calls attention to the loss of logic at its fulcrum. Looking at the razor blade he has picked up in his bleeding palm, Billy realizes he does not have "A GOD-DAMN THING ON THE LINE HERE!" (p. 88). There is no cause to kill. But while in *Pavlo Hummel*, where lives ebb into pink mud in a jungle and where "you can and will, if hit hard enough, gag and vomit and die" (p. 92), in *Streamers* Carlyle can only lash out in anger and warn, "I SAY! CAN'T YOU LET PEOPLE BE?" When Billy then "*hurls his sneaker at the floor at* CARLYLE's *feet*," Carlyle is, according to the stage directions, "*instantly . . . across the room, blocking* BILLY's *escape out the door.*" "Goddamn you, boy!" Carlyle says, switchblade in hand. "I'm gonna cut your ass, just to show you how it feel—and cuttin' can happen. This knife true" (pp. 85–86).

As in *Pavlo Hummel*, then, in this army barracks at the edge of the Vietnam war, "this knife true." And as in *Pavlo Hummel*, the knife is the *only* truth here; it is the only connection possible. Billy's long speech—about his having nothing on the line here and about his refusal to be changed into a violent man even if that means giving up his sovereignty in the house he shares—goes right over Carlyle's head. Carlyle does not understand reasoning; he does not hear Billy's resigned, conciliatory message; he hears only the angry sound of someone in his way. His knifing is an arbitrary spasm, a visceral response to the hostile sound of a logic beyond his ken.

Streamers moves from one emphasis—an emphasis on military routine, a referential demonstration of a way of life—to a more profound emphasis on the hopelessness and despair of those people trapped in the world onstage, which is finally an analogue of our world. Audience expectations are set up (ah, yes, we tell ourselves as we settle in, a slice of army life) and then, as the emphasis shifts to a larger image, to an image of apocalypse now as part of everyday life, audience expectations are broken down. Again, as is common in contemporary plays of impasse, this organization of audience response is intensified in production: by heightening the script's opening emphasis on politics, homosexuality, and race (social issues), the production also heightens the play's final strength, its juxtaposition of these finally inconsequential matters with the tangible process of a bleeding wound.

No matter what happens, in *Streamers*, as in other plays of impasse, the situation endures. Foremost among the factors shaping audience response to *Streamers* (and to *Pavlo Hummel*) are incremental repetition and allusively precipitated violence in a world gone military, a world going to Vietnam, a world gone awry. In a world shot to hell, the yearning for human contact that might propel an old-fashioned play (O'Neill's *The Hairy Ape*, say) is a joke. For everybody finally learns to get by, to live on, like Beckett's tramps dead sure there is nothing to be done, dead sure that everything that acts is, to use Artaud's term, "a cruelty"[46] and, as Albee's *Zoo Story* demonstrates in its depiction of a comparable pathetic attempt to make contact, "what is gained is loss."[47] Human contact is fleeting and it hurts; it is a knife twisted in the belly; it is a song sung to a dying fall.

So the bits and comic routines of *Streamers*—especially its title song—shape our response. As in *Endgame*, when life becomes a terrifying joke at which we can no longer laugh, in *Streamers* and in *Pavlo Hummel*, all those comic segments of Act One are played out again in another key in Act Two, and we are disturbed by narrative returned in form and movement. This is Rabe's risk, and this is where his power lies: in a crystallizing frame of adjustment to a system which promises nothing, a system in which parachutes may not open, a system which can kill a man from within, can wrench his gut or weaken his blood, can deny his sexual or racial identity, and can make a longing for a connection to others the most deadly game—in this context, Rabe replays his jokes and risks our laughter.

But we cannot laugh at that last refrain of *Streamers* sung in nonsense syllables; by then, it has become an energized image, and its closing recurrence is powerful. Like *Pavlo Hummel, Streamers'* final entropic vision catapults the Vietnam experience homeward. In these two plays, especially, Rabe shows that even if some critics worry that "it may turn out, as it so far appears, that the Vietnam War is novel-proof, that only poetry and nonfiction can convey the truths of that mind-numbing debacle,"[48] the Vietnam war is *by no means* drama-proof. Rabe's plays transcend the protest plays' topicality. They go beyond the irritating self-righteousness of protest plays which, as John Lahr aptly described them, "are usually as insistent and as righteously stubborn as the Ancient Mariner: they buttonhole you at the celebration and won't let go."[49] Rabe's Vietnam plays, however, like the phenomenon of war itself, make the rules of a deadly game clear and sharp; they put both body and spirit on the line, and then they explode. A burst of violence in *Streamers*, like Pavlo's transformation into a specter of a soldier in *The Basic Training of Pavlo Hummel* and like the passout parade in *Chips With Everything*, releases tension. But the conditions of a play of impasse—its boundaries and its schemes, the lines beyond which it cannot pass—are aspects of mortality and of real fear, of real space and time that remain fixed and potentially terrifying.

A DREAM OF ORDER

MOST OF THE PLAYWRIGHTS I have discussed in this study are repeaters. Once they set a play in a total institution and explore life within bounds, they tend to do it—or something formally akin to it—again. In addition to *The National Health,* Peter Nichols has written *The Freeway* (1974) about "The Great Traffic Jam" as well as *Privates on Parade* (1977). Peter Weiss has followed his extraordinary *Marat/Sade* with *The Investigation,* pieced together from the transcript of the Auschwitz trial held in Frankfurt from 1963–1965. This list goes on: Jean Genet's *The Balcony* (1956) limits action to a brothel, a grand "House of Illusions." Arnold Wesker confined his first play to a restaurant's *Kitchen* (1956) and a more recent play, *The Journalists* (1971), to a newspaper office. Arthur Kopit's *Indians* (1968) is a Wild West show. And David Storey has practically made a career in the theater out of plays of impasse, set in social Structures. Except for his first play about a homecoming, *In Celebration* (1969), the action of all of Storey's plays—*The Contractor* (1970), *The Changing Room* (1972), *The Farm* (1973), and *Life Class* (1974)—has been rigidly controlled by the laws of the space they inhabit.

In addition to the many referred to in passing throughout this study, other contemporary playwrights have also modeled their plays on social Structures and institutional settings. Plays set in prisons, for example, abound. Slawomir Mrozek's *The Police* is a socialist allegory; Megan Terry's *Keep Tightly Closed in a Cool Dry Place,* like Ronald Ribman's *The Poison Tree,* uses savage games and dreamlike routines to suggest the codes of mechanized men, rotting in a cell (suggesting comparisons with Genet's more comprehensive *Deathwatch*); Maria Irene Fornes's *Promenade* is a vaudevillian version of jail (indebted to Behan's *The Quare Fellow*); John Herbert's *Fortune and Men's Eyes* and Miguel Pinero's *Short Eyes* testify to the unremitting mass appeal of social realism immersed in a prison melodrama; Fernando Arrabal's *And They Put Handcuffs on the Flowers* is a surrealistic treatment of a contemporary Spanish prison; and Athol Fugard's *The Island* depicts Robben Island, South Africa's maximum security prison housing black political offenders.

On the contemporary stage, the asylum setting is similarly ubiquitous. Alluding to Dürrenmatt's *The Physicists* and to John Patrick's *The Curious Savage* in his review of *Marat/ Sade*, Walter Kerr commented on their "use of a madhouse as a means of dislocating and thereby refocusing the action."[1] Joe Orton's *What the Butler Saw*, Dale Wasserman's adaptation of Ken Kesey's *One Flew Over the Cuckoo's Nest*, and Terrence McNally's *Bad Habits* are examples of other recent plays turning mental institutions into social metaphors.

There has also been a slew of plays of impasse set in work places that are not quite *total* institutions, that is, they are not inclusive of all daily activities, as specified in Erving Goffman's model of a total institution. The underlying formal similarity between sickbed plays and plays of barroom revelations, for example, has been noted by Walter Kerr in his *New York Times* article mentioned in the introduction. As Ted Hoffman notes in an essay on recent American drama, the subject of the "paralysis of death and despair" caused Kerr,

> whose three decades of criticism calls for an American drama based on the imaginative power of popular forms and the positive verities of American life, [to observe] in his column, "Confrontations With Mortality" (*The New York Times*, July 2, 1978), that the 1970s drama was preoccupied with the themes of illness, death and dying, and despair. In a society where people live longer

261

and in which many more people die of wasting disease, the subject is much on our minds. It seems as if the characters of the sum of the outstanding plays of the second half of the decade, including *The Shadow Box*, *Wings*, *Ashes*, *Cold Storage*, and *The Gin Game*, had congregated with us for one long last drink at "The Last Chance Saloon" where "we hoist glasses, clink them, and do our broken but earnest best to probe for the conversation we were told we couldn't have, the conversation we'd never had time for, the conversation we know we were born to."[2]

Most prominent among these plays of impasse which glue characters (and audience) to a claustrophobic space—not quite a *total* institution, but nonetheless a place of codified behavior where loss is felt as a condition of survival—are plays set in bars or restaurants, theaters, and schools.

A state of impasse located in bars or restaurants is most profoundly represented by Eugene O'Neill's *The Iceman Cometh*, Tennessee Williams's *Small Craft Warnings*, Athol Fugard's *'Master Harold'* . . . *and the boys*, and Arnold Wesker's *The Kitchen*. Larry, the "foolosopher" of *The Iceman Cometh* (1940), lays it all right on the line when he identifies Harry Hope's saloon:

> What is it? It's the No Chance Saloon. It's Bedrock Bar, The End of the Line Café, The Bottom of the Sea Rathskeller! Don't you notice the beautiful calm in the atmosphere? That's because it's the last harbor. No one here has to worry about where they're going next, because there is no farther they can go. It's a great comfort to them. Although even here they keep up the appearances of life with a few harmless pipe dreams about their yesterdays and tomorrows, as you'll see for yourself if you're here long.[3]

Other, lesser plays of impasse of the past few years that are set in restaurants include: Lee Jackson's *Ladies in Waiting*, Tina Howe's *The Art of Dining*, Ed Graczyk's *Come Back to the Five and Dime, Jimmy Dean, Jimmy Dean*, Mark Medoff's *When You Comin' Back, Red Ryder?*, and Terry Curtis Fox's *Cops*, a play set in the quintessential greasy-spoon diner, detailed like a George Segal sculpture, like what Mark Rothko once called "walk-in Hoppers."[4]

Plays that are self-consciously about life in the theater, following the Pirandellian model, include Genet's *The Blacks*, a performance of funeral rites, Günter Grass's *The Plebians Rehearse the Uprising*, Tom Stoppard's *Rosencrantz and Guildenstern are Dead* and *The Real Inspector Hound*, Joseph Heller's *We Bombed in New Haven*, David Mamet's *A Life in the Theater*, Christopher Durang's *The Actor's Nightmare*, and John Osborne's *The Entertainer*. Goffman has described plays that mock their own theatricality, plays that break down conventional boundaries separating audience from actors and actors from characters, as "the theater of frames." Using *We Bombed in New Haven* and *The Blacks* as immediate examples, Goffman writes:

> The bridge ordinarily available for crossing from one sphere to the other—houselights, prologue, preface, tuning up—is simply absorbed into the inner doings, forcing the audience to drink out of the handle of their cup. Similarly, an attack on any other specific element of the frame can be extended to a whole episode of framed activity, threatening thereby to flood the game into the spectacle and mingle performer with onlooker, character with theatergoer. For example, once a character begins to address the issue of the performer who is sustaining him, it is a small step to extending the syntactical breach by addressing directly the whole matter of the show under presentation.
>
> The so-called theater of the absurd provides many examples of this totalistic attack—in fact, so many that one might better call it the theater of frames.[5]

In this context, the last line of *The Entertainer* (1957) is one of the most powerful frame-breaking, dislocating endings in contemporary drama. Archie Rice, the music hall performer, sings to us one last time; he stops, the music goes on, he puts on his coat, takes his hat, and comes down towards us to say: "You've been a good audience. Very good. A very *good* audience. Let me know where you're working tomorrow night—and I'll come and see YOU."[6]

Notable among the many plays emphasizing the school as a Structure in contemporary drama, especially since Calder Willingham's *End as a Man* and Lindsay Anderson's film, *If*, are such plays as Harold Pinter's *Night School*, Israel Horovitz's *The Primary English Class*, David Storey's art school *Life Class*, Trevor Griffith's *Comedians*, Simon Gray's character study, *Butley*, and Roberto Athayde's *Miss Margarida's Way*. *Miss Margarita's Way*, a one-woman play which Estelle Parsons has performed in actual lecture halls on college campuses across America, is most extreme in its treatment of the school as a Structure. For as Miss Margarita harangues her students/audience, the line between an actual event and a play is blurred.

The documentary aspect of the contemporary mode, with its stress on an accurate rendering of the Structure and of the facts, is evident also in the many documentary-rooted courtroom plays and in some plays set in concentration camps. Giving rise to the popular term "docu-drama" are such plays as Daniel Berrigan's *The Trial of the Catonsville Nine*, Eric Bentley's *Are You Now or Have You Ever Been*, Peter Weiss's *The Investigation*, Donald Freed's multi- media *Inquest*, and Rolf Hochhuth's *The Deputy*. Audiences at Jerzy Grotowski's *Acropolis* were surrounded by actors recreating the experience of a concentration camp. On Broadway, Martin Sherman's *Bent* moved melodrama into a concentration camp. For television, Arthur Miller adapted the memoirs of a camp survivor, *Playing for Time*. There has even been a play, *Laughter!* by Peter Barnes, set for the first half in Tsarist Russia, then for the second half in Auschwitz.

Further, there has been an onslaught of plays of impasse which frame restricted action in the workplace. In *The New York Times* in 1981, Mel Gussow speculated about the abundance of what he dubbed "occupational dramas." Gussow wrote:

Taking a cue from Britain's David Storey, dramatists have increasingly been writing plays about shared work activities. The method is not as easy as it seems. The result can be simply a slice of life rather than a microcosm rising into metaphor. In the words of a character in a recent example of the genre, "What you see is what you get." Plays have taken place in a second-hand resale shop, an all-night diner, bars, a gourmet restaurant, an art gallery and a shoeshine parlor. In each case, one can learn something new and useful. By that, I do not mean moral or philosophical truths, but simple, everyday lessons, such as how to steam a bass, spit-shine shoes or mix colors in a dye factory.[7]

The key phrase here is "microcosm rising into metaphor." Plays of impasse begin with a slice of contemporary life, bounded by the controls of what Malina called "The World As It Is." But that is just the start. From there on, such plays attempt to use the familiar to explore larger issues of the self in society. Often using total institutions such as hospitals, insane asylums, prisons, or military training camps as both setting *and* subject, the plays upon which I have focused in this book (Nichols's *The National Health*, Weiss's *Marat/Sade*, Storey's *Home*, Genet's *Deathwatch*, and Rabe's *The Basic Training of Pavlo Hummel*, for example) tend to engulf and then to exclude the audience, turning an encompassing stage setting—a closed, controlling, absolute system—into a protagonist and turning the theater itself into a psychosocial model. There has been a major shift in focus from modern drama to contemporary plays of impasse: the shift is from the active hero (in the past he might have been the kind doctor, the thought-tormented psychiatrist, the reformist warden, or the brave general) to reactive groups (patients, inmates, prisoners, conscripts) who are objects of the actions taken by the Structure, which looms larger than them all.

The form and effect of such plays often depend upon directorial or ensemble decisions, which sometimes negotiate anew the boundaries separating actors and audience. Central to this study, therefore, has been a focus on the dynamics of drama, on how audience response is shaped by a theatrical event, how that event is itself shaped by its historical frame of reference and by rehearsal methods, and how the audience, the script, and the preparation for performance fit into Peter Brook's equation that reads: Theater $= R$ (repetition or rehearsal) $\times r$ (representation or performance) $\times a$ (assistance or audience attendance). Such a study of the *process* of theater, a kinetic art, is quite a challenge; after all, even Peter Brook acknowledges the insufficiency of his Theater $= Rra$ formula. These interacting elements precipitate a theatrical experience; but, as Brook notes, "the essence is still lacking, because any three words are static. . . . Truth in the theater is always on the move."[8] Central to the discussions here, then, have been considerations of such productions as Joan Littlewood's music hall treatment of Behan's *The Quare Fellow*, John Dexter's stylization of movement in Wesker's *Chips With Everything*, Judith Malina's rigid control of Brown's *The Brig*, and Peter Brook's harrowing version of Weiss's *Marat/Sade*.

It is remarkable that such a list of contemporary plays whose action is driven forward and circumscribed by a dominating Structure can be assembled. Even more remarkable is the name I would put at the top of the list: Samuel Beckett. The action of his plays evoke what Peter Brook calls the "essence" of theater and what Artaud calls the "cruelty" of theater, its formal truth. Moreover, the action of his plays, particularly *Endgame*, expresses the contemporary mode in a distilled form.

A MODAL PICTURE of plays of impasse can now be outlined. The characteristics of plays of impasse are especially apparent in the most straightforwardly purgatorial plays set in total institutions (*Deathwatch* and *Streamers*, for example), where locked-in characters endure each other's presence in a claustrophobic no man's land. As characteristics of plays of impasse are outlined, characteristics of contemporary plays in general will also emerge.

Plays of impasse are modeled, then, along the following lines:

1. The ground (or basis for action) is established the moment we see the set; it is a recognizable milieu, with boundaries and proprieties familiar to us; we are freighted with knowledge of its codes and rules, of its laws.

2. Stereotypical characters are pitted against each other and against the Structure. Squabbles and individual differences ensue. Sequences of everyday action, games, and redundant fights occur.

3. Gradually, the impelling agent seems to be the barracks, the prison, the madhouse, the hospital, the enclosed space, the Structure, rather than any of the figures onstage. This is a crucial point. The set is protagonist; characters react rather than act; individuals are ineffectual, finally powerless. A corollary of this is that the quality and kind of resistance becomes more complex as individuals seem to resist immersion in The World-As-It-Is onstage. They fight with each other often to avoid facing the situation, the futility that engulfs them.

4. A communal project, a spine—to make contact or to get away, finally, just to get by and to go on—emerges.[9] By indirection, using songs, stories, chores, etc., the characters grope towards each other, trying to realize this project. Action is attenuated; characters tell anecdotes, clean up, fulfill duties, engage in nondramatic repetitious tasks (in *Streamers*, they do pushups, for example, and in *The Brig*, they wash the floor). Typically, characters tell anecdotes to pass the time. Characters in plays of impasse want to *kill* time.

5. There is a moment of violence that seems to emerge

from the conflicts of the characters, but is really a rebellion against the Structure. The rebellion, an explosion against the system which generates it, fails. It tests the Structure and loses. Plays of impasse push on, going against the traditional idea of a dramatic climax.

6. After the tension is released, there is a return to normal. Characters return to their earlier pattern of activities, but their actions are performed in a somewhat sadder key once they realize there is no way out. Though survivors onstage seem shattered, the now clearly abysmal Structure endures.

Plays set in total institutions, the most evident Structures with suggestive power in post-World War II western culture, typify this model of contemporary drama.

The further contention of this book—that contemporary plays set in more subtle, more philosophical, or even homey Structures also conform to this model, that this model is as common among contemporary playwrights as was the five-act form among French classical playwrights—is borne out by a consideration of *Endgame*, the definitive postmodern play by our greatest playwright. Growing out of the tradition of Yeats's *Purgatory*, but conceived in a world whose horrors Yeats's age could not have fathomed, *Endgame* combines in a nutshell all the aspects of the types of plays of impasse I have identified in this book: (a) the contemporary Structure—an oppressive, enclosing set, rendered with naturalistic precision; (b) the thematic metaphor—the entropic world, presented ironically; and (c) the controlling image—impasse.

Endgame

ONE WORD keeps cropping up in this study. Time and again it describes the irresolute endings of institutional plays of impasse. The word is "endgame." Samuel Beckett's *Endgame* is a play of impasse abstracted. The contemporary mode of waiting to get out yet not moving, a mode made clear in plays set in institutions, is stripped bare, expressed directly in Beckett's *Endgame*, in the minimal world of that play winding down towards isolation and death. *Endgame* is the quintessential contemporary play: it conforms to the modal picture outlined in the discussion above as it abstracts a Structure to the walls of a room and two tiny windows out of reach, facing nothing, a "corpsed" earth.[10]

Endgame begins with the phrase "Finished, it's finished, nearly finished, it must be nearly finished" (p. 1), a refrain echoing throughout the play. Hamm, bleeding and in pain, is dependent on Clov—his servant, sometimes like his found son, his amanuensis, his complement, his sight, his legs— for everything. Precisely because he depends on Clov, Hamm despises him. He barks his needs at Clov as if they had the power of commands. And Hamm wants more than serv- ice—his painkiller, his dog; he wants Clov to listen to his novel-in-progress, to join in his repartee, to bring him his toy dog, to touch him, to care. For his part, Clov is in bad shape, too: there are no more bicycle wheels, no more rat poison, no more food, no more painkillers, Clov's legs ache, he has a "*stiff, staggering walk*" (p. 1).

Together, Hamm and Clov get on with it. Early in the play, Hamm asks Clov about the choices in a cul-de-sac world. Here, as elsewhere in the contemporary mode, either one gets used to the world or one grows to hate it more and more:

HAMM. Have you not had enough?
CLOV. Yes!
    (*Pause.*)
    Of what?
HAMM. Of this . . . this . . . thing?
CLOV. I always had.
    (*Pause.*)
    Not you?
HAMM (*gloomily*). Then there's no reason for it to change.

CLOV. It may end.
(*Pause.*)
All life long the same questions, the same answers.

(p. 5)

This sameness carries over to the stories recounted: the old stories are the best stories as the dying of the light, or "something"—whatever it is—is "taking its course" (p. 13). "I love the old questions," Hamm says "*with fervour*" later. "Ah the old questions, the old answers, there's nothing like them!" (p. 38).

Hamm and Clov are not alone in their shell of a Structure. Hamm's parents—"accursed progenitor!"—Nagg and Nell, "the old folks at home," live in this "shelter," too, outside of which "it's death" (pp. 9, 3). Nagg and Nell live in Beckett's theater poem in their own Structures, coffin-like boxes, ashbins. Though still barely alive, they are entombed in their ashbins, a concrete metaphor—like the "end beds" of *The National Health* or the Happy Haven itself—for a social phenomenon, the discarding of the aged.

The ashbins also objectify an inner state: they are a projection of Hamm's mental picture of his parents' place in his little, shrinking life. Like the props and sounds of *Wings*, filtered through one character's consciousness, like Winnie's being buried very much alive in the sand of *Happy Days*, the ashbins housing Nagg and Nell resonate as psychological as well as social metaphors made actual: in Hamm's mind—his only remaining site for action—this is where and how his parents live. Side by side, but in separate compartments, they are locked, imprisoned inches apart.

Unable to reach each other for an embrace, for a scratch, Nagg and Nell also make the best of a bad situation. Bound together by a lifetime of shared memory and desire, Nagg and Nell entertain each other with private jokes, and they share whatever pap, sugarplums, or biscuits are tossed their way. And it is up to Nell to articulate the idea of the cosmic joke at the heart of *Endgame*, the definitive post-modern play. "Nothing is funnier than unhappiness, I grant you that," she says. "Yes, yes, it's the most comical thing in the world. And we laugh, we laugh, with a will, in the beginning. But it's always the same thing. Yes, it's like the funny story we have heard too often, we still find it funny, but we don't laugh any more" (pp. 18–19).

At the exact center of *Endgame* is Hamm. In Hamm's cranky misery, Beckett locates an ironic image of loss and degeneration. Physically, Hamm is limited to his wheelchair, according to the opening stage directions, *"an armchair on castors, covered with an old sheet"* (p. 1), a kind of throne on wheels. The wheelchair is limited to one room. "Take me for a little turn," he tells Clov, "Right round the world!" (p. 25). With effort, then, Clov pushes Hamm about his shrinking world, his room. And even within this limited space, there is room for variation. Hamm, the invalid, wants everything just so. Aiming to end up smack in the center of his domain, after their tour of the walls of his world, Hamm fussily calls for slight adjustments of his unwieldy chair. He explains:

> I feel a little too far to the left.
> (*Clov moves chair slightly.*)
> Now I feel a little too far to the right.
> (*Clov moves chair slightly.*)
> I feel a little too far forward.
> (*Clov moves chair slightly.*)
> Now I feel a little too far back.
> (*Clov moves chair slightly.*)
> Don't stay there,
> (*i.e. behind the chair.*)
> you give me the shivers.
> (*Clov returns to his place beside the chair.*)
>
> (p. 27)

Tied together like the tramps in *Waiting for Godot*, bound within "Hollow bricks!" (p. 26), Clov and Hamm get along by means of games, memories, anecdotes, and activities like going "right round the world!" Clov usually humors his boss's whims. After adjusting the chair "Bang in the center!" he says aloud to us and to himself, "If I could kill him I'd die happy" (p. 27).

Hamm ignores Clov's role-distancing asides. Moving towards immobility, towards the completely unknowable shapelessness of God—suffering from "the heights of divine apathia divine athambia divine aphasia," according to Lucky's sputtered pronouncement in *Waiting for Godot*[11]— Hamm wants attention paid to himself alone. At the end of his rope in a world where, he is informed by Clov, all is "corpsed" outside (p. 30), Hamm foresees Clov's parallel decline. When Clov grudgingly acknowledges that though his eyes are bad he sees, and though his legs are bad he walks, he can "come . . . and go," Hamm reminds him, "In my house." Then, according to the stage directions, "*with prophetic relish*" Hamm describes the process of aging, wearying of life, waiting alone:

> One day you'll be blind, like me. You'll be sitting there, a speck in the void, in the dark, for ever, like me.
> (*Pause.*)
> One day you'll say to yourself, I'm tired, I'll sit down, and you'll go and sit down. Then you'll say, I'm hungry, I'll get up and get something to eat. But you won't get up. You'll say, I shouldn't have sat down, but since I have I'll sit on a little longer, then I'll get up and get something to eat. But you won't get up and you won't get anything to eat.
> (*Pause.*)
> You'll look at the wall a while, then you'll say, I'll close my eyes, perhaps have a little sleep, after that I'll feel better, and you'll close them. And when you open them again there'll be no wall any more.
> (*Pause.*)
> Infinite emptiness will be all around you, all the resurrected dead of all the ages wouldn't fill it, and there you'll be like a little bit of grit in the middle of the steppe.
> (*Pause.*)

Yes, one day you'll know what it is, you'll be like me, except that you won't have anyone with you, because you won't have had pity on anyone and because there won't be anyone left to have pity on. (p. 36)

In this bitter prophecy about being imprisoned in a body, about the breakdown of a body's ability to respond to stimuli, Hamm described the "infinite emptiness" all around, enveloping the dying in a diminishing world. He describes here a state of impasse, of imprisonment in one's own dying body—the "heart fastened" (as Yeats puts it in "Sailing to Byzantium") to a "dying animal."

At moments like this one, Hamm's short temper, his grouchiness and bossiness make naturalistic as well as symbolic sense. He is in anguish; the play is his death cry, his rage against what Dylan Thomas names "the dying of the light." "I see my light dying," says Clov early on. In response Hamm explodes: "Your light dying! Listen to that! Well, it can die just as well here, *your* light. Take a look at me and then come back and tell me what you think of *your* light" (p. 12). *Endgame* is Hamm's dirge for the joy of life wasted, consumed, petrified in a dream of yesterday. In this Structure enlivened now only by feeble squabbles and hasty apologies, Hamm sighs, "Yesterday! What does that mean? Yesterday!" and Clov responds *"violently,"* "That means that bloody awful day, long ago, before this bloody awful day. I use the words you taught me. If they don't mean anything any more, teach me others. Or let me be silent" (pp. 43–44).

In this almost unspeakable spot of time, Hamm reminisces about perspective. He creates an analogy for this isolation, for this inner endgame, each man finally alone, having to fend for himself in a larger Structure, each man finally seeing only the ashes:

I once knew a madman who thought the end of the world had come. He was a painter—and engraver. I had a great fondness for him. I used to go and see him, in the asylum. I'd take him by the hand and drag

273

him to the window. Look! There! All that rising corn!
And there! Look! The sails of the herring fleet! All
that loveliness!
(*Pause.*)
He'd snatch away his hand and go back into his corner.
Appalled. All he had seen was ashes.
(*Pause.*)
He alone had been spared.
(*Pause.*)
Forgotten.
(*Pause.*)
It appears the case is . . . was not so . . . so unusual.

(p. 44)

On this "day like any other day. . . . As long as it lasts. . . .
All life long the same inanities" (p. 45), then, Hamm and
Clov keep trying to make a connection with the past, to
make order. They even try unsuccessfully to pray. In this
place of impasse—this place between the living and the
dead—Hamm knows, "The end is in the beginning and yet
you go on" (p. 69), while Clov tries to make some order.
"I love order. It's my dream," he says. "A world where all
would be silent and still and each thing in its last place,
under the last dust" (p. 57).

This world where, if only Clov could have his way, "all
would be silent and still," is a minimal version of the stifling
Structure common to plays of impasse. According to the
play's opening stage directions, the set consists of:

Bare interior.
Grey light.
Left and right back, high up, two small windows, curtains
drawn.
Front right, a door. Hanging near door, its face to wall, a
picture.
Front left, touching each other, covered with an old sheet,
two ashbins.
Center, in an armchair on castors, covered with an old sheet,
Hamm.

Motionless by the door, his eyes fixed on Hamm, Clov. Very red face.
Brief tableau. (p. 1)

In this minimal Structure, a room with a king and his pawn, two ashbins, and little else, Beckett plays out the moves of impasse: the tired jokes, the attempts at contact, the pecking order, the "corpsed" world outside, the fragmented life sustained by memories of art, a dream of order.

The tension between entropy and order, between strength sapped and the tenacity of will, between physical restraints or incapacities and the energy to play—the tension of a play of impasse—is central in *Endgame*. This tension is objectified in the relationship between Hamm and Clov. Finally dying not just of bloody wounds, but simply "of darkness" (p. 75), Hamm asks for "A few words . . . from your heart." Clov's answer, delivered "*tonelessly, towards auditorium,*" is a vision of the beauty of art and order:

> They said to me, That's love, yes, yes, not a doubt, now you see how. . . . How easy it is. They said to me, That's friendship, yes, yes, no question, you've found it. They said to me, Here's the place, stop, raise your head and look at all that beauty. That order! They said to me, Come now, you're not a brute beast, think upon these things and you'll see how all becomes clear. And simple! They said to me, What skilled attention they get, all these dying of their wounds. . . . Then one day, suddenly, it ends, it changes, I don't understand, it dies, or it's me, I don't understand, that either. I ask the words that remain—sleeping, waking, morning, evening. They have nothing to say.
> (*Pause.*)
> I open the door of the cell and go. . . . I say to myself that the earth is extinguished, though I never saw it lit. (pp. 80–81)

This vision of art and order disintegrating beyond language's capacity to explain or even to chronicle it holds the

275

stage. Hamm cannot match it and he concedes defeat. "Old endgame lost of old, play and lose and have done with losing," he says "*wearily*" (p. 82).

Clov watches Hamm end. Clov says he is leaving the "cell," the Structure, but we see him silhouetted in the shadows, "*his eyes fixed on* HAMM, *till the end*" (p. 82). Thinking himself alone, Hamm "*gives up*," he discards his whistle, his toy dog, he covers his face with his handkerchief, and he succumbs to the throbbing in his head. Thinking himself alone in the Structure, Hamm dies alone.

This Structure in which Hamm finally dies has been variously described as Hamm's head, a chessboard, a prison cell, a post-atomic shelter. There is room here for all of these responses, for the overdetermined Structure outside of which "it's death" (p. 9)—the Structure to which Hamm is sentenced—is an abstract, condensed version of what I have been describing throughout this book as a place of impasse. Whether an old age home, a prison, or a chessboard, the setting of plays in the contemporary mode is final, and it is the boldest thing onstage.

Epilogue

The poem of the mind in the act of finding
What will suffice. It has not always had
To find: the scene was set; it repeated what
Was in the script.
       Then the theatre was changed
To something else. Its past was a souvenir.
It has to be living, to learn the speech of the place.
It has to face the men of the time and to meet
The women of the time. It has to think about war
And it has to find what will suffice. It has
To construct a new stage. . . . The actor is
A metaphysician in the dark. . . .
       Wallace Stevens, "Of Modern Poetry"

Wallace Stevens's poem is oddly prophetic in the light of this book: the contemporary theater has indeed had "to construct a new stage." Throughout this book, as I have considered the recurrent spatial and temporal patterns in post-World War II drama, I have also considered the correlation between a mode of art and its time, trying to see, in formal terms, just how contemporary drama has found "what will suffice" as it gropes about, its actors "metaphysicians in the dark" of our time, having "to think about war" and about questions of humanity haunting us in a post-World War II world. "What will suffice" is a mode of impasse, plays set in closed systems, where the splintered self, like the divided society, strives to endure against enormous, codified odds. The contemporary dramatic mode finally seems to be characterized by sparse, introspective action in an onstage model of a world gone awry, a world without reprieves.

Each chapter has emphasized a different aspect of this mode in which we are witness to the onstage "insurrection of subjugated knowledges," as defined by Michel Foucault. Foucault means two things by subjugated knowledges: first, he means "meticulous, erudite, exact historical knowledge," and second, he means "local and specific . . . naive knowledges, located low down on the hierarchy, beneath the required level of cognition or scientificity." Discussing criticisms of asylums and prisons, Foucault writes:

> I . . . believe that it is through the re-emergence of these low-ranking knowledges, these unqualified, even directly disqualified knowledges (such as that of the psychiatric patient, of the ill person, of the nurse, of the doctor—parallel and marginal as they are to the knowledge of medicine—that of the delinquent etc.), and which involve what I would call a popular knowledge (*le savoir des gens*) . . . a differential knowledge incapable of unanimity and which owes its force only to the harshness with which it is opposed by everything surrounding it—that it is through the re-appearance

of this knowledge, of these local popular knowledges, these disqualified knowledges, that criticism performs its work.[12]

A parallel approach is taken by contemporary playwrights. They rediscover for us a world we thought we knew; they show us by means of marginal, low-ranking knowledges the way the power of the Structure works. In the hospital plays, the idea of Structure as metaphor is central; in the asylum plays, the "secular myth of self-transcendence" is mocked, made ironic; in the prison plays, the ritualistic feeling of a routine is stressed; and in the military plays, the idea of warfare as a game, the image of man the player, locked in a combat zone, takes the stage. And *Endgame* seems almost to be a meta-play of impasse: the *Endgame* Structure is at once a metaphor, an exploded myth, a space for ritualistic action, and a chance for self-conscious theatricality, for play. In its ironic discussion of the way things are as well as in its silhouette of action, its tableau of stasis—a dying man in a wheelchair, the servant at the door—it distills the action of plays in the contemporary mode. In every play, characters have been props, living and fading, but with a subjugated knowledge to impart to us about their place in the world onstage. The Structure itself has seemed purgatorial, like a wasteland, delineating contemporary life in a parenthesis, at an impasse.

The state of impasse permeates the Structure by means of the stilled action. Always literally depicted, the Structure is first an actual, then a metaphor, an idea, and finally an image. We move from a sense of nonfictive, naturalistic presentation, that is, from a documentary rendering which digests the meaning of life in an institution, towards a fictive construct, that is, towards an image of life ebbing, towards a sense of being in the presence of life consumed by a Structure. A final dislocating action—sometimes direct address to the audience breaking the frame of action, sometimes a bizarre plot twist, sometimes a cycle spiraling—ends these plays, jolting us into a sense of the irreparable distinction between play and reality, between a theatrical construct that seems actual and the social model on which it is based.

The impulse for this mode has to do with its tensions: between naturalism and symbolism, between actual and play. Jean Duvignaud's overview of contemporary theater's place in life is useful in this context. Duvignaud writes:

> [A] characteristic feature of artistic creation in industrial societies is the change which has taken place in the collective perception of representations of human facts. The cinema and television (particularly the latter), ever since they have become influential, have given a theatrical dimension to human affairs. In other words, the detailed presentation of living history has actually become a factor in the way history is perceived, and this in turn implies an intense dramatization of man's life in the universe. . . . To a large extent, contemporary history has become a great theatrical event which is observed from a distance and in which one can no longer participate except as an enlightened amateur. . . . Because developments in the theatre have accustomed the spectator's eye to changes which do away with all that was essentially artificial in the . . . theatre, and because the cinema once again created a picture of the world as it is, the general public has now come to regard the work of art as an event which re-enacts the actual event as it originally took place. . . .
>
> But the close relationship between a work of art and an event has other important results, because "event" means that which is real and unexpected, harsh and unusual, all that is unforeseeable. An event has all the impact created by life, by an object or by a colour. . . .
>
> The event which contemporary art focuses on is not only the exalted form of an art which equates the real representation of history with aesthetic representations and which joins life and the imaginary in all as-

279

pects of existence; it is also the outcome of a desire which extends beyond the framework of art itself.[13]

This desire extending "beyond the framework of art itself" to give art the impact of an "event" is, as Duvignaud suggests, a way of reconciling our theater to a world where, as Robert Brustein has put it, we perceive history as "news theatre."[14]

R. D. Laing has seen the other side of this impulse towards giving art the impact of an event. If life itself has been siphoned of intrinsic value, then: "If there are no meanings, no values, no source of sustenance or help, then man, as creator, must invent, conjure up meanings and values, sustenance and succor out of nothing. He is a magician."[15] Out of nothing, or worse, out of a world where, as novelist Jerzy Kosinski says, "real events have been far more brutal than the most bizarre fantasies," an artist needs to "examine 'this new language' of brutality and its consequent new counter-language of anguish and despair."[16] In Kosinski's early fiction, this new language of brutality finds expression in a dispassionate account of a world emptied of meaning:

> Rats aren't murdered—we get rid of them; or, to use a better word, they are eliminated; this act of elimination is empty of all meaning. There's no ritual in it, no symbolism; the right of the executioner is never questioned. That's why in the concentration camps my friend designed, the victims never remained individuals; they became as identical as rats. They existed only to be killed.[17]

Its consequent new counter-language of anguish and despair is expressed in the action of a boy who wedges himself between the rails with a locomotive train passing above so that he might find "at the very bottom of this experience the great joy of being unhurt."[18] Onstage, this new language of brutality and its counter-language of anguish and despair translate into Artaudian poetics, for the theater today is charged with the task of teaching us to feel again.

After all, if nothing can shock us any more in this age when we have seen the worst and we have still gone on, the theater must clarify for us a world which can devastate the spirit, leaving man only "the great joy of being unhurt."

At once outer and inner signs of our age, plays in the contemporary mode, particularly those set in total institutions, do just that. These plays acknowledge the way things are: petrified. Then they try to find some way to touch us, to move us beyond the fourth wall. These plays attempt to go beyond easy, comfortable suspension of disbelief towards actual immersion in experience depicted onstage. The social Structure takes the stage; like a Duchamp "readymade," it usurps the world, and it engulfs the action evoking "all the impact" of an event. It carries us to an intense involvement with a Structure made metaphorical and with everyday behavior made ritualistic. And then it expels us, ending the action with a piercing reminder of the vast gap between an actual event and a play, an object and its image. In these plays, an actual environment is rendered, explored, turned into a mental construct, and realized in the image of an endgame, lost of old.

By redefining a social Structure, by distilling experience in a model of reaction, stressing memories, dreams, anecdotes, games, chores, and routines of everyday, such plays seek to grapple with the inquietude of our age. First, the Structure is bracketed onstage, placed on solid, naturalistically charted territory. Then, its action is displaced, objectified, exposing its hollow core of play, its vacuum of meaning, its bereaved language. In such a Structure, to escape or to win is impossible. The only objective is to make contact, to get by, or to go on in a world getting smaller, closer. Finally, each play expresses in its Structure, in the stillness of impasse, we can't go on. We go on. Beckett describes the dilemma in his story, *The Lost Ones*. Here, even inside a flattened cylinder fifty meters round and eighteen inches high for the sake of harmony, ladders are in great demand among the roaming miniscule lost bodies. "For the need to climb is too widespread. To feel it no longer is a rare deliverance."[19]

NOTES

>>>>>>>>>> NOTES TO CHAPTER 1 <<<<<<<<<<

1. Walter Kerr, "Stage View: Confrontations With Mortality," *New York Times*, July 2, 1978, sec. 2, pp. 1, 4.
2. Roger Copeland, "Theater in the 'Me Decade,'" *New York Times*, June 3, 1979, sec. 2, pp. 1, 20.
3. Mel Gussow, "The Time of the Wounded Hero," *New York Times*, April 15, 1979, sec. 2, pp. 1, 30.
4. George Steiner, *In Bluebeard's Castle: Some Notes Towards the Redefinition of Culture*, p. 54 (et passim).
5. Victor Brombert, "Sartre and the Drama of Ensnarement," in *Ideas in the Drama: Selected Papers from the English Institute*, ed. John Gassner, pp. 170, 155–156, 155, 160, 172, 158. This essay is reprinted in a slightly different form in Victor Brombert, *The Romantic Prison: The French Tradition*, pp. 185–199. See also Jean-Paul Sartre, *Situations II*, pp. 112, 245, 312–313 (et passim).
6. Erving Goffman, *Asylums: Essays on the Social Situation of Mental Patients and Other Inmates*, pp. 4–5, 12, 13.
7. Ibid., p. 6.
8. Judith Malina, "Directing *The Brig*," in Kenneth H. Brown, *The Brig*, pp. 83, 85.
9. Goffman, *Asylums*, p. 4.
10. Julian Beck, "Storming the Barricades," in Brown, *The Brig*, pp. 6–7, 26.
11. Stanley Kauffmann, "Notes on Naturalism: Truth Is Stranger As Fiction," *Performance*, 1 (March/April 1973), 34–35.
12. Antonin Artaud, *The Theater and Its Double*, trans. Mary Caroline Richards, pp. 85, 37, 44.
13. Susan Sontag, "The Image-World," in *On Photography*, p. 154.
14. Quoted in an interview with Lawrence M. Bensky, in *Theatre at Work: Playwrights and Productions in the Modern British Theatre*, ed. Charles Marowitz and Simon Trussler, p. 104.
15. Harold Pinter, *The Hothouse* (London: Eyre Methuen, 1980),

pp. 18, 27. Subsequent page references to this edition of *The Hothouse* will appear in the text.

16. Robert Jay Lifton, *The Broken Connection: On Death and the Continuity of Life*, pp. 367–368.

NOTES TO CHAPTER 2

1. Alexander Solzhenitsyn, *Cancer Ward*, trans. Nicholas Bethell and David Burg, p. 25.

2. Erving Goffman, *Asylums: Essays on the Social Situation of Mental Patients and Other Inmates*, p. 4.

3. Like all the plays Nichols has written for the stage, including his *Privates on Parade* (before he began writing for the stage, he wrote two screenplays—*Catch Us If You Can* and *Georgy Girl*—as well as sixteen plays for British television), *The National Health* is drawn from the playwright's personal experience. When the playwright was hospitalized repeatedly because of a collapsed lung, he made observations which would later be translated into stage terms. In an interview (Catherine Stott, "Plays in the Life of Joe Egg's Dad," London *Guardian*, January 26, 1970, p. 8), Nichols explained the semi-autobiographical roots of *The National Health*. The playwright stated that unlike *Joe Egg*, his first stage play which was drawn from personal experience with medical experts as the parent of a brain-damaged child, *The National Health* was "more like a number of phenomena. Like going along in a train and looking at the different things people are doing behind the windows of their houses . . . a series of observed moments and episodes which is exactly what I observed in the four hospitals I was in." In another interview (Ronald Bryden, "Playwright Peter Nichols: The Comic Laureate of Bad Taste?" *New York Times*, November 10, 1974, sec. 2, p. 5), Nichols says that even the soap-opera parodies are based on his own experience as a patient. He wanted to achieve a double-take "between the romantic sort of thing the nurses used to read in magazines and us just lying there all day in our beds." And when Bryden mentions that some critics accused Nichols of "inventing his hospital patients arbitrarily to represent the British welfare state's range of social types," Nichols responds, "I didn't invent any of them. They were all people I'd known."

For additional information concerning the autobiograph-ical aspect of much of Nichols's playwriting, see, for example, Vincent Canby, "Peter Nichols, 'Joe Egg' Author, Found Humor in Desperation," *New York Times*, February 3, 1968, p. 22; and Elizabeth Tate, "Program Notes" from the Amer-ican Long Wharf Theater production of *The National Health* in Spring 1974 (concerning the autobiographical nature of *Forget-Me-Not Lane* and *Joe Egg*). See also Benedict Night-ingale, "Unsoldierly Soldiers in New Nichols Play," *New York Times*, March 6, 1977, sec. 2, p. 6.

Kopit's *Wings* is also rooted in his own experience. The playwright goes into this in depth in the preface to *Wings* (New York: Hill and Wang, 1978), pp. vii–xvii. He writes of how "In the spring of 1976, seven months before Earplay was to commission me to write on a subject of my choosing, my father suffered a major stroke which rendered him in-capable of speech. Furthermore, because of certain other complications, all related to his aphasia, and all typical of stroke, it was impossible to know how much he compre-hended." In this preface, Kopit goes on to discuss the Re-habilitation Center and the two brave women who served as models for the central character of his play. One of these women was, in fact, a former wingwalker.

4. Quoted in *Barnard's*, 1970. See also John Russell Taylor, *The Second Wave: British Drama for the Seventies* (New York: Hill and Wang, 1971), p. 30; and Bryden, "Playwright Peter Ni-chols."

5. The popularized image of the dashing medicine-man in twentieth century screen sagas was chronicled in a series of still photographs included in the original program for *The National Health* distributed at the National Theatre. Pictures in the playbill reminded the audience of the Dr. Kildare film series (1930s), *The Citadel* (1937), *Four Girls in White* (1939), *The Courageous Dr. Christian* (1940), *Dr. Erlich's Magic Bullet* (1940), the BBC Dr. Finley TV series, the ATV's *Emergency Ward 10*, and the Dr. Kildare TV series. For an excellent, wide-ranging discussion of the image of doctors and patients in American television series, see Sharon L. Rosen and Joan Liebmann-Smith, "The Presentation of Illness on Televi-sion," in *Deviance and Mass Media*, pp. 79–94.

6. Anthony Astrachan, "Life Can be Beautiful/Relevant: There's

a Schism in the World of the Grand Old Soap Opera," *New York Times Magazine*, March 23, 1975, p. 62.

7. Peter Nichols, *The National Health (or Nurse Norton's Affair)* (New York: Grove Press, 1970), p. 101. Subsequent page references to this edition of *The National Health* will appear in the text.

8. Peter L. Berger, "Sociological Perspective—Society as Drama," in his *Invitation to Sociology: A Humanistic Perspective*, p. 146.

9. See Goffman, *Asylums*, pp. 27–28.

10. Ibid., pp. 82, 178.

11. Minna Field, *Patients are People: A Medical-Social Approach to Prolonged Illness*, pp. 57, 70. See also Polly Toynbee, *Patients*, on London hospital life.

12. Erving Goffman, "Role Distance," in his *Encounters: Two Studies in the Sociology of Interaction*, pp. 129–130, p. 114. For an alternative contemporary dramatic vision of role-distancing devices employed by subordinate staff members in a hospital setting, see Edward Albee's *The Death of Bessie Smith*, in *"The Sandbox" and "The Death of Bessie Smith,"* pp. 41–42. The orderly in Albee's play distances himself from his demeaning role with sullenness and sarcasm—as opposed to Barnet's joking and irony in *The National Health*. In a hostile encounter with the Nurse, for example, Albee's orderly bitterly announces, "I've told you I don't intend to stay here carrying crap pans and washing out the operating theatre until I have a . . . a long gray beard . . . I'm . . . I'm going beyond that."

13. Goffman, "Role Distance," pp. 132–133.

14. Donald M. Kaplan, "The Psychopathology of Television Watching," *Performance* 1: 21–29. See also Martin Esslin, "The Global Village and the Mass Mind," *Theatre Quarterly* 2: 39–43, for an analysis of TV series as "the sagas of the twentieth century" whose heroic protagonists are "neo-mythological figures" and the "archetypes of twentieth-century man's collective unconscious" (p. 43).

15. Ronald Bryden, "Having An Extravaganza on National Health," *Observer Review*, October 19, 1969, p. 32.

16. *London Evening Standard*, January 5, 1970, p. 1.

17. *Variety*, March 14, 1973, p. 21.

18. "Stage: 'National Health': Play with 27 Actors Arrives From Britain," *New York Times*, April 7, 1974, p. 50.

19. Goffman, "Role Distance," pp. 125–126.

20. See David Sudnow, "The Occurrence and Visibility of Death," in *Passing On*, especially pp. 33–38, 43–44, 48, 85, on the staff attitudes and "non-person treatment" of corpses.

21. Walter Kerr, "Two More From Britain: Not Good Theater," *New York Times*, October 20, 1974, sec. 2, p. 7; see also Walter Kerr, "Kerr on 'The National Health': 'Joe Egg,' Soft," *New York Times*, April 14, 1974, sec. 2, p. 14.

22. For an objective picture of the procedure intentionally travestied in "Nurse Norton's Affair," see Roberta G. Simmons and Richard L. Simmons, "Organ-Transplantation: A Societal Problem," *Social Problems* 19: 36–57. See also Aubrey C. McTaggart, *The Health Care Dilemma*, pp. 30–31.

23. Though this song is not included in the Grove Press edition of *The National Health*, it was sung in the American as well as in the British production of the play. (It is in the Samuel French edition of *The National Health* [New York, 1970], p. 96.)

24. John Arden, *The Happy Haven*, in *Three Plays* (New York: Grove Press, 1964), p. 193. Subsequent page references to this edition of *The Happy Haven* will appear in the text.

25. Edward Albee, *The Sandbox*, in *"The Sandbox" and "The Death of Bessie Smith,"* pp. 11, 13; and Edward Albee, *"The American Dream,"* in *"The American Dream" and "The Zoo Story,"* pp. 67, 82–83, 114.

26. Megan Terry, *The Gloaming, Oh My Darling*, in *Four Plays by Megan Terry*, pp. 214, 231, 244.

27. "John Arden: interviews with Tom Milne and Clive Goodwin, and with Simon Trussler," reprinted in *Theatre at Work: Playwrights and Productions in the Modern British Theatre*, ed. Charles Marowitz and Simon Trussler, pp. 41–42.

28. Goffman, *Asylums*, pp. 102–103.

29. See Edna Nicholson, "Nursing and Convalescent Homes," in *Housing the Aging*, ed. Wilma Donahue, p. 123.

30. Dulcy B. Miller, *The Extended Care Facility: A Guide to Organization and Operation*, p. 93.

31. Marowitz and Trussler, "Interviews with Tom Milne and Clive Goodwin," p. 41. See also John Russell Taylor, *Anger and After: A Guide to the New British Drama*, p. 84.

32. Nicholson, "Nursing and Convalescent Homes," p. 126.

33. Goffman, "Role Distance," p. 86.

34. Arthur Kopit, *Wings* (New York: Hill and Wang, 1978), pp.

7–8. Subsequent page references to this edition of *Wings* will appear in the text.

35. Harold Pinter, *The Homecoming*, p. 28.
36. Arthur Kopit, quoted in Robert Berkvist, "Playwright Arthur Kopit Tells How 'Wings' Took Flight," *New York Times*, June 25, 1978, sec. 2, pp. 1, 5.
37. Dale Harris, "A Broadway Bravo for Constance Cummings," *Guardian*, April 8, 1979, p. 21.
38. Samuel Beckett, *Endgame*, p. 57.
39. Susan Sontag, *Illness as Metaphor*, pp. 72, 85, 3, 58.
40. Ibid., pp. 86–87.
41. John Leonard, "Books of The Times," *New York Times*, June 1, 1978, sec. C, p. 19.
42. Sontag, *Illness as Metaphor*, pp. 87–88.

NOTES TO CHAPTER 3

1. Ken Kesey, *One Flew Over the Cuckoo's Nest*, pp. 19, 34, 29, 48–49.
2. Phyllis Chesler, *Women and Madness*, pp. 34–35. Chesler mentions Goffman's *Asylums* in this connection.
3. Bruce Ennis and Loren Siegel, *The Rights of Mental Patients: The Basic ACLU Guide to a Mental Patient's Rights*, pp. 36–37.
4. Lewis Carrol, *Alice's Adventures in Wonderland*, in *The Annotated Alice*, Introduction and Notes by Martin Gardner, pp. 27–30, 89.
5. See Erving Goffman, *Relations in Public: Microstudies of the Public Order*, p. 241. See also his "Information Control and Personal Identity," in *Stigma* (Englewood Cliffs, New Jersey: Prentice-Hall, 1963), p. 94.
6. Eugene Heimler, *Mental Illness and Social Work*, p. 62.
7. Peter Brook, quoted in Joseph Roddy, "*Marat/Sade* Stuns Broadway Playgoers with Sanity from the Asylum," *Look*, February 22, 1966, p. 110.
8. Peter Brook, "Introduction," in Peter Weiss, *The Persecution and Assassination of Jean-Paul Marat as Performed by the Inmates of the Asylum of Charenton Under the Direction of the Marquis de Sade*, English version by Geoffrey Skelton, verse adaptation by Adrian Mitchell (New York: Atheneum, 1975), p. vi. Subsequent page references to this edition of *Marat/Sade* will appear in the text.

9. Howard Taubman, "Theater: The Assassination of Marat," *New York Times*, December 28, 1965, p. 35.

10. Walter Kerr, "Texts and Non-Texts," in his *Thirty Plays Hath November*, p. 60.

11. Bosley Crowther, "Screen: Weiss's 'Marat/Sade' in Eerie Close-Up; Camera Provides for New Involvement," *New York Times*, February 23, 1967, p. 41.

12. Joseph Roddy, *Look*, February 22, 1966, p. 110.

13. Antonin Artaud, "The Theater of Cruelty (First Manifesto)," in *The Theater and Its Double*, p. 89.

14. Henry Hewes, "The Weiss/Brook," *Saturday Review*, January 15, 1966, p. 45.

15. Erving Goffman, *Asylums*, pp. 308–310.

16. Goffman, *Encounters*, p. 132.

17. Jack Kroll, "No Refuge," *Newsweek*, May 20, 1968, p. 114.

18. See Mel Gussow, "From Prison, 'Nowhere Being Nobody,' A Young Playwright Emerges to Fame," *New York Times*, March 27, 1974, p. 45.

19. A. Alvarez, "Peter Weiss: The Truths That Are Uttered in a Madhouse," *New York Times*, December 26, 1965, sec. 2, p. 3.

20. Margaret Croyden, *Lunatics, Lovers and Poets: The Contemporary Experimental Theatre*, p. 240.

21. Steven Hopkins, "Playwright as Politician: The Revolutionary World of Peter Weiss," *Playbill*, March 1966, pp. 6–7.

22. This exchange between the Herald and Sade in Episode 32, "The Murder," is not in the Atheneum or the Pocket Book edition (New York, 1968). It was printed in the Dramatic Publishing Company edition (Chicago: 1965), pp. 109–110.

23. Goffman, *Asylums*, pp. 109–110.

24. Jean Genet, *The Balcony*, p. 75.

25. Artaud, "Preface," in *The Theater and Its Double*, p. 13.

26. Taubman, "Theater: The Assassination of Marat," p. 35.

27. Artaud, *The Theater and Its Double*, pp. 85, 37, 44.

28. Artaud, "No More Masterpieces," in *The Theater and Its Double*, pp. 82–83.

29. See Goffman, *Asylums*, pp. 188, 306, 315–320.

30. Johan Huizinga, *Homo Ludens: A Study of the Play-Element in Culture*, pp. 2–4.

31. Eugen Fink, "The Oasis of Happiness: Toward an Ontology

of Play," in *Game, Play, Literature*, ed. Jacques Ehrmann, pp. 19–30.

32. Peter Weiss, quoted in Oliver Clausen, "Weiss/Propagandist and Weiss/Playwright," *New York Times Magazine*, October 2, 1966, p. 132.

33. Jerzy Grotowski, *Towards a Poor Theatre*, pp. 17–18; also quoted in John Lahr and Jonathan Price, *Life-Show: How to See Theater in Life and Life in Theater*, p. 60.

34. Quoted in Martin Esslin, "The Neurosis of the Neutrals: Friedrich Dürrenmatt," in *Brief Chronicles: Essays on Modern Theatre*, p. 121.

35. Ibid., p. 120.

36. Friedrich Dürrenmatt, "Problems of the Theatre," trans. Gerhard Nellhaus, *The Tulane Drama Review* 3: 3–26, especially pp. 19–21.

37. Friedrich Dürrenmatt, *The Physicists*, trans. James Kirkup (New York: Grove Press, 1964), p. 12. Subsequent page references to this edition of *The Physicists* will appear in the text.

38. Tom Stoppard, quoted in Mel Gussow, "Stoppard's Intellectual Cartwheels Now With Music," *New York Times*, July 29, 1979, sec. 2, p. 22.

39. Bamber Gascoigne, "Fable and Fiction," *Spectator*, January 18, 1963, quoted in Michael Morley, "Dürrenmatt's Dialogue with Brecht: A Thematic Analysis of *Die Physiker*," *Modern Drama* 14: 233.

40. Timo Tiusanen, *Dürrenmatt: A Study in Plays, Prose, Theory*, p. 277.

41. Henry Hewes, "Theater in England," *Saturday Review*, July 25, 1970, p. 20, and Stanley Kauffmann, "On Theater: *Home*," *The New Republic*, December 12, 1970, p. 33. According to Hewes, "The Theater: Knights at a Round Table," *Saturday Review*, December 12, 1970, p. 16, however, "Storey has stated that he has never seen a Beckett or Pinter play and has not been influenced by them."

42. T. E. Kalem, "Duet of Dynasts," *Time*, November 30, 1970, p. 48.

43. The term "new naturalism" was coined to describe the mode of Storey's *The Changing Room* and *The Contractor* in Stanley Kauffmann, "Notes on Naturalism: Truth is Stranger as Fiction," *Performance* 1: 33–39.

44. Anton Chekhov, quoted in David Magarshack, *Chekhov the Dramatist*, p. 84.
45. John Russell Taylor, *The Second Wave: British Drama for the Seventies*, p. 151.
46. David Storey, *Home* (New York: Random House, 1971), p. 3. Subsequent page references to this edition of *Home* will appear in the text.
47. Indeed, the dramatic use of an ambiguous resort setting that is gradually revealed as some kind of asylum is not unique to this play. A suggestive parallel to Storey's setting in *Home* may be found in Ibsen's last experimental play, *When We Dead Awaken*, as well as in Marguerite Duras's new wave novel of elliptical reality, *Destroy, She Said*, trans. Barbara Bray (New York: Grove Press, 1970). Terrence McNally's play, *Bad Habits* (1974), parodied this kind of sanatorium.
48. A congruent situation is described in Goffman's "Focused Interaction: Face Engagements," in *Behavior in Public Places: Notes on the Social Organization of Gatherings*, p. 109. Goffman describes patients who "were fearful and anxious of their whole setting, but who none the less made elaborate efforts to show that they were still what they had been before coming to the hospital and that they were in poised, business-like control of the situation. One middle-aged man walked busily on the grounds with the morning newspaper folded under one arm and a rolled umbrella hooked over the other, wearing an expression of being late for an appointment. A young man, having carefully preserved his worn grey flannel suit, bustled similarly from one place he was not going to another. . . . The management of a front of middle-class orientation in the situation, in these circumstances, was so precarious and difficult that (for these men) it apparently represented the day's major undertaking."
49. This powerful aspect of *Home*—its use of the character Alfred—is, like its restful environment, not unique to Storey's play. The traditional dramatic use of the "natural fool" as oracle has elsewhere also been translated into twentieth-century theater through the playwright's use of the modern taboo term, "lobotomy." See, for examples of medical experiments as stage villains, Dennis Reardon's *The Happiness Cage* and Dale Wasserman's adaptation of Ken Kesey's *One Flew Over the Cuckoo's Nest*. For an exceptional treatment of

this stage image of induced metamorphosis, see Allen Ginsberg's stage adaptation of his poem, *Kaddish*. In his *The Contractor*, as in Peter Nichols's *Joe Egg* and *The National Health*, Storey breaks another social taboo by dramatizing a situation involving a brain-damaged or defective character. Harold Pinter also makes use of such a character in *The Caretaker*; Aston's speech in that play (pp. 54–57) is a vivid account of the confused terror of a mental patient probably slated for shock treatment. Before *The Caretaker*, Pinter attempted to write a satirical play about a total institution very much like *Home*. Pinter's *The Hothouse* is discussed in detail in the introductory chapter.

50. Quoted in Tom Prideaux, "Playwright for a Torn-Apart Time: The Art of David Storey," *Life*, February 12, 1971, p. 10R.

51. Goffman, *Asylums*, pp. 68–69.

52. Bernard Beckerman, *Dynamics of Drama: Theory and Method of Analysis*, pp. 16–17. Beckerman is here citing Suzanne Langer, *Feeling and Form*, pp. 46–48.

53. Susan Sontag, *Illness as Metaphor*, pp. 35–36.

54. Genet, *The Balcony*, p. 96.

55. R. D. Laing, *Knots*, p. 39.

NOTES TO CHAPTER 4

1. Alexander Solzhenitsyn, *One Day in the Life of Ivan Denisovich*, p. 160.

2. Of the three plays to be examined here, *The Brig* is perhaps most obviously rooted in real experience. It is a stark and total recreation of a singular experience. According to Julian Beck, in his essay "Storming the Barricades" which prefaces Kenneth H. Brown's *The Brig* (New York: Hill and Wang, 1965), p. 33, "Brown, in a brig in Japan, staring straight ahead at attention or exhausted falling asleep at night, but with a writer's canny feel, said to himself, 'What a thing all this is.' And getting out of the place, he made accurate diagrams of the architecture and tried first to cast the happenings into the form of a novel, but his instincts sharpened and he turned it into 'A concept for the stage or film.' " See also Richard Schechner, "Interviews With Judith Malina and Kenneth H. Brown," *Tulane Drama Review* 8 (1964): 212–213.

According to John Russell Taylor, *Anger and After*, p. 105, Behan "joined the I.R.A. in 1937, and was sentenced to three years in Borstal for political offences by a Liverpool Court in 1939. Out of Borstal, he was sentenced again, by a Military Court, in Dublin in 1942, this time for fourteen years, also for political offences, and served nearly six years of his sentence." Behan's autobiographical account of his prison experience as a youth, *Borstal Boy*, was itself adapted for the stage by Frank McMahon in 1967; these early memoirs are also often cited by Erving Goffman as supportive material in his *Asylums*.

Genet, too, served time in prison. As Tom F. Driver notes in *Jean Genet*, Columbia University Essays on Modern Writers #20 (New York: Columbia University Press, 1966), p. 4, "In France Genet was locked up at various times in the Maison Centrale at Fontrevault, La Santé and Prison des Tourelles at Paris, and the prison at Fresnes. It was at Fresnes that he began to write. There, in 1942, he completed his first book, *Notre-Dame-des-Fleurs*. There he also wrote, perhaps first, a long, incantatory poem called 'Le Condamné à mort,' dedicated to his friend and fellow criminal, Maurice Pilorge, who had been executed the seventeenth of March, 1939. By the year 1948 Genet was the author of three published novels . . . two published plays (*Les Bonnes* and *Haute surveillance*), and two long poems. . . . He was in prison, sentenced for life at his tenth conviction for theft." Genet is the artist as criminal: in the confines of a cell he created his art, and his art (through the petitioning led by Sartre) finally set him physically free.

3. Like the Royal Shakespeare Company's production of *Marat/Sade*, the Living Theatre's production of *The Brig* has been preserved on film. In his account of *The Living Theatre: A History Without Myths*, trans. Robert Meister (New York: Avon, 1972), p. 230, Pierre Biner describes the film: "*The Brig*, directed by Jonas and Adolphas Mekas. Screenplay by Kenneth H. Brown, based on his play; produced by David C. Stone for White Line Productions, 1964, 68 minutes in black and white. (The Mekas brothers shot the film on the stage of the Midway Theatre [on West 42nd Street where *The Brig* played for two months after the seizure of the 14th Street Theater] in a matter of hours at a cost of $800. They had

full cooperation from the Becks, who are very fond of the film. In contrast to the financial arrangements of *The Connection*, the company has been receiving regular, appreciable royalty payments from the producers of this enterprise.)"

4. Kenneth H. Brown, *The Brig: A Concept for Theatre or Film*, with an Essay on The Living Theatre by Julian Beck and Director's Notes by Judith Malina (New York: Hill and Wang, 1965), p. 48. Subsequent page references to this edition of *The Brig* will appear in the text.

5. Antonin Artaud, "The Theater of Cruelty (First Manifesto)," in *The Theater and Its Double*, p. 99.

6. Erving Goffman, *Strategic Interaction*, pp. 133, 144, 39.

7. Biner, *The Living Theatre*, p. 64.

8. Ibid., pp. 139–141.

9. Erving Goffman, *Asylums*, pp. 22–23.

10. See Solzhenitsyn, *One Day in the Life of Ivan Denisovich*, p. 93. See also Eugene Heimler, *Mental Illness and Social Work*, pp. 107–109. Martin Sherman's *Bent* (1980), a melodrama set primarily in a concentration camp, also tries to suggest the horror of inmates' experiences by means of a repeated meaningless activity, moving a pile of stones, one by one, back and forth across the stage.

11. Artaud, "The Theater and Cruelty," in *The Theater and Its Double*, p. 85.

12. Taylor, *Anger and After*, p. 107.

13. Martin Esslin, *The Theatre of the Absurd*, p. 377.

14. See Alan Simpson, *Beckett and Behan and a Theatre in Dublin*, pp. 112–117, for a recounting of anecdotes concerning *The Hostage* as a "very fine theatrical abstract which Miss Littlewood mounted and framed in such a way as to make it acceptable to a wide international audience that was neither interested by nor informed on the Irish political scene or 'ways of life.' " When interviewed by Margaret Croyden, in *Behind the Scenes: Theater and Film Interviews From the Transatlantic Review*, ed. Joseph F. McCrindle, pp. 3–4, Littlewood recalls her role in encouraging Behan to revise *The Hostage*:

> Interviewer: Are you responsible for *The Hostage*?
> Littlewood: Well, yes, because Brendan had a nine-year imprisonment—he was aiming to blow up Buckingham Palace. He never got as far as Buckingham Palace. He'd

get to the pub and he'd have *The Irish Republican* (that was a newspaper) in his pocket, and bright green tweeds. . . . So he'd always be arrested. . . . He came to London, and I suppose we were the only people who were noisy enough for him. And we said, "Come on Brendan, let's have it—let's have the play." He was a great, great talker and *The Hostage* came like that, from my old man, my husband, who put a gun in his pants and said, "Now look here you dirty Irish so-and-so. You write that play." And mainly he improvised a lot with us. He had written a beautiful one-act version in Gaelic.

For a discussion of *An Giall*, the Gaelic version of *The Hostage* which opened in 1958, see Ulick O'Connor, *Brendan Behan*, pp. 193–208. O'Connor notes the difference between this play and Littlewood's version, and attributes it both to Littlewood's ingenuity and to Behan's carelessness:

. . .By the middle of September [1958] he had done so [finished the commissioned translation], but in a rather ramshackle way, leaving gaps in the dialogue and plot that were to be filled in as the play went into production.

It was Brendan's own fault that portions of the play had to be extemporized after he had delivered the manuscript to Theatre Workshop. He had been woefully late with the script. But his procrastination left him open to pressures which it would have been much better to avoid. As rehearsals proceeded, it became clear that what was emerging was a different work from the one he had written in Dublin. Additional characters were written in who had no special relevance to the theme. Rio Rita, a homosexual navvy, and "her" Negro boyfriend, Princess Grace, materialized, to use a phrase of Alan Simpson's, "somewhere between Stephen's Green and King's Road." They belonged to Chelsea camp, not Dublin bawdy. Miss Gilchrist, a social worker, and Mr. Mulleady, a Civil Servant, two other additions, are caricatures of English and not Irish prototypes.

This was Littlewood's method of working. Once she got a script, she went into instant collaboration with the cast and, as their views of the play unfolded during rehearsal, she allowed them to interpolate suggestions for dialogue and even scenes that were later incorporated in it. (pp. 195–196)

Though O'Connor believes that "*The Hostage* as it was performed in the West End ... version is a blown-up hotch-potch compared with the original version which is a small masterpiece," he nevertheless acknowledges that one year after Genet's *The Balcony* caused a sensation in London, "Littlewood's Brechtian approach, the popular songs, the cabaret dialogue, the topical references, the theatrical surprises she provided, were acceptable to an international audience and helped to ensure the success of the play which might otherwise have failed commercially through being too local in its theme and treatment" (p. 200).

15. Taylor, *Anger and After*, pp. 104–105.
16. Simpson, *Beckett and Behan*, pp. 115, 44–45.
17. O'Connor, *Brendan Behan*, pp. 166–169, 182–188. It should also be noted in passing that despite various critics' assessments of the differences between Behan's original script and its incarnations onstage, to the playwright's brother all those revisions seemed negligible. "I saw four productions of *The Quare Fellow*," writes Dominic Behan, in *My Brother Brendan* (New York: Simon and Schuster, 1965), p. 138, "and the only difference was three producers' names."
18. Quoted in "Working With Joan: Theatre Workshop Actors Talking to Tom Milne and Clive Goodwin," in *Theatre at Work*, ed. Charles Marowitz and Simon Trussler, pp. 116–117. (The piece was first published in *Encore* in 1960.)
19. Simpson, *Beckett and Behan*, p. 103.
20. Miriam Allen deFord, *Stone Walls: Prisons from Fetters to Furloughs*, pp. 144–145.
21. Brendan Behan, *The Quare Fellow*, in *The Complete Plays* (New York: Grove Press, 1978), p. 39. Subsequent page references to this edition of *The Quare Fellow* and *The Hostage* will appear in the text.
22. O'Connor, *Brendan Behan*, p. 182.
23. Goffman, *Asylums*, pp. 54–55.
24. Taylor, *Anger and After*, p. 107.
25. Quoted in Dominic Behan, *My Brother Brendan*, p. 88. For an alternative version of why the title was changed from *The Twisting of Another Rope* to *The Quare Fellow*, see Simpson,

Beckett and Behan, p. 41. Simpson states, "Taking into consideration—as I did when naming the Pike—the fact that publicity accounts for a high proportion of the running costs of a small theatre, I felt that a title as long as *The Twisting of Another Rope*—visualized in terms of newspaper advertising rates—would make the economic disaster presaged by the huge cost of the play a certainty. It wasn't long before the phrase *The Quare Fellow*, which is the Dublin prison jargon for a condemned man came to mind. Brendan had used it frequently throughout the play and it was both terse and interesting. As it happened, he was in London at the time, in connection with some newspaper work, and I phoned him there for permission to retitle the new play. To my delight, he agreed immediately."

Incidentally, the original title, *The Twisting of Another Rope*, was, as O'Connor notes, in *Brendan Behan*, p. 166, "a pun on the title of a one-act work by Douglas Hyde—*The Twisting of the Rope*, which was the first Gaelic drama to appear on the Irish stage." Hyde's *The Twisting of the Rope* is available in *Three Irish Plays* (Boston: International Pocket Library, 1936), pp. 37–50. For mention of the first production of *Casad-an-Sugan* (Hyde's play), see Lady Gregory, *Our Irish Theatre* (1913; rept. ed., New York: Capricorn Books, 1965), p. 29.

26. Gabriel Fallon, quoted in Mary Lodge, "The First Play," in Sean McCann, ed., *The World of Brendan Behan*, p. 86, says that Behan "writes didactically—and his play in essence is a plea for the abolition of capital punishment."

27. Richard N. Coe, *The Vision of Jean Genet: A Study of His Poems, Plays and Novels*, p. 225.

28. Keith Botsford, "Thief; male prostitute; pimp; trafficker in drugs; deserter; stool pigeon; traitor; glorifier of violence, torture, perversion . . . But He Writes Like an Angel," in *New York Times Magazine*, February 27, 1972, p. 61.

29. See deFord, *Stone Walls*, p. 149.

30. Jean Genet, *Deathwatch*, in *The Maids* and *Deathwatch*, rev. ed., trans. Bernard Frechtman, Introduction by Jean-Paul Sartre (New York: Grove Press, 1962), p. 103. Subsequent page references to this edition of *Deathwatch* will appear in the text.

31. Lucien Goldmann, "The Theatre of Jean Genet: A Socio-

logical Study," in *Genet/Ionesco: The Theatre of the Double, A Critical Anthology*, ed. Kelly Morris, pp. 96, 94.

32. Artaud, "The Theater of Cruelty (First Manifesto)," in *The Theater and Its Double*, p. 89.
33. Artaud, "The Theater and Culture," in *The Theater and Its Double*, pp. 8–9.
34. Genet, *The Balcony*, p. 49.
35. Artaud, *The Theater and Its Double*, pp. 37, 32.
36. Genet, "A Note on Theatre," in *Genet/Ionesco*, p. 21.
37. Artaud, "The Theater of Cruelty (First Manifesto)," p. 89.
38. Artaud, "The Theater and the Plague," in *The Theater and Its Double*, p. 30.
39. Botsford, "But He Writes Like an Angel," p. 70.
40. Genet, "Letters to Roger Blin," in his *Reflections on the Theatre and Other Writings*, trans. Richard Seaver, pp. 40–41.
41. Botsford, "But He Writes Like an Angel," p. 61.
42. Genet, "The strange word *Urb* . . . ," in *Reflections on the Theatre*, pp. 65–66.
43. Bruno Bettelheim, "Schizophrenia as a Reaction to Extreme Situations," in his *Surviving and Other Essays*, p. 115.
44. Julian Beck, in *The Brig*, p. 34.

NOTES TO CHAPTER 5

1. Joseph Heller, *Catch-22*, p. 47.
2. Jonas Mekas, commenting on a screening of his 1964 film of *The Brig* at A Festival of American Independent Feature Films, New York City, September 25, 1979. Mekas went on to say that in filming the Living Theatre's production of the play, "I wanted to approach it as reality, supposing I am a newsreel man. . . . I eliminated conversations, melodramatic bits, so the film is concentrated; the essence is there."
3. Judith Malina, "Directing *The Brig*," in Kenneth H. Brown, *The Brig*, p. 83.
4. Wesker served in the R.A.F. from 1950 to 1952; writing *Chips With Everything*, he drew upon his own experience in national service. In an interview with Simon Trussler in *Theatre at Work: Playwrights and Productions in Modern British Theatre*, ed. Charles Marowitz and Simon Trussler, p. 82, Wesker recalls the genesis of *Chips With Everything*. He states:

I hated national service. I hated the idea of it because it seemed a waste of two years. But because most of us tend in retrospect to make virtues of necessity, I am sort of glad it happened. I knew I wanted to get something out of it—a work out of it—and every day of the first eight weeks of square-bashing I sent a letter to a relative or a friend, in which I detailed what happened throughout the day. And at the end of square-bashing I got all the letters together, put them in chronological order, and proceeded to write a novel, which I can remember writing in the lighthouse near where we were stationed. This was a very bad novel. But, glancing through it . . . it occurred to me that the chapters were a good basis for scenes in a play, and I became preoccupied with this idea of the way in which the rebel is absorbed in English society.

In an interview with this writer in London, August 25, 1978, Wesker recalled further:

I can see it [*Chips*] could have been a three act play or . . . a two act play focusing just in one hut with all the parade going on outside, but the material dictated the shape. Its history, of course, was when I went into the air force, I was determined to write something. And I used to write letters home every day to someone or other, long, long letters, just writing everything that went on in the course of the day. I gathered these letters at the end of the eight week square-bashing period, and wrote a novel called *The Reed That Bent*, my first and only novel, and not a very good novel. It was never published. It was written long before I wrote *The Kitchen*, and I put it away in a bottom drawer. And it was after the trilogy [*Chicken Soup With Barley, Roots*, and *I'm Talking About Jerusalem*] and *The Kitchen* that I realized there was material for a play. Each chapter of the novel became a scene of the play. That's the way the material felt.

Rabe's plays are also firmly rooted in real experience. He was drafted into the United States army in 1965. In his introduction to the published texts of *"The Basic Training of Pavlo Hummel" and "Sticks and Bones,"* pp. xvi–xvii, David

Rabe describes his futile attempts at keeping a journal while stationed in Vietnam. He writes:

> I remember once sitting more or less paralyzed over the phrase "artillery rounds" scribbled on a yellow-lined page. Cannon were booming a few miles across the nearby road and dust shook loose in puffs from the tentfolds. My phrase sat on the page like a husk. I was aware acutely, and in a way that makes writing impossible, of the existence of language as mere symbol. In no way could I effect the cannon, the shuddering tent flaps. In an utterly visceral way, I detested any lesser endeavor. The events around me, huge and continual, were the things obsessing me. So I sat staring at the words on the page and the page was yellow on a cot standing on a wooden floor.

Even here, removed from the war he remembers, Rabe's description is itself visceral rather than analytical. The image of him isolated, even from language, by events huge and continual, is powerful, and sensate rather than narrative. Like Wesker, Rabe later began to write a novel about his experience in the service (Introduction, p. xii), but as this concrete vision suggests, his subject demanded theatrical shape.

5. Interview with this writer, London, August 25, 1978.
6. Arnold Wesker, *Chips With Everything*, in *The Plays of Arnold Wesker* (New York: Harper and Row, 1976), I, 307. Subsequent page references to this edition of *Chips With Everything* will appear in the text.
7. Wesker, "Introduction and Notes for the Producer," *The Kitchen*, in *The Plays of Arnold Wesker*, I, 3.
8. Wesker, *The Kitchen*, p. 20.
9. Wesker, "Introduction," in *The Journalists: A Triptych*, pp. 11–12.
10. Interview with this writer, London, August 25, 1978.
11. Wesker, quoted in Harold U. Ribalow, *Arnold Wesker*, Twayne's English Authors Series, p. 71.
12. Quoted from an article in *The Transatlantic Review* in John Russell Taylor, *Anger and After: A Guide to the New British Drama*, p. 146.
13. Wesker, "From a Writer's Notebook," *Theatre Quarterly* 2:13.

14. Interview with this writer, London, August 25, 1978.

15. See, for example, Erving Goffman's discussion of "role-releases" occasioned by an annual party at which staff and "inmates" (in Goffman's terms) may mix in *Asylums*, pp. 93–99. Wesker has himself noted the inhibitions of his characters in this social environment. In this scene, for example, the class war is made evident at the expense of characterization. The conscripts whisper together about the officers; meanwhile, the officers denigrate "the good old working class of England . . . the salt of the earth" (p. 323). Questioned about the "conventionalized characters" in *Chips With Everything*, Wesker replied, "However rounded I might make them, they still stood for what they did. And even so, the way they spoke and the way they behaved is not caricatured, it is very real" (Marowitz and Trussler, *Theatre at Work*, p. 90).

16. Interview with this writer, London, August 25, 1978.

17. Judith Malina, in *The Brig*, p. 83.

18. Interview with this writer, London, August 25, 1978.

19. Kai T. Erikson, quoted in Erving Goffman, *Relations in Public: Microstudies of the Public Order* (New York: Harper and Row, 1972), p. 341.

20. Interview with this writer, London, August 25, 1978.

21. Ironically enough, in any social situation outside of a total institution a permanent smile might serve a person well. For a discussion of the applicability of his aphorism, "Indeed, when in doubt, play a smile," see Goffman, *Relations in Public*, pp. 160–161.

22. Goffman, *Asylums*, pp. 56–58. For illustrations of supportive "bond formations" specific to an R.A.F. hut, see also T. E. Lawrence, *The Mint* (London: Jonathan Cape, 1955), pp. 59, 91. (This work is also cited by Goffman.)

23. Interview with this writer, London, August 25, 1978.

24. Ibid.

25. Ibid.

26. In contrast to the Living Theatre's total revolutionary stance, and in contrast to the Open Theatre's emphasis on archetypal and social patterns, other theater groups, aiming more at political action than at ritual transcendence, focused steadily and *politically* on the Vietnam war alone. Notable among such groups were The Bread and Puppet Theatre, founded at the start of the 1960s by Peter Schumann; The San Fran-

cisco Mime Troupe, whose member Peter Berg first used
the term "guerrilla theatre" to describe "a hit-and-run affair
composed of unexpected action, and accompanied by chants,
signs, political slogans, and a quick dispersal before the police
could break up the unauthorized performance; or else an
extended performance in the streets or in a park" (Arthur
Sainer, *The Radical Theatre Notebook*, p. 63); and The Pageant
Players, founded in 1965 by young people who, as Sainer
notes, used innovative, rough theater "as a forum for their
political beliefs." According to Sainer:

> there was a certain rough edge to the first offerings of
> the Pageant Players. They had a kind of inspired am-
> ateurishness, relying heavily on energetic beliefs and a
> simple, anti-illusionistic rhetoric. Their initial produc-
> tion was *The Paper Tiger Pageant*, first presented in No-
> vember of 1965, a "dance/movement and music" piece,
> as Michael Brown, one of the founders of the Players,
> describes it, a kind of "anti-imperialist analysis," per-
> formed at peace rallies. . . . In the fall of 1966, the
> *Laundromat* play was developed, treating U.S. aggression
> in Vietnam in allegorical terms. Several performers,
> pretending to be customers in a laundromat, begin to
> quarrel among themselves in front of legitimate laun-
> dromat customers who become, unknown to themselves,
> audience members. (pp. 23–24)

In his chronicle of radical theater groups of the sixties, Sainer recounts many such instances of guerrilla theater. As he
points out:

> The performances were often one-shot or random oc-
> casions, e.g., Schechner's group performing Robert
> Head's *Kill Viet Cong* at the Port Authority Bus Terminal
> in New York, asking passersby to "kill the enemy" (a
> performer). Sometimes the performances were part of
> a continuing repertoire . . . Often the police would arrive
> before the group could disperse and thus become part
> of the performance or event. Sometimes when the group
> was not dispersed, political discussions would ensue.
> Sometimes there were angry confrontations. The meth-
> ods were provocative, designed to call attention to a
> condition. (pp. 63–64)

Understandably, given the immediacy and free form of guerrilla theater—its element of surprise and currency—documentation is scarce. Still, suggestive of the power and possible grace of anti-Vietnam war presentations of this kind are The Bread and Puppet Troupe's antiwar vigil in front of St. Patrick's Cathedral and their *Fire*, conceived and developed by Peter Schumann in 1965. *Fire*, a speechless series of images using masks and sounds such as a bell tolling and a "shrieking, metallic whine," leading finally to a tableau of Vietnamese sacrifice, was described by one spectator as exhibiting "the quality of prayer" as it "*responds* to the horrors of Vietnam" as, "to some extent, it is a service for the dead." To evoke the memory of *Fire*, that spectator recalls its final ritualistic scene:

The last placard names the scene *End*. The robed, masked figures are seated. A Vietnamese woman, whose mask is like the face of death in old age, and whose white robes are like the splendor of a sacred celebration, stands alone just off center of the stage. And now in perfect silence something shocking occurs. Two figures enter, bare-armed and bare-handed, dressed in blue jeans and scivvy shirts, wearing masks of Western faces. They are lugging cinderblocks. Their motions are the motions of workmen at work—and they appear brutal. . . . They place the cinderblocks around the white-robed woman, and surround her with a little fence of wire . . . and then withdraw. There is silence again . . . The aged woman holds a roll of bright red tape. With deliberate movements—movements at once practical, prosaic, and ceremonious—she tears long strips of the tape and fastens them on her robe near her feet. The red strips become numerous, and move higher, beginning to entwine her. . . . The strips cross her mouth now, and her cheeks, and finally lie across her eyes. She folds in upon herself and topples forward, sagging heavily against the fence. There is a long silence. Something has been restored. The bell tolls. (George Dennison, in *The Drama Review* 14 [1970], quoted in Sainer, pp. 154–159.)

27. Roy Bongartz, "Pitchman for Free (and Freewheeling) Theater," *New York Times Magazine*, August 15, 1971, p. 18.

28. Interview with this writer, London, August 25, 1978.
29. Jack Kroll, "Greek Salad," *Newsweek*, April 30, 1973, p. 87.
30. Mel Gussow, "Rabe is Compelled 'to Keep Trying,' " *New York Times*, May 12, 1976, p. 34.
31. David Rabe, *The Basic Training of Pavlo Hummel*, in *"The Basic Training of Pavlo Hummel" and "Sticks and Bones"* (New York: Viking Press, 1973), p. xxv. Subsequent page references to this edition of *The Basic Training of Pavlo Hummel* will appear in the text.
32. Bertolt Brecht, *Mother Courage and her Children*, trans. Eric Bentley, p. 67.
33. John Lahr, "On-Stage," *Village Voice*, May 27, 1971, p. 57.
34. See Stanley Kauffmann on "new naturalism" in Storey's plays in his "Notes on Naturalism: Truth is Stranger as Fiction," *Performance* 1: 33–39.
35. Lahr, "On-Stage," p. 57.
36. Quoted in Robert Wahls, "Footlights: Onstream with Rabe," *New York Sunday News*, April 25, 1976, Leisure sec., p. 4.
37. Michael Herr, *Dispatches*, p. 260.
38. Wahls, "Footlights: Onstream with Rabe," p. 4.
39. Gussow, "Rabe is Compelled 'to Keep Trying,' " p. 34.
40. Quoted in Robert Berkvist, "How Nichols and Rabe Shaped 'Streamers,' " *New York Times*, April 25, 1976, sec. 2, p. 12.
41. David Rabe, *Streamers* (New York: Knopf, 1977), pp. 72, 58–59. Subsequent page references to this edition of *Streamers* will appear in the text.
42. Quoted in Chris Chase, "The Audience Can Almost Hear Him Ticking," *New York Times*, June 13, 1976, sec. 2, p. 5.
43. See Walter Kerr, "When Does Gore Get Gratuitous?" *New York Times*, February 22, 1976, sec. 2, pp. 1, 7.
44. Quoted in Gussow, "Rabe is Compelled 'to Keep Trying,' " p. 34.
45. Quoted in Berkvist, "How Nichols and Rabe Shaped 'Streamers,' " p. 12.
46. Antonin Artaud, *The Theater and Its Double*, p. 85.
47. Edward Albee, *The Zoo Story*, p. 36.
48. Ivan Gold, "Vietnam, Grunt's-Eye View," a review of Larry Heinemann, *Close Quarters*, in *New York Times Book Review*, June 26, 1977, p. 15. This reviewer's opinion seems to be borne out so far by the fact that the most powerful nondramatic writing to come out of the Vietnam experience has

been nonfiction, most notably Michael Herr's *Dispatches*; Philip Caputo's *A Rumor of War*; and more recently, two compiled oral histories, Mark Baker's *Nam: the Vietnam War in the Words of the Men and Women Who Fought There*, and Al Santoli's *Everything We Had: An Oral History of the Vietnam War by Thirty-Three American Soldiers Who Fought It*.

49. Lahr, "On-Stage," p. 57.

NOTES TO CHAPTER 6

1. Walter Kerr, "*Marat/Sade*: All Work and No Play," *New York Herald Tribune*, January 16, 1966, p. 19.
2. Quoted in Ted Hoffman, "Introduction," in *Famous American Plays of the 1970s*, p. 18.
3. Eugene O'Neill, *The Iceman Cometh*, p. 25.
4. Rothko quoted in Robert Hughes, *Shock of the New*, p. 377.
5. Erving Goffman, "The Manufacture of Negative Experience," in *Frame Analysis: An Essay on the Organization of Experience*, pp. 388–412, esp. p. 399.
6. John Osborne, *The Entertainer*, p. 89.
7. Mel Gussow, "Critic's Notebook: The Hazard in Occupational Dramas," *New York Times*, November 19, 1981, p. C24.
8. Peter Brook, *The Empty Space*, pp. 125, 127.
9. Some of the terms used here, such as "impelling agent" and "project," have been influenced by Bernard Beckerman, *Dynamics of Drama: Theory and Method of Analysis*.
10. Samuel Beckett, *Endgame*, in *Endgame* and *Act Without Words* (New York: Grove Press, 1958), p. 30. Subsequent page references to this edition of *Engame* will appear in the text.
11. Beckett, *Waiting for Godot*, p. 28B.
12. Michel Foucault, *Power/Knowledge: Selected Interviews and Other Writings 1972–1977*, ed. Colin Gordon, pp. 81–92.
13. Jean Duvignaud, *The Sociology of Art*, trans. Timothy Wilson, pp. 132–135.
14. See Robert Brustein, "News Theatre," in *The Culture Watch: Essays on Theatre and Society, 1969–1974*, pp. 173–189.
15. R. D. Laing, *The Politics of Experience*, p. 24. Also quoted in John Lahr, "The New Theater: A Retreat from Realism," in his *Up Against the Fourth Wall: Essays on Modern Theater*, p. 215.

16. Jerzy Kosinski, "Afterward," in *The Painted Bird*, rev. ed., pp. 254, 256.
17. Kosinski, *Steps*, p. 64.
18. Kosinski, *Painted Bird*, p. 231.
19. Samuel Beckett, *The Lost Ones*, pp. 7, 10.

Albee, Edward. *"The American Dream" and "The Zoo Story."* New York: Signet, 1961.

———. *"The Sandbox" and "The Death of Bessie Smith."* New York: Signet, 1960.

Alvarez, A. "Peter Weiss: The Truths That Are Uttered in the Madhouse." *New York Times*, December 26, 1965, sec. 2, p. 3.

Arden, John. *Three Plays.* New York: Grove Press, 1964.

Artaud, Antonin. *The Theater and Its Double.* Translated by Mary Caroline Richards. New York: Grove Press, 1958.

Astrachan, Anthony. "Life Can Be Beautiful/Relevant: There's a Schism in the World of Grand Old Soap Opera." *New York Times Magazine*, March 23, 1975, p. 62.

Baker, Mark. *Nam: The Vietnam War in the Words of the Men and Women Who Fought There.* New York: Morrow, 1981.

Beckerman, Bernard. *Dynamics of Drama: Theory and Method of Analysis.* New York: Drama Book Specialists, 1979.

Beckett, Samuel. *"Endgame" and "Act Without Words."* New York: Grove Press, 1958.

———. *The Lost Ones.* New York: Grove Press, 1972.

———. *Waiting for Godot.* New York: Grove Press, 1954.

Behan, Brendan. *Borstal Boy.* London: Hutchinson, 1958.

———. *The Complete Plays.* New York: Grove Press, 1978.

Behan, Dominic. *My Brother Brendan.* New York: Simon and Schuster, 1965.

Berger, Peter L. *Invitation to Sociology: A Humanistic Perspective.* Garden City, New York: Doubleday Anchor, 1963.

Berkvist, Robert. "How Nichols and Rabe Shaped Streamers." *The New York Times*, April 25, 1976, sec. 2, p. 12.

———. "Playwright Arthur Kopit Tells How 'Wings' Took Flight." *New York Times*, June 25, 1978, sec. 2, pp. 1, 5.

Bettelheim, Bruno. *Surviving and Other Essays.* New York: Knopf, 1979.

Biner, Pierre. *The Living Theatre: A History without Myths.* Translated by Robert Meister. New York: Avon, 1972.

Bongartz, Roy. "Pitchman for Free (and Freewheeling) Theater." *New York Times Magazine*, August 15, 1971, p. 18.

Botsford, Keith. "Thief; male prostitute; pimp; trafficker in drugs; deserter; stool pigeon; traitor; glorifier of violence, torture, perversion . . . But He Writes Like an Angel." *New York Times Magazine*, February 27, 1972, p. 61 ff.

Brecht, Bertolt. *Mother Courage and Her Children*. Translated by Eric Bentley. New York: Grove Press, 1966.

Brombert, Victor. "Sartre and the Drama of Ensnarement," in *Ideas in the Drama: Selected Papers from the English Institute*, edited by John Gassner, pp. 155–174. New York: Columbia University Press, 1964.

———. *The Romantic Prison: The French Tradition*. Princeton, N.J.: Princeton University Press, 1978.

Brook, Peter. *The Empty Space*. New York: Avon, 1969.

Brown, Kenneth H. *The Brig*. New York: Hill and Wang, 1965.

Brustein, Robert. *The Culture Watch: Essays on Theater and Society, 1969–1974*. New York: Alfred A. Knopf, 1975.

Bryden, Ronald. "Playwright Peter Nichols: The Comic Laureate of Bad Taste?" *New York Times*, November 10, 1974, sec. 2, p. 5.

———. "Having An Extravaganza on National Health." *Observer Review*, October 19, 1969, p. 32.

Canby, Vincent. "Peter Nichols, 'Joe Egg' Author, Found Humor in Desperation." *New York Times*, February 3, 1968, p. 22.

Caputo, Philip. *A Rumor of War*. New York: Holt, Rinehart and Winston, 1977.

Carroll, Lewis. *Alice's Adventures in Wonderland*, in *The Annotated Alice*. Introduction and Notes by Martin Gardner. New York: World Publishing Company, 1968.

Chase, Chris. "The Audience Can Almost Hear Him Ticking." *The New York Times*, June 13, 1976, sec. 2, p. 5.

Chesler, Phyllis. *Women and Madness*. Garden City, New York: Doubleday, 1972.

Clausen, Oliver. "Weiss/Propagandist and Weiss/Playwright." *New York Times Magazine*, October 2, 1966, p. 132.

Coe, Richard N. *The Vision of Jean Genet: A Study of His Poems, Plays and Novels*. New York: Grove Press, 1968.

Copeland, Roger. "Theater in the 'Me Decade.' " *New York Times*, June 3, 1979, sec. 2, pp. 1, 20.

Crowther, Bosley. "Screen: Weiss's 'Marat/Sade' in Eerie Close-

Up; Camera Provides for New Involvement." *New York Times*, February 23, 1967, p. 41.

Croyden, Margaret. *Lunatics, Lovers and Poets: The Contemporary Experimental Theatre*. New York: McGraw-Hill, 1974.

deFord, Miriam Allen. *Stone Walls: Prisons from Fetters to Furloughs*. Philadelphia: Chilton, 1962.

Donahue, Wilma, ed. *Housing the Aging*. Ann Arbor: University of Michigan Press, 1954.

Driver, Tom F. *Jean Genet*. Columbia University Essays on Modern Writers, no. 20. New York: Columbia University Press, 1966.

Duras, Marguerite. *Destroy, She Said*. Translated by Barbara Bray. New York: Grove Press, 1970.

Dürrenmatt, Friedrich. *The Physicists*. Translated by James Kirkup. New York: Grove Press, 1964.

———. "Problems of the Theatre." *Tulane Drama Review*, no. 3, October, 1958, pp. 3–26.

Duvignaud, Jean. *The Sociology of Art*. Translated by Timothy Wilson. London: Paladin, 1972.

Ehrmann, Jacques, ed. *Game, Play, Literature*. Boston: Beacon Press, 1971.

Ennis, Bruce and Siegel, Loren. *The Rights of Mental Patients: The Basic ACLU Guide to a Mental Patient's Rights*. New York: Avon, 1973.

Esslin, Martin. "The Global Village and the Mass Mind." *Theatre Quarterly* 2:39–43.

———. *Brief Chronicles: Essays on Modern Theatre*. London: Temple Smith, 1970.

———. *The Theatre of the Absurd*. Rev. ed. Garden City, New York: Doubleday Anchor, 1969.

Field, Minna. *Patients are People: A Medical-Social Approach to Prolonged Illness*. 3rd ed. New York: Columbia University Press, 1967.

Foucault, Michel. *Power/Knowledge: Selected Interviews and Other Writings 1972–1977*. New York: Pantheon, 1980.

Gascoigne, Bamber. "Fable and Fiction." *Spectator*, January 18, 1963.

Genet, Jean. *The Balcony*. Rev. ed. Translated by Bernard Frechtman. New York: Grove Press, 1966.

———. *The Maids* and *Deathwatch*. Translated by Bernard Frechtman. New York: Grove Press, 1962.

Genet, Jean. *Reflections on the Theatre and Other Writings.* Translated by Richard Seaver. London: Faber, 1972.

Goffman, Erving. *Asylums: Essays on the Social Situation of Mental Patients and Other Inmates.* Garden City, New York: Doubleday Anchor, 1961.

———. *Behavior in Public Places: Notes on the Social Organization of Gatherings.* New York: Free Press, 1963.

———. *Encounters: Two Studies in the Sociology of Interaction.* Indianapolis: Bobbs-Merrill, 1961.

———. *Frame Analysis: An Essay on the Organization of Experience.* New York: Harper and Row, 1974.

———. *Relations in Public: Microstudies of the Public Order.* New York: Harper and Row, 1972.

———. *Stigma.* Englewood Cliffs, N.J.: Prentice-Hall, 1963.

———. *Strategic Interaction.* 1969. Reprint. New York: Ballantine Books, 1972.

Gold, Ivan. "Vietnam, Grunt's-Eye View." *New York Times Book Review,* June 26, 1977, p. 15.

Gregory, Lady. *Our Irish Theatre.* 1913. Reprint. New York: Capricorn Books, 1965.

Grotowski, Jerzy. *Towards a Poor Theatre.* New York: Simon and Schuster, 1968.

Gussow, Mel. "Critic's Notebook: The Hazard in Occupational Dramas." *New York Times,* November 19, 1981, p. C24.

———. "From Prison, 'Nowhere Being Nobody,' A Young Playwright Emerges to Fame." *New York Times,* March 27, 1974, p. 45.

———. "Rabe is Compelled 'to Keep Trying.' " *New York Times,* May 12, 1976, p. 34.

———. "Stoppard's Intellectual Cartwheels Now with Music." *New York Times,* July 29, 1979, sec. 2, p. 22.

———. "The Time of the Wounded Hero." *New York Times,* April 15, 1979, sec. 2, pp. 1, 30.

Harris, Dale. "A Broadway Bravo for Constance Cummings." *Guardian,* April 8, 1979, p. 21.

Heimler, Eugene. *Mental Illness and Social Work.* Baltimore: Penguin, 1969.

Heller, Joseph. *Catch-22.* New York: Dell, 1965.

Herr, Michael. *Dispatches.* New York: Avon, 1978.

Hewes, Henry. "Theater in England." *Saturday Review,* July 25, 1970, p. 20.

———. "The Theater: Knights at a Round Table." *Saturday Review*, December 12, 1970, p. 16.

———. "The Weiss/Brook." *Saturday Review*, January 15, 1966, p. 45.

Hoffman, Ted. Introduction to *Famous American Plays of the 1970's*, pp. 9–27. New York: Dell, 1981.

Hopkins, Steven. "Playwright as Politician: The Revolutionary World of Peter Weiss." *Playbill*, March 1966, pp. 6–7.

Hughes, Robert. *Shock of the New*. New York: Alfred Knopf, 1981.

Huizinga, Johan. *Homo Ludens: A Study of the Play-Element in Culture*. 1949. Reprint. Boston: Beacon Press, 1968.

Hyde, Douglas. *The Twisting of the Rope*, pp. 37-50, in *Three Irish Plays*. Boston: International Pocket Library, 1936.

Kalem, T. E. "Duet of Dynasts." *Time*, November 30, 1970, p. 48.

Kaplan, Donald M. "The Psychopathology of Television Watching." *Performance* 1: 21–29.

Kauffmann, Stanley. "Notes on Naturalism: Truth Is Stranger As Fiction." *Performance* 1: 33–39.

———. "On Theater: *Home*." *The New Republic*, Dec. 12, 1970, p. 33.

Kerr, Walter. "Marat/Sade: All Work and No Play." *New York Herald Tribune*, January 16, 1966, p. 19.

———. "Kerr on 'The National Health': 'Joe Egg,' Soft." *New York Times*, April 14, 1974, sec. 2, p. 14.

———. *Thirty Plays Hath November*. New York: Simon and Schuster, 1969.

———. "Two More From Britian: Not Good Theater." *New York Times*, October 20, 1974, sec. 2, p. 7.

———. "When Does Gore Get Gratuitous?" *New York Times*, February 22, 1976, sec. 2, pp. 1, 7.

Kesey, Ken. *One Flew Over the Cuckoo's Nest*. New York: Signet, 1962.

Kopit, Arthur. *Wings*. New York: Hill and Wang, 1978.

Kosinski, Jerzy. *The Painted Bird*. Rev. ed. New York: Bantam, 1978.

———. *Steps*. New York: Bantam, 1977.

Kroll, Jack. "Greek Salad." *Newsweek*, April 30, 1973, p. 87.

———. "No Refuge." *Newsweek*, May 20, 1968, p. 114.

Lahr, John and Price, Jonathan. *Life Show: How to See Theater in Life and Life in Theater*. New York: Viking Press, 1973.

Lahr, John. "On-Stage." *The Village Voice*, May 27, 1971, p. 57.

Lahr, John. *Up Against the Fourth Wall: Essays on Modern Theater.* New York: Grove Press, 1970.

Laing, R. D. *Knots.* New York: Pantheon, 1970.

——. *The Politics of Experience.* New York: Pantheon, 1967.

Langer, Suzanne. *Feeling and Form.* New York: Scribner, 1953.

Lawrence, T. E. *The Mint.* London: Jonathan Cape, 1955.

Leonard, John. "Books of the Times." *New York Times*, June 1, 1978, p. C19.

Lifton, Robert Jay. *The Broken Connection: On Death and the Continuity of Life.* New York: Simon and Schuster, 1979.

McCann, Sean, ed. *The World of Brendan Behan.* New York: Twayne, 1966.

McCrindle, Joseph F., ed. *Behind the Scenes: Theater and Film Interviews from the Transatlantic Review.* New York: Holt, Rinehart and Winston, 1971.

McTaggart, Aubrey C. *The Health Care Dilemma.* Boston: Holbrook Press, 1971.

Magarshack, David. *Chekhov the Dramatist.* London: John Lehmann, 1952.

Marowitz, Charles and Trussler, Simon, eds. *Theatre at Work: Playwrights and Productions in the Modern British Theatre.* New York: Hill and Wang, 1967.

Miller, Dulcy B. *The Extended Care Facility: A Guide to Organization and Operation.* New York: McGraw-Hill, 1969.

Morley, Michael. "Dürrenmatt's Dialogue with Brecht: A Thematic Analysis of *Die Physiker*." *Modern Drama* 14: 232–242.

Morris, Kelly, ed. *Genet/Ionesco: The Theatre of the Double, A Critical Anthology.* New York: Bantam, 1969.

Nichols, Peter. *The National Health (or Nurse Norton's Affair).* New York: Grove Press, 1970.

Nightingale, Benedict. "Unsoldierly Soldiers in New Nichols Play." *New York Times*, March 6, 1977, sec. 2, p. 6.

O'Connor, Ulick. *Brendan Behan.* London: Hamish Hamilton, 1970.

O'Neill, Eugene. *The Iceman Cometh.* New York: Vintage, 1957.

Osborne, John. *The Entertainer.* New York: Criterion, 1958.

Pinter, Harold. *The Caretaker.* New York: Grove Press, 1965.

——. *The Homecoming.* New York: Grove Press, 1966.

——. *The Hothouse.* London: Eyre Methuen, 1980.

Prideaux, Tom. "Playwright for a Torn-Apart Time: The Art of David Storey." *Life*, February 12, 1971, p. 10R.

Rabe, David. *The Basic Training of Pavlo Hummel* and *Sticks and Bones*. New York: Viking Press, 1973.

———. *Streamers*. New York: Alfred Knopf, 1977.

Ribalow, Harold U. *Arnold Wesker*. New York: Twayne, 1965.

Roddy, Joseph. "*Marat/Sade* Stuns Broadway Playgoers with Sanity from the Asylum." *Look*, February 22, 1966, p. 110.

Rosen, Sharon L. and Liebmann-Smith, Joan. "The Presentation of Illness on Television." In *Deviance and Mass Media*, edited by Charles Winick. Beverly Hills: Sage, 1978, pp. 79–94.

Sainer, Arthur. *The Radical Theatre Notebook*. New York: Avon, 1975.

Santoli, Al. *Everything We Had: An Oral History of the Vietnam War by Thirty-Three American Soldiers Who Fought It*. New York: Random House, 1981.

Sartre, Jean-Paul. *Situations II*. Paris: Gallimard, 1948.

Schechner, Richard. "Interviews With Judith Malina and Kenneth H. Brown." *Tulane Drama Review* 8: 207–220.

Simmons, Roberta G. and Simmons, Richard L. "Organ-Transplantation: A Societal Problem." *Social Problems* 19: 36–57.

Simpson, Alan. *Beckett and Behan and a Theatre in Dublin*. London: Routledge and Kegan Paul, 1962.

Solzhenitsyn, Alexander. *Cancer Ward*. Translated by Nicholas Bethell and David Burg. New York: Bantam, 1972.

———. *One Day in the Life of Ivan Denisovich*. Translated by Ralph Parker. New York: Dutton, 1963.

Sontag, Susan. *Illness as Metaphor*. New York: Farrar, Straus, and Giroux, 1978.

———. *On Photography*. New York: Farrar, Straus, and Giroux, 1977.

Steiner, George. *In Bluebeard's Castle: Some Notes Towards the Redefinition of Culture*. New Haven: Yale University Press, 1971.

Storey, David. *Home*. New York: Random House, 1971.

Stott, Catherine. "Plays in the Life of Joe Egg's Dad." *London Guardian*, January 26, 1970, p. 8.

Sudnow, David. *Passing On*. Englewood Cliffs, New Jersey: Prentice-Hall, 1967.

Taubman, Howard. "Theater: The Assassination of Marat." *New York Times*, December 28, 1965, p. 35.

Taylor, John Russell. *Anger and After: A Guide to the New British Drama*. Baltimore: Penguin, 1963.

Taylor, John Russell. *The Second Wave: British Drama for the Seventies.* New York: Hill and Wang, 1971.

Terry, Megan. *Four Plays by Megan Terry.* New York: Simon and Schuster, 1967.

Tiusanen, Timo. *Dürrenmatt: A Study in Plays, Prose, Theory.* Princeton: Princeton University Press, 1977.

Toynbee, Polly. *Patients.* New York: Harcourt Brace Jovanovich, 1977.

Wahls, Robert. "Footlights: Onstream with Rabe." *New York Sunday News*, April 25, 1976, Leisure sec., p. 4.

Weiss, Peter. *The Persecution and Assassination of Jean-Paul Marat as Performed by the Inmates of the Asylum of Charenton Under the Direction of the Marquis de Sade.* English version by Geoffrey Skelton, verse adaptation by Adrian Mitchell. New York: Atheneum, 1975.

————. *The Persecution and Assassination of Jean-Paul Marat as Performed by the Inmates of the Asylum of Charenton Under the Direction of the Marquis de Sade.* English version by Geoffrey Skelton, verse adaptation by Adrian Mitchell. Chicago: The Dramatic Publishing Company, 1965.

Wesker, Arnold. "From a Writer's Notebook." *Theatre Quarterly* 2: 8–13.

————. *The Journalists: A Triptych.* London: Jonathan Cape, 1979.

————. *The Plays of Arnold Wesker.* New York: Harper and Row, 1976.

LIBRARY OF CONGRESS CATALOGING IN PUBLICATION DATA

Rosen, Carol, 1950–
  Plays of impasse.

  Bibliography: p.   Includes index.
  1. Drama—20th century—History and criticism.
2. Setting (Literature)   I. Title.   II. Title: Contemporary drama set
in confining institutions.
PN1861.R65 1983   809.2'04   82-61381   ISBN 0-691-06565-9

Carol Rosen is Associate Professor of Theatre Arts at the State
University of New York at Stony Brook, where she is also chair-
man of the Committee for the Graduate Programs in Theatre Arts
and Dramaturgy.